Human Relations: Law Enforcement In A Changing Community

Human Relations: Law Enforcement In A Changing Community

Third Edition

ALAN COFFEY

EDWARD ELDEFONSO

WALTER HARTINGER

Prentice-Hall, Inc., Englewood Cliffs, New Jersey 07632

Library of Congress Cataloging in Publication Data

Coffey, Alan.
    Human relations.

    Bibliography: p.
    Includes index.
    1. Public relations--Police. I. Eldefonso,
Edward. II. Hartinger, Walter.
III. Title.
HV7936. P8C62 1982   363.2   81–12090
ISBN 0–13–445700–5   AACR2

Editorial/production supervision
and interior design by Esther S. Koehn
Cover by Tony Ferrara Studio
Manufacturing buyer: Ed O'Dougherty

Printed in the United States of America

10 9 8 7 6

ISBN 0-13-445700-5

Prentice-Hall International, Inc., *London*
Prentice-Hall of Australia Pty. Limited, *Sydney*
Prentice-Hall of Canada, Ltd., *Toronto*
Prentice-Hall of India Private Limited, *New Delhi*
Prentice-Hall of Japan, Inc., *Tokyo*
Prentice-Hall of Southeast Asia Pte. Ltd., *Singapore*
Whitehall Books Limited, *Wellington, New Zealand*

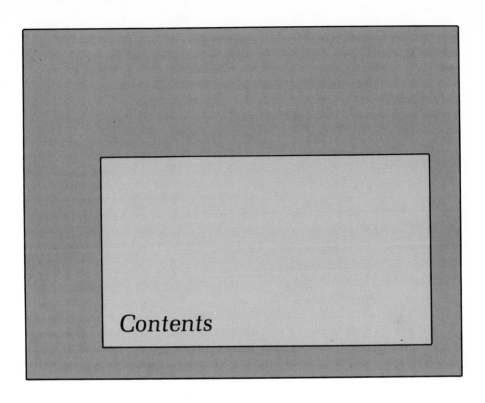

Contents

APPENDICES

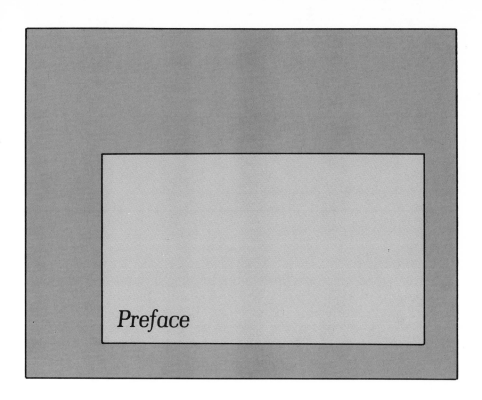

Preface

There is nothing new about the fact that the field of law enforcement is seeking to anticipate and prevent violation of law or the disturbance of peace. Nor is there anything new about deliberate efforts to keep the public informed about law enforcement. What *is* new, however, is an emerging law enforcement concept of *active* involvement in programs designed to reduce community tensions in general.

With the emphasis on constitutional rights steadily increasing, the law enforcement methods used to anticipate and prevent disturbance have shifted toward community-relations and human-relations programs. The relatively uncomplicated function of dealing with traditional crime may well prove one of the policeman's lesser responsibilities as the tensions mount between various segments of the population.

Although it is addressed to a complex subject, the purpose of the third edition of this volume remains the same: to describe the development of the community social forces and the resultant problems they present to the effective enforcement of law. And because our context is the broadest possible definition of law enforcement, we also seek to suggest and define appropriate avenues of solution.

This, the third edition of *Human Relations: Law Enforcement in a Changing Community,* still retains the psychological, sociological, and anthropological approach to the problem of policing in the twentieth century. Also retained is the point of view that police are *primarily* responsible for enforcing law and only *indirectly* responsible for the resolution of social problems. But out of deference to the courage and dignity with which police have confronted the enormous social contest of this era, this text seeks to isolate the nature and scope of police–community relations.

ACKNOWLEDGMENTS

With the usual proviso that they cannot be held accountable for either errors of omission or commission, the authors express their gratitude for the advice, counsel, and encouragement tendered by B. Earl Lewis, Professor, Department of Law Enforcement Education, DeAnza College and the Administration and Staff of the Santa Clara County Juvenile Probation Department, San Jose, California. Also, we wish to express our gratitude to the International Association Chiefs of Police, specifically Mr. Charles E. Higginbotham, Consultant, Professional Standards Division, for his generosity in permitting us to utilize some of the late N. A. Watson's excellent material on "Threats and Challenges in Police Work"; and the Los Angeles, San Francisco and Berkeley, California, Police Departments for many of the photos used in this volume.

As far as the authors are concerned, acknowledgments are not complete without some mention of our wives and children. Actually, without their firm support and understanding, this volume, like the others we have written, would not have been possible, so to *Mildred Ann Eldefonso, Beverly May Coffey, and Patricia Hartinger, we express our gratitude and appreciation: We thank you.*

Alan Coffey

Edward Eldefonso

Walter Hartinger

Human Relations: Law Enforcement In A Changing Community

PART ONE

RACE AND
COMMUNITY TENSION

Some Comments on Race and Prejudice

Man is a complex animal—so complex, in fact, and so baffling that since the beginning of recorded time, the average person has responded to the riddle, "What is man?" only in glib and totally erroneous generalizations. Not only is such erring all too human, it is further compounded by a set of contradictory facts: Human behavior is characterized by (1) an *essential sameness,* and (2) *multifold differences.*

Race: myth and reality

Race, as the term is popularly defined, evolves from three factors:

1. *Mutations*—markedly different specimens that appear in a species for no apparent reason and then pass on their unusual characteristics to their offspring through hereditary forces

2. *Isolation*—whether geographical, self-imposed, or whatever, resulting in interbreeding that tends to perpetuate and magnify the original characteristics

3. *Inbreeding*—the usual outcome of a combination of mutation and isolation

The most frequently used criteria for racial identification are skin color; hair color; hair form; eye color; ratio, multiplied by 100, of head width to length (cephalic index); ratio of nose width to nose height times 100 (nasal index); distribution of body hair and beard; stature; and prognathism (lower facial projection). These criteria are used because it is assumed that they are (1) relatively stable—that is, more or less unmodified by the environment and essentially inherent in the genes; and (2) easily measured.

But in the study of the distribution of these characteristics in the human species, it has been discovered that there is a *wide variation* in each of them; thus, human types range through every conceivable combination of such factors—see Figure 1–1. Are there not, however, large numbers of people who have a *combination* of these characteristics in common? Earlier research did suggest that the world population could be divided into three distinct "clusters" of people, each distinguishable by the fact that those in it shared a combination of physical characteristics not shared by

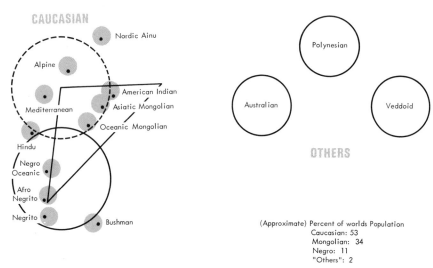

FIGURE 1–1. *That "races" differ from one another only slightly and through a continuing series of graduation (i.e., differences of degree or intensity, not of kind) is apparent. From the strictly genetic standpoint, there can be no such thing as a pure race or human type, because every single individual is a mixture of genes. The graphs above indicate the general groupings and subracial groupings of mankind. There are some groups ("Others") that defy accurate classification, owing to overlapping of physical characteristics.*

people in other clusters. The following types were suggested by such early theorists:

1. *Negroid*—long-headed, wide-nosed, dark-skinned, dark-haired, dark-eyed, more or less hairless, tending toward tall stature, having tightly coiled hair, highly prognathous

2. *Mongoloid*—medium stature, straight-haired, yellow-skinned, "slant-eyed" (the Mongolian fold is merely a drooping of the eyelids), medium-headed, medium-nosed, medium-eyed, mildly prognathous, and relatively free from body hair and beard

3. *Caucasoid*—light-haired, light-eyed, light-skinned, medium or tall stature, round to medium head shape, relatively hairy, long-nosed, wavy- or curly-haired, nonprognathous

Those groups that did not fit into any of these clusters were either ignored or squeezed into one of the three racial pigeonholes, regardless of their lack of conformity.

We now know that no individual fits exactly into the definition of a particular race, because the definition itself is a *statistical average* of traits of the whole group. Thus, if we say a man is Negroid, we imply that, to some degree, he has all the Negroid characteristics listed above. In actuality, we find among the so-called Negroids the tallest and the shortest people on earth; people with light tan skins and bluish-black skins; those with long, thin noses and flat, broad noses; and people having heads that are elongated and heads that are "round." The same scattered array of racial traits marks the Mongoloid and Caucasoid.

In the last analysis, more people do *not* fit these type descriptions than do fit them! Most people are neither distinctly Mongoloid nor Negroid nor Caucasoid but show some mixture of all the listed characteristics. Whatever the origin of man—multiple or single—biologists and anthropologists concur on one point: *There is no "pure" race.* A pure race could exist only if its people had lived throughout its history in complete and total isolation, with no cross-breeding whatsoever with other groups.

We find, then, that there are no pure races in any serious sense of the word and no large numbers of people who are reasonably identifiable as distinct types (who share numerous characteristics in common). We are left, therefore, only with the fact that many small groups may share in common certain genetic features by which they are identifiable and distinguishable. The biological fact of race and the myth of "race" should and must, then, be distinguished. *For all practical social purposes, "race" is not so much a biological phenomenon as a social myth.* We cannot, therefore, scientifically account for differences in group behavior in terms of differences in group biology. The events overwhelmingly point to the conclusion that "race" and "race differences" are not valuable concepts for the analysis of similarities and differences in human group behavior.

Whatever classification of races an anthropologist might concur with,[1] mental characteristics are never included as part of the classifications. It is generally recognized in today's social science circles that intelligence tests do not in themselves enable us to differentiate safely between what is due to innate capacity and what is the result of environmental influences, training, and education (the usual estimate is 65 to 70 percent inheritance). In fact, wherever it has been possible to make allowances for differences in environmental opportunities, the tests have shown essential similarity in mental characteristics among all human groups.

One of the more famous studies in this area provided conclusive data on the point: Blacks newly arrived in New York City from the Deep South obtained far lower intelligence quotients than did American-born whites when *they* first arrived in the city. But several years later—acclimated to the city's competitive, literacy-stressing, fast-geared environment—the same blacks' IQs were statistically identical with those of the whites!

As another example of the huge role of cultural conditioning in structuring intelligence, consider the numerous well-documented cases of identical twins (who have identical intelligence) reared apart. IQ differences of 20 and 30 points have separated twins reared in favorable versus unfavorable environments. In short, *given similar cultural opportunities to realize their potentialities, the average achievements of the members of each and every ethnic group are virtually identical.*

Not only are there no innate cultural, social, or intellectual differences among the races; there is no evidence whatsoever that race mixture produces biologically "bad" results. As was stated earlier, each race is in fact an intricate amalgam of cross-breeding with other racial strains. No race (or nation), then, is biologically any more or less pure than any other; races are "inferior" only in the sense that they are defined as inferior by the ethnocentric values of people such as white supremacists.

The idea of race, as one authority has noted, represents one of the greatest errors—if not the greatest—of our time, and the most tragic. Everyone seems to know, and is only too eager to tell, what race is. Well-intentioned or otherwise (the latter is most often the

---

[1] For more detailed and illustrative data on the weakness of racial classifications, see R.W. Mack, *Race, Class and Power*, 2nd ed. (New York: American Book Co., 1973), pp. 33–94; and H.S. Becker, ed., *Social Problems: A Modern Approach*, 3rd ed. (New York: John Wiley, 1977), pp. 339–56.

case), the "man on the street" is abysmally ignorant and almost totally ill-informed on the matter. For the student in particular, the facts must be put straight.

"Though the concept of race is genuine enough," famed anthropologist Clyde Kluckhohn once observed, "*there is perhaps no field of science in which the misunderstandings among educated people are so frequent and so serious.*" One of the basic misunderstandings to which Kluckhohn refers is the confusion between *racial* and *ethnic* groupings of mankind.

ETHNIC GROUP

Whereas race refers, of course, to hereditary ties, the term *ethnic* connotes social and cultural ties. Thus, when people confuse racial and ethnic traits, they are confusing what is given by nature and what is acquired through learning. What, then, is an ethnic group? The Jews, the American Indians, and the Nordics are not racial entities but ethnic units, in the sense that they largely *share a common cultural heritage* and set of values. But even the label *ethnic* is conducive to gross oversimplification. Take for example, the category *Jew*. Jews of German, Russian, Spanish, English, and Polish descent (who together make up some 95 percent of American Jewry) differ radically from one another, not only in cultural terms but in the realms of religious belief and dogma, too. Further, there is a profound split within the Jewish religion, among Orthodox, Conservative, and Reformed. Also, in America, fewer offspring of Jewish parents are Jews in the *religious* sense than are Protestants' children Protestant or Catholics' children Catholic. Similarly, the generic term *Indian* encompasses a people whose original tribes differed from one another linguistically and culturally as much as modern Americans differ from ancient Chinese.

Racial prejudice

We have all known people whom we can justly label prejudiced. Many of the readers of this book, in fact, are in all probability quite intolerant toward one or more of the ethnic or racial groupings—toward Jews, blacks, or some group of "foreigners." Prejudice and bias (bias is an important extention of prejudice because if biases are not displayed, prejudices are not necessarily negative) toward outsiders (out-groups) is so frequent an aspect of American society—and of all other known societies—that it is literally a universal phenomenon. Despite the contention of many racialists, however, prejudice is *not* inherent in man as man; it is *not* a biogenic trait. To effectively probe the how and why of prejudice, then, it is crucial to recognize that like stature or IQ, prejudice is not something a person either has or does not have, but is a matter of degree and intensity. We cannot, for example, legitimately assert that a man whose height is 6 feet is "tall" and a man who is 5 feet, 11 inches is "short," or that a person with a recorded IQ of 140 is "near-genius," while one whose IQ is 139 is merely "bright." Nevertheless, there are tall people, geniuses, and highly prejudiced persons. And the authors' concern throughout the remainder of this chapter will largely be with the highly prejudiced.

DEFINITION OF PREJUDICE

Prejudice is, specifically, thinking ill of a person or a group without sufficient justification; a feeling (favorable or unfavorable, although we shall be concerned with the latter aspect here) that is prior to, or not based on, actual experience. Of course, it is not easy to say how much "fact" is required to justify a judgment. A prejudiced person will almost certainly claim to have sufficient cause for his or her views, telling of bitter experiences with refugees, Koreans, Catholics, Jews, blacks, Mexicans, Puerto Ricans, or Indians. But in most cases, it is evident that these "facts" are both scanty and strained. Such a person typically resorts to a selective sorting of his or her own memories, mixes them up with hearsay, and then overgeneralizes. No one can possibly know *all* refugees, Koreans, Catholics, and so on. Hence, any negative judgment of these groups as a whole is, strictly speaking, and instance of thinking ill without warrant or justification.

We can further elaborate our basic definition of prejudice to include an avertive (avoiding) or hostile attitude toward a person simply because he or she belongs to a certain group and is, therefore, presumed to have the objectionable qualities ascribed to the group. Another essential attribute of prejudice is that of giving and applying a stereotyped name or *label of difference* to members of a given group.[2]

TARGETS OF PREJUDICE

Historically, the targets of prejudice have been determined by the particular configuration of conflicting values and opposing

[2] A *stereotype* is a conception of a particular group held by the general public in the absence of specific knowledge of the characteristics of the individual members of that group. Stereotypes function, in a sense, as a substitute for knowledge.

groups, largely because of the cultural and social situation of the time and place. *And the most evident targets of prejudice have been those groups whose relationships with the prejudiced are marked by competition or other forms of opposition.* Often a group has been singled out as a target for a period of time and then replaced by another group.

At the outset of American history, the targets of strong prejudice were the British, who opposed our efforts toward independence. But there was also a certain amount of sectional division among the states. As the struggle for the extension of slavery became more and more a factor in national politics, a split between the industrial North and the agrarian, slave-geared South became evident. After the Civil War, the whole situation changed in the South, with the appearance of the color-caste system, which still continues. Later, as blacks moved into the North in response to sordid conditions at home and the lure of freedom and economic betterment, they came into direct competition with the northern urban whites. A certain amount of antiblack prejudice began to emerge in such places as Chicago, Detroit, Los Angeles, and New York City. Then, with the flood of immigrants fleeing poor political and economic conditions in Europe, new objects of prejudice entered the scene.

The black and immigrant groups constituted a handy set of specific targets of intolerance, discrimination, and prejudice on the part of native-born or longer-established American citizens. Economic competition was a crucial factor in the earlier outbreaks of prejudice; immigrants willing to work for lower wages often eased American workers out of jobs in this era of rapid industrialization and explosive capitalism. But one of the symbols of hostility pertained to an ideological conflict between the Protestantism of most of the Americans and the Catholic faith of the immigrants. This was especially true after 1890, when southern Europeans began to outnumber immigrants from Germany, Great Britain, and Scandinavia. The Protestant–Catholic friction—with native enmity less often directed toward Catholicism per se than toward the very different southern European brand of culture—erupted in the growth of "Native American" or nativist movements. Foremost among these movements was the Ku Klux Klan.

TWO BASIC TYPES OF PREJUDICE

Granted that prejudice is so widespread that it is "normal," who are likely to manifest the *most* prejudice? Although prejudice is essentially a matter of degree, there are two basic types of prejudice: culture-conditioned and character-conditioned.[3]

Culture-Conditioned Prejudice. We shall consider the former first, for it is by far the most typical. As its name might imply, culture-conditioned prejudice is primarily learned or acquired in the normal process of social interaction. Thus most people raised in an environment verbalizing antipathy toward blacks assume prejudicial behavior, for they have been taught—deliberately and by subtle examples—that the black is both different and inferior; they have known no other explanation from childhood on.

It cannot be overemphasized that typically the formation of prejudiced attitudes is not a product of distorted personality development. Prejudiced attitudes are, in fact, formed through the same process as other attitudes; they are derived from group norms. Within a group when patterns of prejudice prevail, it is the person who *conforms* to the group (that is, the most "normal" or "well-adjusted" person) who is likely to be the most prejudiced; conversely, lack of prejudice in such a group implies nonconformity. And studies of the growth of ethnic prejudice in children indicate that such prejudice arrives largely through contacts with prevailing social norms rather than through individual contacts with members of the out-group in question. Once a small child accepts the prejudicial norms of his parents and, through osmosis, his schoolmates, the negative stereotypes he has learned become internalized; that is, they slide into his subconscious mind and become a functioning part of his personality configuration. In his adult years, when he "feels" an aversion for the out-group he learned to dislike in childhood, he will defend his attitude with all manner of "reasonable" rationalizations.

There are, however, differences in susceptibility to the culture-conditioned brand of prejudice even among people reared in the same general culture. Thus, the more highly prejudiced person, in contrast with those less prejudiced, is more likely to (1) be older; (2) have had less formal education; (3) be either a farmer or in an unskilled or semiskilled occupation; (4) live on a farm or in a very small town; (5) take less interest in civic affairs, be less informed on public issues, and vote less often; and (6) receive a smaller income. Many of these sociological factors, it is apparent,

---

[3] For a lucid analysis of culture- and character-conditioned prejudice, see T.W. Adorno et al., *The Authoritarian Personality*, 4th ed. (New York: Harper & Row, 1970); G. Allport, *The Nature of Prejudice*, 2nd ed. (Reading, Mass.: Addison-Wesley, 1965); and H.M. Hodges, Jr., *Social Stratification*, 3rd ed. (Cambridge, Mass.: Schenkman Publishing Co., 1975).

are intercorrelated; that is, they almost automatically "go with one another" (education, age, income, occupation, and so on). Closer analysis has revealed that of all these sociological variables, *formal education* is the most crucial. Other social cultural determinants appear to be downward mobility and socioeconomic insecurity.[4]

The particular target of prejudice will depend upon a number of factors; but it is currently most likely to be the black in the North and South; the Puerto Rican, Mexican, and Jew in large urban areas; and in the more rural sectors of the Middle West, the big-city eastern intellectuals or "aristocrats." The *scapegoat* or object of prejudice will often, however, be a group sanctioned as "inferior" by people in general, or a person or group too weak to strike back when attacked.[5]

Culture-conditioned prejudice *can* be "unlearned," although the process is not as effortless as many well-intentioned and naive people believe. Because such attitudes are not formed in a piecemeal way and are usually deeply ingrained within the personality structure, attempts to legislate prejudice out of existence have, on some occasions, had the opposite effect. Almost as unsuccessful have been efforts to "educate" people, to shame them (by appeals to their religious ethics or Americanism), or to bring them into contact with minority groups. Lecturing, like legislation, requires expert and subtle direction if it is to avoid alienating its subjects. Social contact and situations such as living in an interracial housing project have often, when poorly handled, increased friction and hostility. Because highly prejudiced people are conformistic and attuned to their group's values, they are unlikely to alter their basic beliefs unless the group's beliefs change too.[6]

To lessen prejudice with any degree of effectiveness, then, either we must change the basic values or attitudes of entire groups, or we must somehow transfer the prejudiced person's allegiance to another group (or "reference group"). Educating the young child is, of course, a far simpler undertaking than changing ossified adult attitudes. However, such educational programs must

---

[4] Adorno, *The Authoritarian Personality.*

[5] Scapegoating has always been with us; people have traditionally found it uncomfortable to blame themselves when things are going wrong. Projecting blame onto another source (displaced aggression) has long been a popular way to ease such unpleasant tensions.

[6] The authors do not intimate that such legislation (Civil Rights Act, 1964) is inappropriate; active government intervention in areas of unjustified ethnic prejudice is an absolute must. However, such efforts will only cause frustration or false hopes if the laws are unenforceable or are not intelligently executed.

reach the child during his lower elementary-school years, must be skillfully handled (preferably with the help of visual aids), and must strongly compete against extracurricular influences, such as the family and lower-culture values, which are frequently enormously potent.

Character-Conditioned Prejudice. This type of prejudice is quite firmly imbedded in the personality makeup, and attempts to rid people of it must be, needless to say, far more formidable than the just-cited techniques of eradicating culture-conditioned prejudice. As will become clearer later in this chapter, people with character-conditioned prejudice almost *have* to hate, and if one of their scapegoats or objects of venom is somehow eliminated from focus, they will inevitably seek out some other victim.

A psychologically prejudiced person (one having character-conditioned prejudice) is more dangerous than the sociologically or culture-conditioned prejudiced person in a twofold sense. He or she is (1) present in all areas of the population—among the educated, wealthy, and influential as well as the poor and ill-educated; and is (2) more likely to be actively prejudiced and in a position to translate hatred into effective political or social action. Postwar studies of the more avid Nazis and of potent native American Fascists have uncovered all the earmarks of the *character-conditioned* brand of prejudice.

Like culture-conditioned prejudice, the character-conditioned variety has its roots in childhood. But unlike the former, specific sets of prejudice, such as antiblack or anti-Semitic, are seldom acquired in the early years. Rather, a basic outlook on life is learned during this formative period—an outlook that will warp the entire life of its victim. How does the childhood of such a psychologically prejudiced person differ from the normal person's? It differs at many crucial points, as the subconscious will affirm. We must recognize how vitally important the formative years are in shaping one's entire personality.

It is abundantly clear, in summation, that the more deeply prejudiced person—one who looks down on *many* minority groups rather than one or two specific out-groups—is marked by a distinct personality makeup. These people are, in short, "sick." Their sickness is not of their own doing but rather the outcome of a strict and undemocratic upbringing. As a result, their entire lives will be marred by deeply imbedded frustrations, vague hatreds, and insecurity. They are already targets for demagogues of the far Right and far Left. They will be unhappy with both the Republicans and the Democrats, and can be satisfied only with a totalitarian order.

FORMS OF PREJUDICE

What is racism? The word has represented daily reality to millions of racial minorities for centuries (particularly the black people), yet it is a difficult term to define. *Racism* may be defined as the prediction of decisions based on considerations of race. Furthermore, such decisions or policies are intended to subjugate a minority racial group for the purpose of maintaining or exerting control of that group.

Minority problems are problems of intergroup relations, in which each minority is the subject of prejudice and discrimination by the majority. The majority itself is made up of many minorities and, indeed, is sometimes but the dominant minority of a group of minorities holding key positions. As previously indicated, prejudice is an attitude arrived at without sufficient exploration of the facts—see Figure 1–2. It is prejudging, in the sense of making a judgment before knowing or independently of, the relevant facts in the matter. *Discrimination*, although related to prejudice, is not the same thing. Discrimination implies the unequal treatment of different people according to the group to which they belong.

THE FUNCTIONS OF PREJUDICE

Among the functions performed by prejudice against minority groups are the following:

1. It provides a source of egotistic satisfaction, through invidiously comparing others with oneself.

2. It affords a convenient grouping for people one is ignorant of. Lumping such people together under a popular stereotyped description saves time and thought and affords a convenient grouping.

3. It provides someone to blame when things go wrong in one's personal life or in the community (scapegoating).

4. It provides an outlet for projecting one's tensions and frustrations onto other people.

5. It symbolizes one's affiliation with a more dominant group.

6. It furnishes justification for various types of discrimination that are thought to be of advantage to the dominant group.[7]

---

[7] For a thorough analysis of minority-group problems, see J.S. Roucek and R.L. Warren, *Sociology, An Introduction,* 4th ed. (Totowa, N.J.: Littlefield, Adams & Co., 1978), pp. 146–48.

FIGURE 1-2. *Equal treatment by the courts and the police—as well as society in general—is a necessary ingredient in our American way of life. Courtesy Wide World Photos.*

THE FUNCTIONS OF DISCRIMINATION

Among the functions performed by discrimination against minority groups are the following:

1. It tends to reinforce prejudice concerning the group's alleged inferiority.
2. It ensures members of the majority group various types of economic advantages.
3. It limits the effectiveness of possible competition from members of the minority group in business, education, political office, and so forth.
4. It affords an avenue to economic exploitation of the minority group.[8]

ELIMINATION OF PREJUDICE

Because much prejudice is based on stereotyped thinking, education in the matter of group differences—where they are found—should provide the necessary intellectual basis for a change of attitude. It is for this reason that various organizations like the National Conference of Christians and Jews, the National Association for the Advancement of Colored People, the Urban League, and the Anti-Defamation League carry on extensive educational programs.

However, as we mention in another section, prejudice is almost by definition an irrational attitude. Knowledge is not enough. A change of attitudes—attitudes conditioned by norms found acceptable by the group—must be the ultimate goal. Several techniques have been found to be successful in achieving this goal, notably (1) changing group norms (values, folkways, mores) through discussion, lectures, and the use of communication media (TV, newspapers, books, radio); and (2) encouraging association with members of the minority group. Quite often, the removal or suspension of discrimination subsequently provides an opportunity for experiencing social participation and leads to a reconsideration of the prejudiced conception held by majority-group members. Because prejudice is largely irrational and emotional in nature, emotional appeals to the alleged values of democracy are sometimes effective, although they seldom have permanent effect.

[8] Roucek and Warren, *Sociology*, pp. 146–48.

Educational campaigns seem to be effective over a longer period of time.[9]

REDUCTION OF DISCRIMINATION

Most sociologists and social psychologists are of the opinion that the attempt to eliminate prejudice under conditions of widespread discrimination is almost destined to fail, "for it separates verbal symbols and behavior, and the verbal symbols of tolerance and understanding are largely ineffective if daily life reinforces habits of discrimination. Hence, many people see the resolution of the problem in a constant agitation to defeat discrimination wherever possible, and to make it illegal where this is within the power of the law.[10]

Therefore, antidiscriminatory laws have proved to be effective, although not without conflict. There are some indications of an improvement in the conditions surrounding minority groups—particularly the black minority. The U.S. Supreme Court has made several important decisions pertaining to desegregation—in education, housing, use of public facilities, and voting. Because blacks are becoming much more sophisticated politically and their vote is growing larger with every election, politicians are taking cognizance of the black's might. Also, many new types of employment were opened up for large number of blacks during World War II, the Korean conflict, and the Vietnam War; these jobs have "opened the door," and labor unions have displayed a willingness to admit black workers to their membership. Nevertheless, the range of discrimination is still great and constitutes a challenge to any country claiming to be a democracy.

PREJUDICE: RELATED EFFECTS

There are some segments of our population—notably blacks and other nonwhite minorities—that have been systematically excluded for generations from effective participation in the society. They have been locked into a self-perpetuating pattern of poverty, substandard living conditions, inadequate education, lack of skills, and unequal protection of the law, all mutually reinforcing one another. Their efforts to break out of this vicious circle have been frustrated by subtle and not-so-subtle biases that have denied them

[9] Roucek and Warren, *Sociology.*
[10] Roucek and Warren, *Sociology.*

access to educational opportunities, to jobs, to unions, to loans—in short, to all potential points of entry into the system.

Members of these groups have now gone beyond the earlier civil-rights movement in insisting that their right to full participation in the society implies not merely the removal of legal barriers, but active affirmative efforts to open up opportunities to them and to ensure that they will be in a position to take advantage of those opportunities. Moreover, they are insisting on the right to their own identity—the right to be included in the system on their terms, without having to adopt the values, lifestyles, and other cultural trappings of the white middle-class majority.

Two black assistant professors of psychiatry at the University of California Medical Center, William H. Grier and Price M. Cobbs, conclude in their book that riots express personal pain and rage provoked by the severe psychological and emotional pressures of living in a racist society.[11] Many other authorities in the field of race relations are of the same opinion. The psychological pressures and fear derive from a history of oppression and capricious cruelty. This is clearly pointed out by Louis E. Lomax:

> The American Negro spent the first half of the twentieth century adjusting to and recovering from the all-pervasive reality of legalized segregation. Fear of white people being advanced was the basic motivation of Negroes during those years, and I suppose there is some validity in the analysis. But I doubt that fear was the only force shaping Negro activities and behavior; self-realization in an essentially hostile world, I suggest, is a no more accurate description of what the Negro was about. Fear, to be sure, was one of the techniques of that self-realization. After all, when the entire legal structure is against you and your very life is in daily peril, fear is an understandable emotion. Denied modern weapons with which to defend yourself, and hauled before openly hostile courts when you fight back with sticks and stones, you will do well to pretend fear even when you are not afraid.[12]

Not surprisingly, according to Grier and Cobbs, paranoid psychosis (or persecution complex, quite exaggerated) is the most typical kind of serious mental illness among blacks. The authors assert that the problem has its genesis during the formative years at the most crucial stage of development—sexual identity. A black mother, because she is afraid of the "penalties" of white society, will strive to maintain stringent control of her son. She must "intuitively cut off and blunt his masculine assertiveness and aggression lest they put the boy's life in jeopardy." Furthermore, this pattern

---

[11] *Black Rage,* (New York: Basic Books, 1968). See also E.E. Thorp, *The Mind of the Negro* (New York: Ortlieb Press, 1968); and F.K. Berrien, *Comments and Cases in Human Relations* (New York: Harper & Row, 1971).

[12] Louis E. Lomax, *The Negro Revolt* (New York: Harper & Row, 1963), p. 12.

of attempting to eliminate assertiveness and creativeness does not stop when the child reaches the adolescent stage but continues under the guise of the parents' discouragement of education. Black families, Grier and Cobbs write, tend to discourage their sons from seeking degrees by using hostility, scorn, and hatred as well as praise. Black families feel that having a degree may force the child into direct and dangerous competition with whites.

Unable to withstand the pressure of daily living in the ghetto, many black families are simply unable to function. This disintegration can be seen in the high percentage of fatherless homes. Sociologist Daniel P. Moynihan, in a well-publicized report, argues that lack of job opportunities prevents the black father from asserting authority in his household, so that, *psychologically emasculated* and humiliated, he leaves his family. The emasculating force is not economic but social; the father feels impotent and helpless because, living in a prosperous American society, he is unable to provide for his family and protect it from harm.

For many blacks, self-respect has become almost impossible. Traditionally, a large number were preoccupied with hair straighteners, skin bleaches, and the like, illustrating a most tragic aspect of American racial prejudice—blacks coming to believe in their own inferiority. Recently, however, there have been some encouraging signs. For instance, blacks have begun to advocate the beauty of dark skin and kinky hair, and have developed a new culture pride (natural Afro hair styles and African style of dress), which has had a positive effect on their mental health.

DISCRIMINATION AGAINST MINORITY GROUPS

Discrimination takes several forms as it applies to minority groups. *Economic discrimination* involves unequal treatment in the economic sphere of members of certain minorities. *Educational discrimination* results in school segregation and inferior facilities for educating those who reside in poorer school districts owing to economic deprivation. This is particularly true in the case of the blacks and the Spanish-speaking Mexican-Americans and Puerto Ricans. Because of "apathy in enforcement procedures," *political discrimination* is exercised against minority groups despite constitutional amendments designed to ensure all citizens the right to vote. Political discrimination is particularly important because it is largely through federal legislation that minorities can expect to gain protection against the many other types of discrimination.

Another aspect of political discrimination is the manipulation of political boundaries and the devising of restrictive electoral systems. In areas where there is a large bloc of minority-group residents, it is not unusual for the political machinery of the dominant group to have gerrymandered such neighborhoods so that their true voting strength is not reflected in political representation.

Social discrimination is perhaps the most difficult form to eliminate through legislation, since many people believe strongly that it is their basic democratic right to associate with whom they please and to bar whom they please from membership in associations to which they belong. So, for example, many fraternities will not admit members of certain minority groups. Also, restrictive covenants in housing operate to exclude minority groups from certain residential areas. The recent Supreme Court decision regarding open housing has not eliminated this problem, nor has the Rumford Act in California. Social discrimination is important because it hinders a closer association between the members of different groups and thus reinforces stereotyped prejudicial thinking that arises through ignorance.

Although racial prejudice and discrimination have been a problem to other racial groups, blacks, who constitute 26.5 million (1980 census) of the U.S. population, have been so victimized by discrimination that they have been referred to as "second-class citizens" and the "underdog's underdog." The difference in life expectancy of blacks and whites is perhaps the best indication of the condition of blacks as a minority group. The average nonwhite male, according to the U.S. Department of Health, Education and Welfare, has a life expectancy at birth $9\frac{1}{2}$ years less than that of the average white male, and the average nonwhite female nearly 11 years less than that of the white female.

Police and prejudice

It is universally agreed that the elimination of police misconduct requires careful selection of police officers for duty in ghettos. Police responsibility in these areas is particularly demanding and sensitive as regards the residents' attitudes, and often it is rather dangerous as well. Only the highest-caliber personnel can overcome residents' feelings of inadequate protection and unfair, discriminatory treatment by the police. Of late there has been some effort to recruit minority-group members into the police department. The feeling is that with such personnel patrolling the ghettos and barrios, the people living in these areas will see the police as a part of the community rather than as an outside occupational force of the white establishment.

POLICEMEN REPRESENTING
MINORITY GROUPS

Generally speaking, if government is to be for all the people, it must be *by* all the people. However, minority groups have tended to be underrepresented in that portion of the government known as law enforcement. Because there has been a great deal of tension between minority-group members and the police, probably one of the better ways of resolving some of this tension would be to encourage minority-group members to be full participants in the governing process. This means that they need to become involved in law enforcement activities. "Not of least importance is the fact that the very stresses and tensions between the protective services and minorities which hinder recruitment are not likely to be resolved until these services are more representative of the minority community."[13]

Generally speaking, recruitment of minority-group members into the police department can come about only if these members do not view the police as enemies of the people. This means that acts of police brutality and police harassment must be punished swiftly by top municipal and police officials. It also means, as discussed in Chapter 4, that police officers must be trained in human relations.

John Herber of *The New York Times* throws some light on the situation:

> Cities have long had trouble recruiting black police officers because, as Nick Trenticosta, a community organizer in New Orleans, said, "People feel the police force is racist whether officers are black or white." Nevertheless, they have had some success. In Chicago, 23 percent of the police force is black: in Philadelphia 19 percent, in Memphis 18 percent, in Baltimore 17 percent, in Detroit 62 percent, and San Francisco 14 percent.

> Yet in some cities black recruitment has slipped. In Tampa, only 19 of 559 sworn officers are black, fewer than were on the force during the 1967 riot in that city. New Orleans, with a Hispanic population of 120,000, reports that it has been unable to recruit a single officer who speaks Spanish. And in some cities, community leaders say minority police officers do not make much difference in behavior.

> "Regardless of color, putting on a badge does something to a person," said Rev. Willie F. Wilson of Washington. "It makes it difficult to distinguish who he is from what he is."

> Many cities still do not have civilian review boards for disciplining police, and the community relations departments set up in police departments have in many incidents—in Miami, for example—been ineffective.

[13] C.E. Pope, "Race and Crime Revisited," *Crime and Delinquency*, 25, No. 3 (July 1979), 347–57.

A few weeks ago, a national conference of black and Hispanic leaders was held in Washington to try to reach a better understanding on police procedures. The minorities wanted a model code to be used nationally that would set standards for shooting a fleeing felon. But attempts at agreement broke down when the minority groups emphasized the need for more restraint and the police emphasized the danger to officers and other persons.

Still, progress is being made in some cities. In Philadelphia, blacks say there has been improvement since William J. Green replaced Frank L. Rizzo as mayor and for the first time in the city's history published a written policy for the use of deadly force by the police.

In Kansas City, Emanuel Cleaver, a black member of the City Council, said the city was "a potential powder keg" until police officials began keeping track of officers who were the subject of most complaints of brutality and, if cause were found, dismissing them.

"That was what brought results," he said, "not the community relations division set up internally in the police department. That is like putting Dracula in charge of the blood bank."[14]

Mounting a one-time minority recruitment campaign by the police department tends to be ineffective. There should be an ongoing recruitment. This, however, is not an easy matter. The problems facing the black police officer are quite extensive and may cut down his or her effectiveness a great deal.[15]

On the other hand, Bannon and Wilt indicate that policemen who are also members of a minority make a substantial contribution:

This should not be such a surprising finding, but much of the current literature on the subject contradicts this statement. In light of that literature, we felt that if further studies by ourselves and others add more data to support the findings concerning the positive characteristics of black policemen, this should help to overcome many of the hesitations which sociologists and policemen alike have concerning black policemen.[16]

MINORITIES IN POLICE WORK: SOME PROBLEMS AND ANSWERS

It is important at this juncture to point out that *the problems of economic, educational, political, and social discrimination have been continually under attack by local, state, and federal govern-*

[14] John Herber, The New York Times, June 8, 1980.

[15] See N. Alex, Black in Blue: A Story of the Negro Policeman, (New York: Century-Crofts, 1960); and J. Margolis, A Report of the U.S. Commission on Civil Rights: Who Will Wear the Badge? (Washington, D.C.: U.S. Government Printing Office, 1971).

[16] D. Bannon and G.M. Wilt, "Black Policemen: A Study of Self-Images," Journal of Police Science and Administration, 1, March 1973, p. 29. See also P.D. Mayhall and D.P. Geary, eds., Community Relations and Administration of Justice (New York: John Wiley, 1979).

ments, not to mention private organizations and groups. The federal, state, and local governments' "affirmative action" hiring policy (hiring of minorities) has had a definite effect on resolving some of the economic problems confronting these racial minorities. Along these lines, the Department of Justice's Law Enforcement Assistance Administration (LEAA) equal opportunity guidelines (see Appendix B) have generated a great deal of concern on the part of police administrators, and the recruitment of minorities has been accorded top priority.

Furthermore, rulings by federal courts relating to the "ratio hiring" of minority personnel, although appearing to civil service commissions and police unions and associations to be discrimination in reverse, have been handed down throughout the states. In San Francisco, for example, entrance-level examinations and the examinations used for promotions to sergeant have been declared discriminatory. According to Federal Judge Robert F. Peckham, they prevented minorities from being able to compete on an equal level with the dominant group in the community. However, "federal court supervision of city employment policies . . . ," Peckham said, "cannot substitute for enlightened leadership by city and police officials. Court intervention, at best, stimulates concerned parties to develop and implement policies which not only comply with the law but would also be an advantage to general community interests."

"Affirmative action" is certainly not the only answer to the hiring of minorities. Its use as a political ploy will defeat its purpose. A strong statement regarding such misuse, which applies to all segments of the criminal justice system, was made in a speech by Robert Weigle:

> There will be a special place in hell for those who knowingly misuse Affirmative Action. Like the hucksters who use Christianity in order to fleece congregations, their sin is made worse because it betrays the trust of honest men and women and does so while hiding behind a worthy cause.
>
> Corrections, because of its ongoing interest in social justice, is particularly vulnerable to the charlatan. To religious zealots, a man's holiness is frequently weighed by how often he shouts "Jesus!" or "Hallelujah!" In corrections there is a tendency to judge a man's social awareness by how often he shouts "Prejudice!" Both groups had better keep an eye on their wallets.
>
> In Ventura County, Affirmative Action was used as an excuse to destroy standards related to the hiring of probation officers. Are "standards" ever used solely for keeping out minorities? Damn right they are, but is it always so? Is it so in Los Angeles County? Standards as applied in Los Angeles

County may not have the same intent and purpose as they do in Jackson, Mississippi.

In some counties, quotas are being set up as the sole criteria for employment or advancement. Merit and ability are being dumped. Personnel departments have become employment offices. Legitimate hiring standards have become troublesome road blocks.

What kind of professional development is being served? Where are we headed? You cannot say, on the one hand, that a job is important and difficult to do and then turn around and say that anyone can do it. You cannot talk about improving the quality of work and, in the next breath, state that *merit* and *ability* are merely secondary virtues. You cannot speak of measuring the quality of the work, but deny that it is possible to measure the quality of the worker. No one, white, black, or brown, can maintain his moral or intellectual balance taking part in that kind of a high wire act. Sooner or later everyone falls off. And there's no safety net to catch them.[17]

Police departments throughout the United States appear to be aggressively pursuing the goal of integration and are seriously concerned about discriminatory practices and behavior within their own organizations. Focusing on the most predominant minority group, blacks, numerous research studies have provided some insight into this problem. Bannon and Wilt investigated the role of the black policeman within two social contexts:[18] "(1) as a member of a specially and institutionally defined bureaucratic functional setting, the police department; and (2) as a person functioning within a dually defined and enacted role of public servant and figure of authority within black communities or residential areas." Regarding the first context:

> Police–community relations can best be improved in black neighborhoods by the department setting up strict rules of courtesy and insisting that they be adhered to. These rules should stress the importance of treating each individual citizen regardless of race or social status with the dignity of a human being. Until such time that a person acts otherwise, decent treatment is his right. Abuse of this right is the basic cause of poor police–community relations. The black community is not well-organized and it is therefore up to the police department, which is well-organized, to move toward gaining the respect and trust of the black community. This is at best a very difficult job, but it is not impossible. The great majority of the black community fully realize that the major beneficiary of community–police dissension is the criminal element of the black community, which is protected by the community and ignored by the police.[19]

---

[17] R. Weigle, in an address for the California Probation, Parole, and Corrections Association, January 1974, p. 4.

[18] Bannon and Wilt, "Black Policemen," pp. 21–25.

[19] Bannon and Wilt, "Black Policemen," p. 25.

Regarding the second issue, a person's functioning in a dual role, the opinion of the study's respondents was that:

Integration is an unrealistic, undesirable red herring invented by whites as a stumbling block to equality. The key to police–community relations is professional, well-trained, adequate police.

I think that police–community relations can definitely be improved by placing more black officers in *all* areas of both the black and white community. This way both communities will begin to trust and have confidence in the police department as a whole, be it black or white officers they have contact with.

[An increase in black policemen is needed] only if these officers are of a high caliber—mediocre personnel who do inadequate work will only worsen a bad situation.[20]

The statements made by the respondents reveal, according to Bannon and Wilt, a deep concern, particularly on the part of black officers, regarding the issue of hiring more black officers:

These men state that they favor the hiring of more black officers, but express a concern that standards not be reduced to facilitate this goal. It appears that the underlying reason for this concern is that present black officers have the attitude that if they could pass the more rigid standards, so should new recruits.

It seems that what is functioning here is an awareness that, as minority officers, their performance has been thoroughly scrutinized by their white counterparts much more critically than for other recruits. Along with this is perhaps the unconscious awareness that the whites tend to identify all blacks as equivalent to each other.

The black officers seemed to be concerned that should standards be lowered and inferior officers hired, then demonstrate deficiencies, their common color will tend to cause all blacks to be equated with the inferior performer. In other words, just because they are black, others will assume that all blacks hired were in fact below standard, regardless of the individual's capacity. On an empirical basis, we suspect that this fear is not altogether groundless.

As blacks have been more and more accepted, their assignments have become much more challenging. Thus, they have been placed in positions which have allowed them to demonstrate their equal or superior abilities vis-à-vis their white counterparts. They naturally do not want to regress because of a new wave of stereotyping. Old-line black officers have seen the painful

[20] Bannon and Wilt, "Black Policemen," p. 26.

and lengthy process of escape from "black jobs" within the law enforcement establishment. They recognize that this progress was only possible through the performance of truly superior black policemen who had to be better than anyone else to escape the stereotype.

It has been a long and tortuous road since it was common to hear "he's a good colored officer" with the implication that this was not only rare, but that it was limiting or relative. He was "good" only in relation to other "colored" officers—he was not being equated with officers who were white. In other words, it was polite variation on an old theme: "That's surprising for a black." Now these officers are more commonly referred to as "good cops," without the limiting adjective.[21]

Some members of the ghetto, most significantly the middle-class residents, are of the opinion that the black officer is a "victim of the system"; lower-class residents are not so kind! The prevailing sentiment is that Mexican-American and Puerto Rican officers will be given the same contempt.

It is an important but often overlooked factor that ". . . black citizens who distrust black policemen essentially do not want any policemen. Others [respondents] felt that those who are going to cooperate will do so with any police officer. The general consensus was that about 95 percent of all blacks have a high regard for black policemen. They believe that distrust exists because many blacks do not view law enforcement as being to their advantage."[22]

A key to the effectiveness of community relations may very well lie in the attitude of black, as well as other minority, members of police agencies, and in whether or not there is active recruiting of young people for the police service. Ongoing recruitment should make police/minority-group relations more effective and meaningful.

Anthropologists, in their studies of varying social groups the world over, have identified and emphasized the importance of recognizing cultural factors in dealing with problems of our own American society. Such groups as Puerto Ricans, Italians, and blacks often maintain their own cultural systems and social groups as completely as do natives of New Guinea. Such cultural systems are composed of and supported by characteristic behavior and attitudes shared by all members. These attitudes and behavior patterns, not those of the surrounding dominant culture, define what is considered right and "moral" by the group members. It is not possible to understand the actions of an individual from a point of view outside his cultural system or subculture, any more than one

[21] Bannon and Wilt, "Black Policemen," p. 26.
[22] Bannon and Wilt, "Black Policemen," p. 23.

can judge an iceberg from its visible fraction above the water. One must know, then, the values a subculture imposes upon its members, especially as those values differ from one's own. A person's actions must be examined in the context of his own group.

Summary

Race is popularly defined as being traceable to (1) *mutations,* (2) *isolation,* and (3) *inbreeding.* There are no *pure* races in any serious sense of the word and no large numbers of people who are reasonably identifiable as distinct types (who share numerous characteristics in common).

The biological fact and the myth of "race" must, then, be distinguished. *For all practical social purposes, "race" is not so much a biological phenomenon as a social myth.* We cannot, therefore, scientifically account for differences in group behavior in terms of differences in group biology. The evidence overwhelmingly points to the conclusion that "race" and "race differences" are not valuable concepts for the analysis of similarities and differences in human group behavior. Whatever classification of races the anthropologist might concur with, he never includes mental characteristics as part of those classifications. Nor do intelligence tests enable us to differentiate safely between what is due to innate capacity and what is the result of environmental influences, training, and education.

The term *ethnic* connotes social and cultural ties. Thus, when people confuse racial and ethnic traits, they are confusing what is given by nature and what is acquired through learning.

Prejudice is defined as thinking ill of others without sufficient justification—a feeling (favorable or unfavorable) toward a person or group that is not based on actual experience.

Essentially, there are two basic types of prejudice: *culture-conditioned* (sociologically prejudiced) and *character-conditioned* (psychologically prejudiced). This chapter discusses fully the manifestations of such prejudices and analyzes the personality makeup of those who fall into each group.

Chapter 1 also discusses the extremely sensitive area of police recruitment of minorities. Minorities in police work are concerned about professionalism; therefore, they regard the hiring of *unqualified* minority-group members as a negative practice.

In the area of politics, education, and economics, there has been improvement, in that discriminatory processes have lessened somewhat.

Discussion topics

1. Briefly discuss mutations, isolation, and inbreeding.
2. Is there pure race? Discuss.
3. Discuss the difference between ethnic groups and race.
4. Discuss prejudice.
5. Discuss culture-conditioned and character-conditioned prejudice.

Annotated references

Adorno, T.W., et al., *The Authoritarian Personality,* 4th ed. New York: Harper & Row, 1973. This book is still a classic in the field of the study of authoritarianism.

Allport, G., *The Nature of Prejudice,* 3rd ed. Reading, Mass.: Addison-Wesley, 1975. This textbook provides an excellent discussion of bias and bigotry.

Anderson, W., *The Age of Protest.* Pacific Palisades, Calif.: Goodyear, 1969. Essays, articles, and studies relating to significant protest movements and actions in the areas of civil rights, education, peace, and religion. Also discussed are the roots of violence in American society.

Grier, W.H., and P.M. Cobbs, *Black Rage.* New York: Basic Books, 1968. This book discusses the role of rage in black violence. The social emasculation of the black male is examined, and an intuitive explanation is given of the severe psychological injury suffered by black male and female servants.

Margolis, R.J., *Who Will Wear the Badge?* A Report of the United States Commission on Civil Rights. Washington, D.C.: U.S. Government Printing Office, 1971. This is an excellent study of minority recruitment efforts in protective services. See also H.G. Locke, *Impact of Affirmative Action and Civil Service on American Police Personnel Systems.* Washington, D.C.: U.S. Government Printing Office, 1979.

Mayhall, P.D., and D.P. Geary, eds., *Community Relations and Administration of Justice.* New York: John Wiley, 1979. This text provides readers with an awareness of behavioral, psychological, social, and other determinants of police–community relations. See also W.T.

Rusinko, K.W. Johnson, and C.A. Hornung, "Importance of Police Contact in the Formulation of Youth's Attitudes toward Police," *Journal of Criminal Justice,* 6, No.1 (Spring 1978), 53–67.

Mexican-Americans and the Administration of Justice in the Southwest, rev. ed., Summary of a Report of the United States Commission on Civil Rights. Washington, D.C.: U.S. Government Printing Office, 1978. This pamphlet investigates the biased treatment that Mexican-Americans receive from law enforcement agencies in the Southwest.

Reese, C.D., "Police Academy and Its Effects on Racial Prejudice," *Journal of Police Science and Administration,* I, No. 3 (September 1973), 257–68. This article is well worth reading by prospective law enforcement officers.

chapter two

Equal Justice
and Minority Groups

In the "Pledge of Allegiance," every American school-child learns the phrase, "liberty and justice for all." These words, if truly accepted as expressing a national goal, carry broad implications not only in regard to equal treatment by the courts and the police but also in regard to the general functions of society.

The courts and the police are the institutions of society generally examined with reference to injustice. However, it would be more logical to start an investigation of injustice by examining minority-group treatment within the general society.

According to a study published in the late 1960s, over 70 percent of minority-group members lived in ghettos.[1] There is no evidence that this percentage has changed much in the ensuing years. The generally accepted definition of a ghetto is an area of a city inhabited, often as a matter of involuntary segregation, by people of an ethnic or racial group who live in poverty and social disorganization. In a discussion of Spanish-speaking minorities, the

---

[1] *Report of the National Advisory Commission on Civil Disorders* (Washington, D.C.: U.S. Government Printing Office, 1968), p. 31.

word *barrio* is often used instead of *ghetto. Barrio* is Spanish for "precinct, district, or quarter." However, it is often used as a shortened form of *barrio bajo,* which translates to "slum."[2]

Keeping these definitions in mind, one soon realizes that slum/ghetto dwellers, because of the limited nature of their environment, do not enjoy liberty or freedom to pursue any goals. In this chapter, to help in our understanding of injustice as it exists for minorities in the United States, we will examine the black ghetto, and later the barrio. Blacks are the largest single minority group in the United States; the Spanish-surnamed minority, often referred to as Hispanics, is the second largest.

The black ghetto

Almost every large city in the United States has a black ghetto. Such ghettos contain a constantly growing concentration of blacks within the central city.

Studies show that during the past four decades, there has been a great shift of blacks from the rural southern areas to the large cities of the North and West. (However, during the 1970s there was a countermigration from the large cities of the North and West to the large cities of the South.) In 1910, the number of blacks in the metropolitan areas of the United States was approximately 29 percent of the total black population.[3] Today, approximately 69 percent live in metropolitan areas, with about 56 percent in the central city.

It is obvious that more and more of the black population has become urbanized during the past sixty years; however, so has most of the population of the United States. The difference is that most blacks have moved into and are concentrated in the inner core of cities, whereas whites have moved to the suburbs.

Furthermore, approximately 1 percent of the total population of the nation consists of poor blacks who come from disadvantaged neighborhoods. This 1 percent represents from 16 to 20 percent of the total black population in the central cities. Therefore, within the central city, there is a high concentration of very poor people of a particular ethnic background—in this case, black people.

It is speculated that the population shifts that have led to the

[2] Ramondero, ed., *The New World Spanish-English and English-Spanish Dictionary* (New York: Signet Books, New American Library, 1969), p. 82.

[3] *Report of the National Advisory Commission,* pp. 115–20.

formation of large black ghettos have been caused by three factors: (1) the migration of southern blacks to the cities in pursuit of employment (this has accelerated during the past thirty years), (2) the concentration of blacks in segregated big-city neighborhoods, and (3) the rapid growth of the black population because of better medical care coupled with a high fertility rate.[4]

By 1966, approximately two-thirds of all black people who lived outside the South were residents of the twelve largest cities of the United States, mostly of the central city. These cities are New York, Chicago, Los Angeles, Philadelphia, Detroit, Baltimore, Houston, Cleveland, Washington, D.C., Milwaukee, St. Louis, and San Francisco. For the most part, blacks move into ghetto-type segregation. Like other migrants and immigrants, they first move into the older sections of cities. But unlike the case with migrants from Europe, the blacks' color historically barred them from leaving these poor neighborhoods even when they became financially able to do so. The predominantly white society that has absorbed the immigrant has, by and large, refused to absorb the black. Until quite recently, this segregation was effected by local housing ordinances and real estate codes coupled with violence and intimidation. Often when a black moved into a white neighborhood, whites moved from the area, causing vacancies that were, in turn, filled by black citizens, and the whole character of the neighborhood was changed. Unscrupulous real estate agents often used this "blockbusting" technique to increase sales and, consequently, real estate commissions.[5]

Racial segregation has existed in American cities for decades. But during the 1950s and 1960s, it seemed to increase in every large city in the United States. A study by Karl and Alma Taeuber shows this quite graphically.[6] These authors, in order to measure the degree of residential segregation, devised an index that indicated the percentage of black Americans who would have to move to other blocks from where they lived to bring about a perfectly proportioned, unsegregated distribution of the population. The average segregation index for 207 of the largest cities of the United States in the year 1960 was 96.2. This means that an average of over 96 percent of all blacks would have had to relocate to create an unsegregated population distribution.

This index indicates quite strikingly that blacks live in segregated areas of the city. Let us examine the housing facilities available in these areas.

[4] Report of the National Advisory Commission.
[5] Report of the National Advisory Commission.
[6] Negroes in Cities (Chicago: Aldine, 1965).

GHETTO HOUSING

Ghetto housing has been described in a federal government report as follows:

> If the slums of the United States were defined strictly on the basis of dilapidated housing, inadequate sanitary facilities, and overcrowding, more than five million families could be classified as slum inhabitants.[7]

> To the inner-city child, home is often characterized by a set of rooms shared by a shifting group of relatives and acquaintances, furniture shabby and sparse, many children in one bed, plumbing in disrepair, plaster falling, roaches and sometimes rats, hallways dark or dimly lighted, stairways littered, air dank and foul.

> In such circumstances, home has little holding power for a child, adolescent, or young adult. Physically unpleasant and unattractive, it is not a place to bring friends; it is not even much the reassuring gathering place of one's own family. Indeed, the absence of parental supervision early in the slum child's life is not unusual, a fact partly due to the conditions of the home.[8]

It should be noted that the number of urban whites in substandard housing, generally known as slums, is $2\frac{1}{2}$ times the number of urban blacks in such housing. However, the *proportion* of the black population in inferior dwellings is much greater; approximately 25 percent of the black population in central cities lives in substandard housing, running from a low of 18.1 percent in Los Angeles to a high of 58.9 percent in Pittsburgh.[9] By contrast, only 8 percent of all Caucasians live in slums. Furthermore, in six of the fourteen largest cities, 40 percent of black housing was below standard in the last 20 to 25 years. Generally speaking, black housing is far more likely than white housing to be substandard, quite old, and overcrowded; only about 8 percent of housing for whites is overcrowded. Proportionately, approximately three times more blacks than whites live in substandard housing.

The overcrowding is directly related to the fact that blacks tend to get far less for their housing dollar than do whites. Often they cannot get housing similar to that of whites without paying much more for it, a situation that seems to prevail in most slum areas. This fact, plus the predominantly low income earned by black ghetto dwellers, results in a large percentage of the family in-

---

[7] See the *Report of the Task Force on Individual Violence, Crimes of Violence* (Washington, D.C.: U.S. Government Printing Office, 1970), Chap. 14.

[8] The National Commission on the Causes and Prevention of Violence, *To Establish Justice, to Insure Domestic Tranquility* (Washington, D.C.: U.S. Government Printing Office, 1969), pp. 30–31.

[9] *Report of the National Advisory Commission*, p. 257.

come being spent for housing—in many cities, from 35 to 40 percent. Needless to say, this severely cuts into the ghetto resident's funds for other items.

Landlords often victimize ghetto residents by ignoring building codes, probably because they know that their tenants are restricted, by economic or ethnic background, to living in the ghetto. Broadly speaking, these circumstances, along with others that will be expanded on later, are those that minority groups refer to when they say they are being treated unjustly by society.

There is some feeling that ghetto dwellers might have a better chance of leaving the ghetto if they were able to earn higher incomes. On the other hand, there is evidence that when they do obtain better incomes, blacks feel uncomfortable moving away from their old neighborhoods; consequently, they may stay in the black neighborhood even though they have the monetary resources to move.[10] And these higher incomes are hard to come by; ghetto residents have problems obtaining jobs.

JOBS AND GHETTO RESIDENTS

Unemployment and underemployment are among the most serious and persistent problems of disadvantaged minorities, and they contribute a great deal to civil disorders in the ghetto. Despite many efforts, and even during times of economic prosperity, blacks tend to have problems getting useful jobs at reasonable wages. Possibly because of the growing demand for skilled people in an economy that is becoming more and more automated, attaining full employment has become increasingly difficult for the ghetto resident.

Even more important than unemployment is the related problem of the undesirable nature of many jobs open to blacks. Black ghetto dwellers are often concentrated in the lowest-paying and the lowest-skilled jobs in the economy. These jobs usually involve substandard wages, great instability, and uncertainty of steady employment. As a result, the income of black families has tended to remain below that of white families.

Because of these factors, residents of black ghetto neighborhoods have been subject for decades to social, economic, and psychological disadvantages. The result is a vicious circle of failure; the employment problems of one generation breed similar problems in the following generation.

[10] J. White and J. Boyce, "America's Rising Black Middle Class," *Time*, June 17, 1974, p. 28.

Getting a good job is harder than it used to be for those without preparation, for an increasing proportion of all positions require an even higher level of education and training. To be a Negro, an 18-year-old, a high school dropout, a resident of the slums of a large city, is to have many times more chances of being unemployed than a white 18-year-old high school graduate living a few blocks away. Seventy-one percent of all Negro workers are concentrated in the lowest-paying and lowest-skilled occupations. They are the last to be hired. Union practices, particularly in the building trades, have always been unduly restrictive toward new apprentices (except those related to union members), and this exclusionary policy has a major impact on young blacks. The unemployment rate, generally down in the last few years, remains twice as high for nonwhites than for whites, and for black teenagers in the central cities in 1968 the unemployment rate was 30 percent, up a third over 1960.

Success in job hunting is dependent on information about available positions. Family and friends in middle-class communities are good sources for obtaining information about employment. In the ghetto, however, information about job openings is limited by restricted contact with the job market. The slum resident is largely confined to his own neighborhood, where there are few new plants and business offices, and unfortunately state employment services have been generally ineffective even when used.

Most undereducated youngsters do not choose a job. Rather, they drift into one. Since such jobs rarely meet applicants' aspirations, frustration typically results. Some find their way back to school or into a job training program. Some drift fortuitously among low-paying jobs. Others try crime, and, if successful, make it their regular livelihood; others lack aptitude and become failures in [the] illegal as well as the legal world—habitués of our jails and prisons. And there are those who give up, retreat from conventional society and search for a better world in the private fantasies induced by drink and drugs.[11]

EDUCATION IN THE GHETTO

So far we have seen that the ghetto is a portion of the central city that is characterized by poor housing, and that people who live there tend to have less education than the average American, consequently have fewer job opportunities, and, in general, are poorer.

The one bright hope most Americans in earlier periods had for their future generations lay in the schools. A good education has traditionally been the means by which people have escaped from poverty and discrimination and, consequently, from the ghetto. Therefore, education within the ghetto is a particularly acute problem. By and large, schools in black ghettos have failed to liberate the people from their plight. This failure has caused resentment by the black community against schools, a resentment that is not wholly unfounded.

An indication of what happens in a ghetto school is summarized in the following excerpt:

[11] National Commission, *To Establish Justice.*

The low-income ghetto child lives in a home in which books and other artifacts of intellectual interests are rare. His parents are usually themselves too poorly schooled to give him the help and encouragement he needs. They have not had the time—even had they the knowledge—to teach him basic skills that are routinely acquired by most middle-class youngsters: telling time, counting, learning the alphabet and colors, using crayons and paper and paint. He is unaccustomed to verbalizing concepts or ideas. Written communication is probably rare in his experience.

The educational system in the slum is generally poorly equipped. Most schools in the slums have outdated and dilapidated buildings, few texts or library books, the least qualified teachers and substitute teachers, the most overcrowded classrooms, and the least developed counseling and guidance services. These deficiencies are so acute that the school cannot hold a slum child's interest. To him it is boring, dull, and apparently useless, to be endured for a while and then abandoned.

The school experience often represents the last opportunity to counteract the forces in a child's life that are influencing him toward crime and violence. The public school program has always been viewed as a major force for the transmission of legitimate values and goals, and some studies have identified a good school experience as a key factor in the development of "good boys out of bad environment."[12]

Unfortunately, the record of public education for ghetto children has never been very good. In the critical verbal skills of reading and writing, black students in the ghetto schools fall farther and farther behind with each year of school completed. The U.S. Department of Health, Education and Welfare published a report indicating that on the average, minority-group children from the ghetto are somewhat below white children in respect to educational levels upon entering first grade. However, by the sixth grade, standard achievement tests indicate that black students from the ghetto are 1.6 grades behind, and by the twelfth grade, they are 3.3 grades behind the white students who have started school with them.[13]

As a result of this, many minority students drop out of school. Black students are three times as likely as white students to do this. A very high proportion of the dropouts are not equipped to enter the normal job market, and when they do, they tend to get low-skilled, low-paying jobs.

The vast majority of inner-city schools are involved in de facto segregation, principally as the result of residential segregation, combined with widespread employment of the neighborhood-school policy. This, of course, transfers segregation from housing to education. Many of the students in the segregated schools are poor.

---

[12] National Commission, *To Establish Justice*, pp. 32–33.

[13] Department of Health, Education and Welfare, *Equality of Educational Opportunity* (Washington, D.C.: U.S. Government Printing Office, 1966).

Many come from families whose adults were products of inadequate rural school systems of the South, which had very low levels of educational attainment. Children from these families most often have limited vocabularies and are not well equipped to learn rapidly. When these disadvantaged children are racially isolated in ghetto schools, they may be deprived of a significant ingredient of quality education—exposure to other children who have strong educational backgrounds. Most educators and sociologists believe that strong socioeconomic backgrounds of pupils in a school exert a powerful effect upon the achievement of other students in that school. By the nature of the ghetto school, this advantage is denied to most of its pupils.

Teachers in inner-city schools say they have many emotionally disturbed, retarded, and maladjusted students and few facilities to deal with them. Another criticism of ghetto schools is that curricula and materials used there are ordinarily geared to middle-class white suburban students, and textbooks make little or no reference to the achievements and contributions of blacks to American life. Because the schoolwork has little or no relevance to the ghetto youngster's life experience, the youth tends to conclude that education is not relevant to his life.

Many black residents of the inner city are angry about the inadequacies of their schools. Unfortunately, communication between the community and the school administrators tends to be poor, probably because the teachers and administrators tend to live outside the ghetto and do not fully understand its problems. On the other hand, most ghetto parents lack much formal education and generally believe they have little voice in changing school matters. However, they do feel the schools are not providing an adequate education for their children, and they regard this as unjust.[14]

Housing, schools, and employment are only a few of the problems in the ghetto. Let us examine some others.

PROBLEMS OF THE TYPICAL GHETTO FAMILY

For years, criminologists have known that crime rates are always higher in poor neighborhoods, whatever their ethnic composition. The black ghetto is no exception. The black resident's sense of personal security is certainly undermined by the frequency of crime in the big-city ghetto. The ghetto may have as

[14] HEW, *Equality*, p. 20.

much as 35 times as much serious crime per 100,000 residents as does a high-income white district.

Crimes in ghettos are committed by a small minority of the residents. Most of the victims are law-abiding people. It is difficult for middle-class whites to understand how insecure these law-abiding ghetto dwellers feel. In poor black areas, a person is 75 percent more likely to be the victim of a major crime than is a resident of a high-income area.[15]

Because of this high crime rate, many blacks have bitter feelings toward the police. The feeling that they do not receive adequate protection by law enforcement agencies tends to be one of their principal grievances against the police. It is important that law enforcement personnel be aware of this.

Poor families are usually found to have poor diets, poor housing, poor clothing, and poor medical care. Generally speaking, about 30 percent of such families suffer from chronic health problems that have adverse effects upon employment possibilities. Although black ghetto residents have many more health problems than white families with comparable incomes, they spend less than half as much per person on medical services. There are several reasons for this: (1) Black families are usually larger than white families; (2) necessities often cost black people more than they do white people (for instance, housing costs); (3) fewer medical facilities and personnel are available to poor blacks, generally because doctors prefer to practice in high-income areas; and (4) general environmental conditions in the black ghetto are not conducive to good health. Among these conditions are poor sanitation and overcrowding, the lack of decent facilities for storing food, and serious rodent problems.

The ghetto neighborhood itself is one of the problems of the ghetto family:

In many center city alleys are broken bottles and snoring "winos"—homeless, broken men, drunk constantly on cheap wine. Yards, if any, are littered and dirty. Fighting and drunkenness are everyday occurrences. Drug addiction and prostitution are rampant. Living is crowded, often anonymous. Predominantly white store-ownership and white police patrols in predominantly black neighborhoods are frequently resented, reviled, and attacked, verbally and physically. Municipal services such as garbage collection, street repairs,—utility maintenance, and the like are inadequate and, at times, all but nonexistent.

Many ghetto slum children spend much of their time—when they are not watching television—on the streets of this violent, poverty-stricken world.

[15] Report of the National Advisory Commission, p. 83.

Frequently, their image of success is not the solid citizen, the responsible, hard-working husband and father. Rather, the "sucessful" man is the cynical hustler who promotes his own interests by exploiting others—through dope, selling numbers, robbery, and other crimes. Exploitation and hustling become a way of life.[16]

The family structure is also affected by residence in the ghetto. Because the men of the family often cannot obtain jobs in legitimate enterprises that enable them to support their wives and children, their status and self-respect are affected. Almost without exception, women are forced to work or go on welfare so that the family can be provided for economically. Often the women earn more money than the men, and this too may affect the status and self-respect of the husband. With the husband feeling inadequate, the possibility of divorce or separation increases. This, in turn, leads to the fact that more and more ghetto families are being headed by females rather than males. A related factor is that welfare payments are often tied to the absence of the father from the home. Therefore, for the mother and children to survive economically, the father often deliberately absents himself from the home.

The result of these two factors is that almost three times as many black families as white families are fatherless, a situation that greatly affects the attitudes of children in these homes. A report of the federal government says this about these families:

Inner-city families are often large. Many are fatherless, permanently or intermittently; others involve a conflict-ridden marital relationship; in either instance the parents may communicate to their offspring little sense of permanence and few precepts essential to an orderly, peaceful life.

Loosely organized, often with a female focus, many inner-city families bestow upon their children what has been termed "premature autonomy." Their children do not experience adults as being genuinely interested or caring persons. These children may, rather, experience adults as more interested in their own satisfactions than those of their children. Consequently, resentment of authority figures, such as policemen and teachers, is not surprising. With a lack of consistent, genuine concern for children who are a burden to them, the parents may vacillate from being unduly permissive to becoming overly stern. Child-rearing problems are exacerbated where the father is sometimes or frequently absent, intoxicated, or replaced by another man; whose coping with everyday life, with too little money for the size of the family, leaves little time or energy for discipline.[17]

It is easy to see why ghetto residents, particularly young people, may believe they have no stake in the "system" and therefore little to gain by patterning themselves by society's rules. In fact, there seems to be little to lose by *not* conforming to those rules. It is

[16] National Commission, *To Establish Justice,* p. 32.
[17] National Commission, *To Establish Justice,* p. 31.

easy for them to believe that the odds against succeeding in a legitimate enterprise are greater than the odds against succeeding in criminal activities. With this sort of conditioning, violence—either individual or group—in the ghetto is understandable.

The Spanish-surnamed minority

The Spanish-speaking minority is the second largest minority in the United States. In many respects, the lot of these people has been similar to that of the blacks. By and large, the Spanish-surnamed minority lives in a separate residential district that has come to be known as the barrio. In the southwestern part of the United States, this is often a residential district separated from the rest of the population center by a highway or railroad track. Housing in the barrio, as in the ghetto, is dilapidated, aged, and substandard.

When discussing this minority group, it is necessary to remember that it is composed of several groups of people with somewhat different backgrounds. In the five southwestern states of Arizona, California, Colorado, New Mexico, and Texas, most of the Spanish-speaking people are Mexican-Americans. This means that they were either born in Mexico rather than in another Latin American country, or that their ancestors originally came from Mexico. The Spanish-surnamed population of New York, New Jersey, and other eastern states, on the other hand, is largely of Puerto Rican descent. And those with Spanish surnames who live in Florida generally trace their ancestry to Cuba.[18]

Besides being from different countries, their racial ancestry tends to be different. They may be Caucasoid, Indian, or Negroid, or any combination thereof. They are sometimes referred to as Latinos or Hispanics. Also, because of their diverse backgrounds, they tend to be less organized than blacks.

> This minority group of the barrio has almost all the problems that are associated with blacks in the ghetto. To compound the difficulty, there is a language problem. Most of this group learns Spanish as a first language. In a limited study in 1968, it was found that only 24 percent of the children and 15 percent of the parents used English all the time. Furthermore, 37 percent of the parents of these children and 15 percent of the children themselves spoke Spanish in their everyday life.[19]

[18] U.S. Commission on Civil Rights, *Mexican-American Education Study* (Washington, D.C.: U.S. Government Printing Office, 1971), p. 15.

[19] J.G. Anderson and W.H. Johnson, *Social and Cultural Characteristics of Mexican-American Families in South El Paso, Texas,* paper prepared for presentation at the Joint Meeting of the American Association for the Advancement of Science with the National Council of Teachers of Mathematics, December 27, 1968, Dallas, Texas, p. 7.

The child who learns Spanish as a first language often has a problem when entering the American public school, where English is the language used. For a time in the 1920s and 1930s, Spanish-surnamed people were considered to be less intelligent because of their problems with schoolwork. Since that time, however, there has developed an awareness of the many variables that affect school achievement, including health and nutritional status as well as language inadequacies.

The problem of overcoming the handicap of learning English as a second language, coupled with segregation of the Spanish-speaking students in school, has had its negative effect. Until the late 1940s, there was segregation of the Mexican-Americans on a de jure (legal) basis in the Southwest.[20] Today there is still de facto segregation of such students within the school system; such segregation is related to residential patterns.

Unfortunately, a member of the Spanish-speaking minority tends to have a problem receiving a good education in English. The result is that this person has problems selling his or her services on the job market, thus continuing the cycle of poverty.

But the solution to the language problem is not rectified by a simple course in English. Many children with Spanish surnames, who are second- and third-generation American citizens, speak Spanish as poorly as they do English. Many of them speak a combination of English and Spanish slang that is quite difficult for language instructors to deal with.

Equal justice in the courts

The problems of both the ghetto and the barrio are sometimes felt to be a reflection of the general social structure of the society and its lack of concern for equal justice among the minority groups. The institutional structure of the courts and their history have had a telling effect upon the present social structure of the ghetto and barrio. Lest it seem, however, that the courts have been wholly responsible for the present situation, one must remember that to a large extent they have been responsible for some of the changes for the better that are happening to minority groups in the community.

The great majority of people accused of crime in this country are poor. The system of criminal justice under which they are judged is rooted in the idea that arrests can be made only for good cause and that those arrested are presumed innocent until proved

[20] Commission on Civil Rights, *Mexican-American Education Study*, pp. 13–14.

guilty. By and large, the accused are entitled to pretrial freedom to aid in their own defense. A plea of guilty should be voluntary, and all the allegations of criminal behavior are to be submitted to the adversary system that is referred to as the "bar of justice."

The importance of the courts is underlined by the fact that even though relatively few criminal matters reach trial, some of those that do so establish the legal rules that affect not only all future cases but the public image of justice as a whole.

To examine this system as it relates to minority-group members, some consideration should be given to the history of the court's treatment of minority groups.

HISTORICAL HIGHLIGHTS OF COURTS AND MINORITY-GROUP MEMBERS

The most appropriate place to start examining minority-group treatment before the courts is the *Dred Scott* decision,[21] which was handed down by the Supreme Court in 1857. This case concerned a Negro slave who had lived with his master for five years in Illinois and Wisconsin Territory. At the time these were free states, whereas the southern states were slave states. The court decided that because Scott was a slave, he was therefore not a citizen. Consequently, he could not even sue in court.

This decision quite plainly indicated that a little under 125 years ago, people of a minority group had no rights whatsoever in court. However, in 1868, the Fourteenth Amendment to the Constitution was passed, stating in part:

All persons born or naturalized in the United States, and subject to the jurisdiction thereof, are citizens of the United States and of the State wherein they reside. No State shall make or enforce any law which shall abridge the privileges or immunities of citizens of the United States; nor shall any State deprive any person of life, liberty, or property, without due process of law; nor deny to any person within its jurisdiction the equal protection of the laws.

The amendment clearly established that members of a minority group were to be treated equally under the law. However, for many years following this, the courts interpreted the law in the light of a doctrine that was known as "separate but equal rights." The case of *Plessy* v. *Ferguson*,[22] decided by the U.S. Supreme Court in 1896, upheld this doctrine as it related to the civil rights of American Negroes. In many areas, especially regarding schools, the

[21] *Dred Scott* v. *Stanford*, 19 How. 393 (1857).

[22] *Plessy* v. *Ferguson*, 163 U.S. 537 (1896).

doctrine of separate but equal was prevalent. In most cases, however, facilities may have been separate but were far from equal. Obviously, for the minority groups, they were inferior.

A study by Guy Johnson, which covers the years 1930 to 1940, indicates that in most southern courts, Negroes who committed offenses against other Negroes were dealt with no more severely than whites who committed crimes against other whites. Differentiation was made when a Negro perpetrated a crime against a Caucasian; the Negro was dealt with quite severely.[23] The Johnson study did not take into account the probability that more accused blacks than accused whites were convicted. This situation was probably related to the fact that blacks in general were poorer than Caucasians, and unfortunately, a great discriminating factor in criminal justice is whether or not the accused has sufficient financial means. People who have money are much more likely to be treated leniently by the courts than people who do not.

More recently, the Supreme Court has made some rulings that should change this. One of the first landmark decisions regarding equality of justice was *Shelly* v. *Kraemer*,[24] which struck down restrictive covenants in housing. Theoretically at least, it enabled members of a minority to legally buy a residence wherever they wished to; from a pratical standpoint, it was necessary to resolve each issue with new litigation. However, part of the reasoning in this case led to another landmark case.

In 1954, the *Brown* v. *Board of Education* ruling declared that the separate-but-equal doctrine that had been used to segregate the public schools was unconstitutional.[25] This case was specifically concerned with the board of education of Topeka, Kansas, but similar cases in Virginia, Delaware, and South Carolina were decided at the same time. This ruling by the Supreme Court began the process of correcting injustice to minority-group members.

It should be noted that segregated schools for Mexican-American youngsters were earlier found to be a violation of due process and equal protection of the law guaranteed under the Fifth and Fourteenth Amendments—in 1947 in California [26] and in 1948 in Texas.[27] Essentially, then, "separate-but-equal" schools have been ruled inappropriate for all minority groups.

The Supreme Court has actively led this country toward a

---

[23] G.B. Johnson, "The Negro and Crime," in M. Wolfgang, L. Savitz, and N. Johnson, eds., *The Sociology of Crime and Delinquency* (New York: John Wiley, 1962), pp. 145–53.

[24] *Shelly* v. *Kraemer*, 68 Sup. Ct. 836 (1948).

[25] *Brown* v. *Board of Education*, 347 U.S. 483 (1954).

[26] *Mendez et al.* v. *Westminister School District in Orange* County et al., 64 Supp. 544 affirmed 161 F, 2d 774 (9th Cir. 1947).

[27] *Delgado* v. *Bastrop Independent School District*, Civ. No. 388 (D.C. WD Tex. 1948).

fuller understanding of the high ideals set forth in the Constitution. Through various decisions, it has begun to equalize a poor person's chances before the bar of justice with those of someone who has more money. This is most important to minority-group members, because they tend to be poorer than members of the white majority. Among the cases that probably did most for minorities in this indirect manner was *Gideon* v. *Wainwright*,[28] decided in 1963. Gideon was charged with breaking and entering a poolroom. At his trial in Florida, he was refused counsel. When the U.S. Supreme Court reviewed the case, it decided that legal assistance is the right of anyone charged with a crime and is fundamental to a fair trial. (It should be noted that when Gideon, with competent counsel, was later retried, he was found not guilty.)

A second case of interest is *Miranda* v. *Arizona*.[29] This case, decided by the Supreme Court in 1966, concerned a confession admitted as evidence in a rape charge. It developed that Miranda had not been informed of his constitutional rights to remain silent and to have legal counsel. The Supreme Court reversed his conviction on the grounds that a person arrested for a crime should be given a fourfold warning before he is questioned: He has a right to remain silent; anything he says may be used against him; he has a right to have an attorney present during the questioning; and if he is indigent, he has a right to have an attorney furnished to him without charge. (Miranda was retried and again found guilty of the crime of rape.)

A third case that was important in bringing about equal justice for minority groups was *in re Gault,* decided in 1967.[30] Gault, a minor, was found to be a "delinquent youngster" and was committed to a state facility in Arizona. However, at the time of his arrest, he was not given the full warning that the court felt reasonable for an adult; furthermore, he had not been provided an attorney and was given no opportunity to face his accusers. All these rights had, before this time, been spelled out for adults. In the *Gault* case, the Supreme Court ruled that they should also be applied to minors being tried in a juvenile court. The *Gault* case is important because from 40 to 50 percent of those arrested for crimes in the United States are juveniles. In addition, as with adults, a disproportionate number come from minority groups and tend to be poor residents of the ghetto or barrio.

The next most important court decision that affects minorities, principally Spanish-surnamed minorities, was a 1974 decision, *Lau*

[28] *Gideon* v. *Wainwright,* 372 U.S. 335 (1963).
[29] *Miranda* v. *Arizona,* 384 U.S. 436 (1966).
[30] *In re Gault,* 387 U.S. 1 (1967).

v. *Nichols*.[31] This case concerned a Chinese youth who spoke only a Chinese dialect. Because of this, it was impossible to educate him in the San Francisco public school system. The Supreme Court ruled that he must be provided an education in his primary language, rather than in English. The long range significance of this ruling to the Spanish-speaking minority can only be estimated. However, it did bring about the development of bilingual educational programs which should be helpful to minorities.

The Bakke decision (*Bakke* v. *State of California*, 1978) indicated that race or ethnic background alone could not be used for setting a quota for admission to college. The decision did say that race/ethnic background could be considered. From a practical standpoint that decision was not important; maybe from a philosophical view it was somewhat of a set back for minorities.

More important has been the affirmative action programs as American companies attempted to deal more equitably with minorities.

During the 1970's, affirmative action began to have some effect in the workplace. The result was that more and more minority members began getting jobs that reflected their education and their abilities.

BAIL AND OTHER METHODS OF RELEASE

Traditionally, criminal cases begin with an arrest. This is followed by detention until a magistrate can decide on the amount of bail the accused may post for release before trial. In its present form, the bail system discriminates against and consequently punishes the poor. The affluent can afford to buy their freedom, but the poor go to jail. Because of this, the defendant without funds may lose his job and his present earning capacity—all this before the trial and before there has been a determination of guilt or innocence. The result may be, in effect, that a person is punished severely for being poor rather than for being guilty.[32]

However, many changes in the bail system have been taking place recently. Some of them show promise of giving more equal justice to the poverty-stricken and, consequently, to minority groups in general.

More and more, law enforcement agencies are coming to the conclusion that in certain circumstances, there are alternatives to arrest. There is no question but that arrest and detention are needed

---

[31] *Lau* v. *Nichols*, 42 U.S. Law Week 4165 (1974).

[32] R. Goldfarb, *Ransom: A Critique on the American Bail System* (New York: John Wiley, 1965).

if the crime is serious or if there is danger of the defendant's fleeing from court jurisdiction. Police may feel that the defendant needs to be fingerprinted and photographed as well as searched and questioned. However, generally speaking, an arrest followed by detention is not usual in traffic matters, and there is reason to believe that arrest for certain other offenses need not be followed by detention. Offenses involving petty crimes and local code violations may well be handled in another way.

Alternatives to routine arrest and detention have been developed by several states and by federal courts. These alternatives generally take two forms. In the first situation, a judicial officer issues a summons upon complaint of the prosecutor; in the second, a police officer issues a citation or a notice to appear, much like a traffic ticket. In a number of areas, citations have been used for misdemeanant offenses. Then, unless an arrest is necessary to protect the community, the court process, or the defendant, a misdemeanor suspect is released at the scene of the offense upon identifying himself or herself. The arresting officer decides upon the summons process after checking with headquarters through the computer-based police intelligence network system.

A number of states and the federal government have developed a second method of processing those arrested for criminal acts without subjecting them to posting of bail. In this method, people are released on their own recognizance.[33]

Moves of this kind by the justice system have somewhat improved the chances of the poor defendant for equal treatment before the court. Furthermore, release before trial of a person accused of crime has apparently not posed a serious threat to the community or the justice system per se.

THE POOR AND CIVIL LITIGATION

As far as can be determined, in many matters of criminal justice, the courts have made an increased effort to treat minority-group members much more fairly. It is possible, however, that the emphasis on criminal-court problems has somehow screened out the need for reform in civil problems that are peculiar to the poor.

According to Thomas E. Willinge, the major barrier to justice for poor people is the inability to receive expert legal counsel.[34]

---

[33] The President's Commission on Law Enforcement and Administration of Justice, *Task Force Report: The Courts* (Washington, D.C.: U.S. Government Printing Office, 1967), pp. 40–41.

[34] T.E. Willinge, "Financial Barriers and the Access of Indigents to the Courts," *The Georgetown Law Journal*, 57, No. 2 (November 1968), 253–306.

Although adequate counsel is a necessity for successful litigation, our efforts to provide it for the poor have not worked out very well. For example, a poor man who believes that his landlord may be right, or that the alleged debt he owes is just, usually does not bother to show up in court. The person who does come to court feels that he has a good case, and that he has been treated unjustly. But for the most part, lawyers represent businessmen, and they usually win judgments against the bewildered, intimidated poor. Too often, the poor leave the courtroom as losers, without any feeling that justice has been done. Consequently, equity in civil matters is often not the case for poor people.

A second factor, of course, is the financial barrier. Under our system of justice, the Constitution guarantees free access to civil courts for all citizens. However, many poor people are frightened by the court system, which they view as being rigged against them because they are frequently unsuccessful litigants. Therefore, they are faced with loss of time and money as well as court costs if they lose a case.

There have been some efforts at changing such inequities. These efforts have come from people who have been involved in organizing consumer-protection agencies. Although consumer protection has generally been a concern of the middle class in the United States, it certainly has great importance for the poor. Its implications are such that continued review of its progress, as well as some knowledge of where a person might go for redress of grievances, would probably be quite useful to all patrol officers. If they were able to direct people with grievances of this sort to the appropriate agencies, this in itself could be a well-appreciated community-relations gesture.

Police, minority groups, and equal justice

In most instances, the decision to initiate criminal prosecution is a matter of police judgment. Supposedly, this judgment is based upon the legal definition of crime. However, in many cases in which a violation of the law has occurred and the police know of this violation, they do not act. Some of the factors that cause this discrepancy are (1) the volume of criminal law violations and the limited resources of the police, (2) the enactment of laws that define criminal conduct in a generalized manner, and (3) various pressures reflecting the attitudes of a particular community.

An example of this dilemma is social gambling. In most jurisdictions, gambling is illegal. Yet there is good reason to believe that complete enforcement of antigambling laws is neither expected nor intended. For example, in 1974, a number of people were arrested for playing penny-ante poker in a senior citizens' home in San Francisco. The court dismissed the charges against these people even though within the definition of the law they were probably guilty.

Law enforcement agencies are left with the responsibility of deciding whether or not to enforce antigambling statutes in the communities they serve. Thus, bingo may be tolerated at church functions, and bookmaking in the community may be prosecuted. Also, the police may be confronted with the problem of deciding whether gambling in a private home constitutes a violation of the antigambling statutes. For the average white middle-class American, a small game of poker within the confines of one's own home is possible because the indoor living space is adequate. On the other hand, in the crowded ghetto, where indoor living space is at a premium, games of chance are often moved to a dead-end street or alley. When police are informed that such a game is taking place in a ghetto, they generally respond and arrest the players. They justify their intervention by saying that such arrests serve to prevent crime because past experience shows that card games in the ghetto frequently end in fights; those played in suburban areas generally do not.[35] Consequently, although the police intention might be quite noble, the practice gives the appearance of improper class and racial discrimination.

Another example of the discrepancy in prosecution is the handling of assaultive-type offenses. These offenses come to the attention of law enforcement agencies quite frequently because they occur in public. Police, therefore, wish to intervene before more harm is done, or because the victim is found by a patrol unit to be in need of medical aid. Although the perpetrator of the assault is known to the victim in a large percentage of the cases, frequently there is no arrest or, if an arrest is made, it is followed by release of the alleged assailant without prosecution. This seems to be especially true in ghetto areas, owing, according to law enforcement personnel, primarily to an unwillingness on the part of the victim to cooperate in the prosecution. Even if the victim should cooperate during the investigation stage, this willingness often disappears at the time of trial. It might be possible for police to achieve some success in assault cases by subpoenaing the victim to testify, but the subpoena process is seldom used. Instead, the path of least resistance—the decision not to prosecute—is followed

---

[35] The President's Commission, *Task Force Report: The Police* (Washington, D.C.: U.S. Government Printing Office, 1967), pp. 21–22.

when the victim appears unwilling to testify. Police justify this action by pointing out the high volume of cases and other compelling demands made upon the agency. It is further rationalized on the grounds that the injured party was the only person harmed and does not wish to pursue the matter. Cases of this sort can be written off statistically as cleared cases, which then constitute an index of police efficiency.

These kinds of police practices, particularly in the ghetto, give rise to the question of the degree to which police tolerance of assaultive conduct results in the formation of negative attitudes by ghetto residents toward law and order in general.[36] How can a ghetto resident consider law enforcement fair when an attack by a ghetto resident upon a person residing outside the ghetto generally results in a vigorous prosecution?

Many minority-group members believe that police brutality and harassment occur repeatedly in black neighborhoods. This is one of the main reasons for minority-group resentment against the police. To a large extent, however, research reported by the federal government seems to show that these beliefs are unjustified:

> One survey done by the Crime Commission suggests that when police–citizen contacts are systematically observed, the vast majority are handled without antagonism or incident. Of 5,339 police–community contacts observed in slum precincts in three large cities, in the opinion of the observer, only 20—about three-tenths of one percent—involved excessive or unnecessary force. And almost all of those subjected to such force were poor, more than half were white.[37]

In another study, conducted by the Center of Research on Social Organization, the data seem to support the same kind of conclusion.[38] In this study, observations of police arrests were made in Boston, Chicago, and Washington, D.C., seven days a week for seven weeks. Professional observers accompanied policemen on their calls and to the stations where bookings and lockups were made. There were 643 white suspects and 751 black suspects in the sample. Twenty-seven of the whites and 17 of the blacks experienced undue use of force when they were arrested. This yields an abuse rate of 41.9 per thousand white suspects and 22.6 per thousand black suspects.

Thus, physical abuse does not seem to be practiced against minority-group members in a greater degree than against majority-group members. However, physical abuse is certainly not the only

[36] The President's Commission, *Task Force Report: The Police*, p. 22.

[37] *Report of the National Advisory Commission*, p. 159.

[38] A.J. Reiss, Jr., "Police Brutality—Answers to Key Questions," *Trans-Action*, 5 (July–August 1968), 10–19.

source of irritation to the ghetto resident. Any police practice that degrades a citizen's status, restricts his freedom, or annoys or harasses him is felt to be an unjust use of powers by police enforcement personnel. A policeman's talking down to a person or calling him or her names is particularly objectionable; this type of treatment strips people of their dignity. Also, police are often inclined to command minority-group members to "get going" or "get home." Because homes in ghetto areas tend to be overcrowded, young ghetto residents are the most likely target of this type of authority, especially during the hot summer months when ghetto youths spend most of their time in public places or walking the streets because they have no other place to go.

An article about an incident that occurred in Washington, D.C., might be construed by minority groups as harassment. This incident involved a man who had been arrested three times in two weeks' time—once for littering when he dropped a paper cup, and twice for drinking in public. The latter occurred when the man was found drinking a beer while sitting behind a laundromat.[39] Incidents of this type are generally regarded as police harassment by ghetto residents.

Everyone agrees that a police officer needs to be able to act in a judicious manner in innumerable situations. However, there seems to be further evidence that for the police as an organization to be better able to deal with the public, the police need to understand all the public they serve. There are those who feel that an ethnic minority cannot be understood by anyone other than a member of that minority. Whether or not this is true—and the authors regard it as very doubtful—is unimportant. What is important is for the public that is served to *believe* that it is understood. Consequently, every effort needs to be made to get fair representation of ethnic minorities into law enforcement.

Summary

The ghetto and barrio are characterized by poverty and social disorganization. Mainly because of poverty and segregation, much of the housing in these areas tends to be substandard, overcrowded, old, and deteriorated. Underemployment and unemployment are critical problems of ghetto and barrio dwellers and may well be the key to their poverty. For example, twice as many black people as white people are unemployed, and black

[39] H. Blum, "The Police," in S. Endleman, ed., *Violence in the Streets* (Chicago: Quadrangle Books, 1968), pp. 417–33.

people are three times more likely to be underemployed. These circumstances help to strengthen the poverty cycle. For the Spanish-speaking minority, the problem of English being a second language affects the ability to succeed in school; this in turn affects job potential—another continuation of the poverty cycle.

Poverty and family disorganization, as well as tension and insecurity, are part of the ghetto and barrio community. Crime rates are far higher than in other areas of the city. Narcotics addiction, juvenile delinquency, venereal disease, poor health services, and dependency on welfare are all prevalent in these areas. The law enforcement student is reminded that the high crime rate causes the residents of these areas to feel bitter toward the police because they believe they do not receive adequate protection.

Neighborhood schools in these areas tend to be the worst in the school system. The result is that far more minority-group students leave school before graduating than do majority-group students. And a good education has traditionally been the means by which people have escaped from poverty and moved toward more equal treatment in society.

Historic court decisions and statutes have been instrumental in changing minority-group treatment and affirming the legal rights of the indigent. Because minority-group members are often without funds, these decisions should have a far-reaching effect on their treatment in courts. Our bail system and the handling of civil cases by the courts show how poor people are often adversely affected by the judicial process.

Police practices greatly affect equal justice regarding minorities—particularly the police tendency to enforce certain types of violations differently in the ghetto and barrio than elsewhere. An example is the enforcement of antigambling laws in poor sections as opposed to the lack of rigid enforcement in the suburbs.

According to research done by the federal government, acts of police brutality are apparently not related as much to minority-group prejudice as they are to poverty. Police harassment, often called police brutality by minorities, is a good example of the problem in communication between police and minority groups. Incidents of police harassment seem to be highest among the youth of ethnic minorities. It is felt that when each law enforcement officer understands some of the minority-group complaints regarding unequal justice, he or she will be better equipped to understand members of minority groups and to communicate better. Such meaningful communication will lead to the solution of many of the problems in the area of police–community relations.

Discussion topics

1. What is a ghetto? What is a barrio?
2. What does a ghetto or a barrio have to do with equal treatment for minorities?
3. Why should the conditions in a ghetto or barrio be of concern to law enforcement personnel?
4. What does learning English as a second language have to do with the poverty cycle?
5. Explain why it is felt that the courts have changed their attitudes toward minorities over the past 125 years.
6. In what area have the courts been slow in acting in the best interests of minorities?
7. How can consumer-protection agencies help alleviate tension in the ghetto and barrio?
8. Explain the difference between police brutality and police harassment.

Annotated references

Clear, Val, and S. Clear, "Horizons in the Criminal Justice System," *Crime and Delinquency,* 20, No. 1 (January 1974), 25–32. A concise treatment of changes in the criminal justice system.

Department of Health, Education and Welfare, *Equality of Educational Opportunity.* Washington, D.C.: U.S. Government Printing Office, 1966. An extensive study of the education received in ghetto schools as it compares with that of suburban schools. This study is often referred to as the Coleman Report.

Endleman, S., ed., *Violence in the Streets.* Chicago: Quadrangle Books, 1968. A collection of essays regarding violence and police response to criminal behavior. The writers represented in this work seem to form a broad spectrum of political persuasion.

Harris, R., *Justice: The Crisis of Law, Order and Freedom in America.* New York: Avon, 1970. An exceptional and perceptive work of political and social analysis.

The National Commission on the Causes and Prevention of Violence, *To Establish Justice, to Insure Domestic Tranquility.* Washington, D.C.:

U.S. Government Printing Office, 1969. This is the final report of several Task Force Reports that were concerned with the problem of violence, both group and individual, in the United States.

The President's Commission on Law Enforcement and Administration of Justice, *Task Force Report: The Courts.* Washington, D.C.: U.S. Government Printing Office, 1967. This is part of the supporting material for the commission's report, *The Challenge of Crime in a Free Society.* It provides a very good description of the criminal courts and how they function.

The President's Commission on Law Enforcement and Administration of Justice, *Task Force Report: The Police.* Washington, D.C.: U.S Government Printing Office, 1967. This is also part of the supporting material for *The Challenge of Crime in a Free Society.* All law enforcement students should take time to familiarize themselves with the materials in this book.

Report of the National Advisory Commission on Civil Disorders. Washington, D.C.: U.S. Government Printing Office, 1968. A comprehensive study of several of the riots that occurred during the 1960s. It is also an extensive investigation of conditions in the ghetto. Often referred to as the Kerner Report.

United States Commission on Civil Rights, *Mexican-American Education Study.* Washington, D.C.: U.S. Government Printing Office, 1971. This report concerns itself with problems of education of Spanish-speaking children, particularly Mexican-American students in the Southwest.

chapter three

Social Problems in Constitutional Government: Impact on Law Enforcement

In this chapter there will be an introduction of two separate concepts that have great influence on how American law is enforced, or in some cases, not enforced. These two concepts are social problems as related to law enforcement, and the constitutional form of government as related to law enforcement. Consideration of these two concepts will be in terms of how they influence each other, as well as how they impact on law enforcement.

The word *government* suggests the concept of enforcement. The very nature of the process of governing implies a capability of enforcing rules for those who are governed. A valid argument could be made that there is no need to govern unless there is a need to enforce. Of course, these considerations are far too philosophical to be of immediate concern in regard to the effect on law enforcement of government reaction to social problems. Nevertheless, thorough understanding of the effect of social problems on law enforcement requires the fundamental understanding that *government* implies enforcement.

In examining the relationship between law enforcement and social problems more specifically, we must give some thought to the type of government that is involved. The so-called totalitarian governments in which police authority is unlimited are affected differently than the "democratic" governments of which the United States is one. Typical of the democratic government is the *constitutional* basis for enforcing government rules. Constitutional government, then, is an important consideration in examining how social problems influence the enforcement of American law.

For our purposes in this discussion, constitutional government can be thought of as simply a governing process controlled by a written constitution that sets forth the rights and powers of citizens as well as the rights and powers of government. In the case of the United States, the powers and rights of citizens are delineated in the Bill of Rights, which also specifies certain limitations on the powers of American government. Both the Constitution itself and the Bill of Rights are interpreted and reinterpreted by higher-court rulings from time to time, but they essentially remain the basis of government power to enforce American law.

By government power is meant the fundamental nature of the social contract that exists between government and the governed. This contract calls for government to confine its power within the limits of the Constitution, and the governed to respect that power so long as it does not exceed the limits of the Constitution. Creating such a contract also creates a kind of give-and-take between government and governed, with the courts intended to settle differences. Recent history has indicated, however, that not all differences can be settled by the courts, and that such unsettled differences are usually classified as social problems.

Such social problems may or may not impact directly on law enforcement. Some of what is called a social problem may actually be a crime problem; for example, riots in urban centers that are sometimes associated with social problems can be naively rationalized as being no different from a wave of armed robberies; both the riots and the robberies are simply a lot of a given violation of the law during a limited period of time. It would be difficult to say how widespread such oversimplification is. However, most veteran police officers with experience in dealing with social unrest would probably contend that law violation associated with social problems differs significantly from "ordinary crime," even though both may be violations of law. Take, for example, the social problems of increasing family strife and the ensuing increase in the divorce rate.

FAMILY CRISIS AS AN EXAMPLE

The last few decades have witnessed an enormous increase in the demand for and the acquisition of human rights. But although the width and breadth of human rights throughout the world have increased, a tremendous strain has been placed on the family as a unit, particularly in the United States. Traditional definitions of roles for men, women, and children give way to often conflicting notions of what is, or should be, expected of each family member—and in some instances, nothing is expected. To no one's surprise, substantial increases in divorce occur as the constitutional government affords every person the "right" to advocate radical changes in the laws dealing with the family. Government could scarcely argue a need for strong powerful controls of family life without raising serious questions regarding the Bill of Rights.

The question of why police even have an interest in the strife a private family may experience can be dealt with only from the perspective of potential problems for police work. The high risk of physical injury to family members as well as to police during such disturbances can be cited as a rationale for police interest in family interaction.

Similarly, the question of police interest in proponents of radical changes can be dealt with only from the perspective of potential police problems . . . violence, even riots, serving as the rationale.

But interest is usually not a cursory thing for police in either family disturbances or radical social activism. Indeed, police increasingly are called upon to recognize ultrasophisticated theories of cause and effect, and to apply these theories to an everchanging, complicated social scene within a community or a family.

In other words, even though the involvement of police in family fights is not a new phenomenon, the degree and the severity of domestic disputes may indeed increase as the social change in the family structure continues. Police have historically dealt with family disputes, but it has become fairly commonplace for police to find severe danger in their efforts to cope with family problems:

> With neighbors peering from behind closed windowshades, a police patrolman emerged from his prowl car, walked to the front door and knocked. Moments later, the officer lay dead—shot by a man involved in a "family fight."[1]

[1] Alan R. Coffey, *Police Intervention into Family Crisis* (Santa Cruz, Calif.: Davis Publishing Co., 1977), p. 1.

Speculation about how much stimulation violent family arguments receive from efforts to change family roles offers little yield. Various interpretations of the phenomenon seem to reflect more the biases and beliefs of the interpreter than hard, cold scientific facts. It is nonetheless clear that police agencies throughout the land have formalized training in dealing with family crises, as well as hostage crises and a host of other specialty crises associated with "social problems."[2] This evolution of police specialties generally seems to coincide with the pace of expanding human rights throughout the world and, in particular, in the democratic constitutional governments.

Of course, evolving a police specialty to deal with something as removed from law enforcement as family life is but one example of a steady increase in the complexity of police work—a complexity that has steadily increased for the police of Western civilization since the Magna Carta. Perhaps the clearest path to further consideration of the effect of social problems on police is the constitutional expectation that police *ensure* orderly government, or at least an orderly environment in which to conduct government.

Orderly environment for government

The idea of creating an orderly environment in which to conduct government requires recognition that the citizen depends on government to *ensure* individual freedom. No person, regardless of wealth or power, is capable of absolutely protecting all his or her own rights without some form of neutral agreement—some form of government. The earliest primitive man recognized this and eventually contrived methods of regulating the behavior of his peers, particularly when it became apparent that doing so was a prime requisite for survival.

Ever since Cain's assault on his brother Abel, society has had the continuing need to regulate behavior. For in the absence of deliberate and concrete efforts at such regulation, man has historically demonstrated an inclination to foster his own survival and well-being at the expense of his fellow man.

An individual's relationship to the society is one of dependence. In exchange for permitting our own behavior to be regulated, we depend on our society to provide personal safety for us.

[2] See, as one example, National Institute of Law Enforcement, *Training Police as Specialists in Family Crisis Intervention,* (Washington, D.C.: U.S. Dept. of Justice, U.S. Government Printing Office, 1975), p. iii.

In this context, society is, or should be, an enforcer. And because human beings present such great variety in their willingness to be regulated, this enforcement function becomes necessary for society's very existence.

SOCIAL CONTRACT AND ENFORCEMENT

Before moving ahead with the discussion of social problems and constitutional government, it might be useful to examine some of the philosophies that relate the enforcement of law to the freedom of the individual. Perhaps the best point to begin such an examination is the recognition that individuals contract (at least implicitly) to *permit* their conduct to be regulated. All societies provide for the personal safety of their members who permit their own behavior to be regulated—despite the fact that certain regulations seem at times to be virtually impossible to either observe or enforce. Consider the myriad regulations inherent in all the many statutes at the state, local, and federal levels.

But in societies that permit great personal freedom, as is the case with modern constitutional governments, the individual can acquire property, or at least property rights. Such societies obviously differ from those in which the state attempts to retain the rights to all property. The question of property rights relates to social problems through government enforcement of rules and the methods used to enforce them. The strain on law enforcement emerges when we consider that the rationale for such enforcement is, at least in part, the retention of an *orderly environment* in which to govern.

Paradoxically, it is this very orderly environment that many who seek to change certain rules feel compelled to attack in order to make the change. The paradox, of course, is that if the rule is changed, then law enforcement supports those who would disrupt the orderly environment for which law enforcement is responsible. It should not be surprising, therefore, that the rules regulating human behavior in a constitutional form of society, along with the standards of enforcing the rules, increase in complexity as the paradox itself increases: The more the orderly environment is jeopardized in order to change the rules to be enforced, the greater the enforcement problem for those charged with keeping the orderly environment. Theoretically, so much effort could be expended in enforcing the orderly environment rules that no enforcement energy would remain for enforcing rules even after they had been changed.

In seeking to promote the orderly environment through law enforcement, government restricts human behavior to protect both the freedom of those who do not wish to experience change and the freedom of those who do. In both cases, impartiality is necessary to convince those of either orientation of the definite relationship between conformity to existing rules and personal freedom to attempt to change rules. The manner in which the rule changes are attempted then becomes a focal point for law enforcement.

Retaining the goal of an orderly society requires government to take into consideration the relationship between society's power and the power of man's will. Much of what is called the wisdom of the ages deals with this very relationship in one way or another. And this relationship defines most of what are called social problems. For, in the final analysis, the power of the individual is equally potent whether in support of or in dissent from the society's system of providing personal safety and property security. Any veteran police officer will surely agree that without general public support, complete law enforcement is not possible.

The question emerges as to whether the general population is for or against the existing government.

THE STATUS OF EXISTING GOVERNMENT

For the most part, popular elections determine whether the general population supports or opposes the government. The presidential elections every four years, the senatorial and congressional elections at the federal level, and the various legislative structures in the fifty states afford the population a continuing method of condoning or rejecting whatever it is that they perceive as the government's activities. Economic recessions, depressions, or excessive inflation, along with wars and other major generators of unrest, accelerate the changes in the public's perception of the government's performance. In the perspective of the effect of social problems on law enforcement, the significance of man's will increases in terms of the individual's support for or opposition to government. If the individual will is committed to, for example, avoiding war, government efforts to promote war will be resisted.

Regardless of whether it is for or against the existing or established government, the individual will is important. When that will is in opposition to the government, it is usually the source of major problems to law enforcement, particularly if the opposition has insufficient numbers to make its point through the election process—by voting against what it perceives as unacceptable government.

This is not to say that law enforcement must necessarily be concerned with all minority viewpoints. However, the constitutional, democratic approach to governing, when structured on the basis of elected representatives, does tend to cause those without a majority viewpoint to "lose" the elective process. And this fact brings attention to whether the individual will is in support of or opposition to the government. Concern for whether people support or oppose the government is necessary, if for no other reason than the jeopardy in which the government's existing system of providing an orderly environment is placed whenever those seeking to change the government disrupt that environment. Not surprisingly, many of those in law enforcement feel they are compressed between two very restrictive alternatives—*suppress change* or *make change*—neither of which is a workable alternative for the police function in a democratic society.

But even though police have no legitimate responsibility to either suppress or to make changes, law enforcement nevertheless retains a crucial interest in government reaction to social problems. Suppression of change may be appropriate in a totalitarian government, but it is totally unacceptable in a constitutional government. The limit of the police role in this regard is usually to determine precisely *what* changes are being sought and *by whom,* and to attempt to remain detached from whether the change is appropriate or inappropriate—monitoring only the orderly environment necessary to continue the government operation.

Emphasis should be placed upon this complete lack of option for law enforcement—upon the fact that orderly environment and law enforcement create the entire scope of the police responsibility. This is not to say that police cannot *promote* the orderly environment for which they are responsible.[3] They have some fairly recent models of efforts in this regard. In the student unrest of the 1960s, for example, police found themselves deeply involved in social change, frequently in a violent manner. Only one of many signs of unrest, this might serve as an example of how police in recent history have been forced to cope with threats to the orderly environment in the name of changing the rules that police enforce.

SOCIAL UNREST: AN EXAMPLE

In any given decade, history for law enforcement may seem to be simply the events of the preceding decade. While this approach

---

[3] Patricia Hunsicker, Community Services Project, Orange County, California, *Better Ways to Help Youth: Three Youth Service Systems* (Washington, D.C.: U.S. Department of Health, Education and Welfare, 1973), p. 29.

to history is academically inappropriate, there *is* merit in recognizing that events of the last few decades were major influences on American law enforcement agencies' relationships to social problems. Consider the sometimes obscure relationship between the student unrest associated with the unpopular Vietnam War and police functions.

Even though this example by no means encompasses the entire complex range of social change that has occurred in the United States in the past several decades, it nevertheless does afford a meaningful perspective for law enforcement. Of course, the notion of student nonconformity is nothing new. Even before panty raids and goldfish swallowing, most college campuses had accumulated a history of incidents in which segments of the student body had drawn attention to themselves via nonconformity. But insofar as the government was concerned, and particularly the orderly environment for which law enforcement is responsible, the questions students began posing in regard to the Vietnam War were a clear challenge to that environment.

A clearly different pattern of student dissent began to emerge on college campuses at approximately the time of enrollment by students whose parents had been directly involved in World War II—and many still believe this was a significant coincidence. By the early 1960s, this new pattern had drawn mass attention through student demonstrations. The demands made by the students ranged from free speech to the prevention of the military from recruiting on a college campus. However, it became clear ultimately that draft card burning and the like were not the central problem for law enforcement—the problem was the gross disruption of the orderly environment.

Student revolt was far from the only source of assault on the orderly environment in the 1960s and 1970s. Many other problems, perhaps of greater immediate concern to law enforcement, took the form of planned civil disobedience in which the law violation was declared, even advertised in advance. It became commonplace for mature people, including prominent citizens, celebrities, and the like, to place themselves in a position of being arrested in order to take part in a "social movement"—a practice that has by no means been eliminated.

The functions of constitutional government in relation to student revolt afford many clues to the interpretation of the kind of social tensions that affect the orderly environment for which law enforcement is responsible. For one thing, constitutional government in relation to student revolt affords an opportunity to examine extremism—and more particularly, the *degree* of extremism.

INTERPRETING THE DEGREE OF EXTREMISM

There was a time when panty raids were thought to be the behavior of extremists, but the nature of student nonconformity during the 1960s and early 1970s clearly modified that perception. From the perspective of law enforcement, the assessment of extremism during the two decades in which "radical" students held forth affords many useful concepts. In contrast to goldfish swallowing and the like, the law enforcement challenges posed by student militancy approached a magnitude similar to that posed by the emergence of Black Muslims, Black Panthers, and a host of other militant approaches to the ever-increasing trend toward human rights. In effect, an era of *demand* evolved in which former concepts of extremism became clearly obsolete, and the interpretation of the degree of extremism reduced, at least for law enforcement, to the degree of demand—the degree to which any given group was demanding a change. From this perspective, extremism could be thought of as demand that incorporated radical and even violent activities on behalf of the demands. Even today, law enforcement continues to profit by understanding this definition for *extremism.*

As an example of extremism, the radical student movements of the 1960s and 1970s, paralleled by many other radical and militant social movements, confronted law enforcement with what was, and what continues to be, a dilemma: Until extremism brings members of a movement into violation of the law, police have no legitimate function to restrain those members. On the other hand, police held responsible for an orderly society have little choice but to acknowledge the growth of movements that disrupt the orderly society.

In contemporary America, student unrest per se may or may not be of concern to law enforcement. But as in the case of the evolution of militant movements against the government, student unrest, just like unrest among any group of the populace, poses a threat to the orderly environment for which police are responsible. Invariably, it is the *degree* of demand for change, as expressed in the degree of militant conduct, that determines the definition of how "extreme" the problem is.

Law enforcement has achieved few definitive guidelines through the evolution of the extremist militant movements in America in recent decades. Court decisions, particularly those of the U.S. Supreme Court, have not contributed a great deal to the concretization of police responsibility: on the one hand, to retain an orderly environment, and on the other hand, to refrain from interfering with the lives of people who do not violate the law. Concrete though some decisions are, they have not always been popular. Consideration of the Court's role is indicated.

SUPREME COURT DECISIONS

There is no one set of sociological or economic reasons that people relate to a government. In theory at least, the American courts influence the relationship between the individual and the government by reconciling grievances—both between government and the individual, and between individuals themselves. The courts, it is generally agreed, have a significant effect on the relationship between the government and the population it serves. With regard to law enforcement, the relationship between the courts and individuals, particularly people accused of crime, is of immediate concern in examining the effect of social problems on constitutional government.

A traditional role of law enforcement in constitutional forms of government is *apprehending* law violators, leaving *punishment* to the judicial process. Philosophically at least, such a role permits crime prevention to be a mutual, although secondary, responsibility of both police and courts. But in recent times, police and courts are increasingly faced with crimes stemming from the growing demands for social reform rather than merely from the violation of criminal statutes. One apparent reaction by the courts, particularly the Supreme Court, has been a number of decisions that greatly affect police procedure in general, and the relationship of police to social change in particular. In effect, the Supreme Court has handed down rulings that judge not only the lower courts' functions but the police function as well.

Much of the basis of the increasing Supreme Court assessment of police practice is the Fourth Amendment and, to some degree, the Ninth Amendment. The implications of the Fourth Amendment to the police function have received more than adequate concern in law enforcement circles in recent decades. Nonetheless, a brief review of the highlights of the more significant court decisions may serve to clarify the implications—implications that continue to this date.

In 1914, the Supreme Court ruled, in *Weeks* v. *United States,* that a federal court could not accept evidence that was obtained in violation of certain seizure protection, which is guaranteed by the Fourth Amendment. In 1963, the Court ruled on the appeal case of

Gideon v. *Wainwright.* The effect of this ruling was that a new trial could be demanded by anyone convicted of crime who had not had legal counsel.

Moving closer to the function of police, in 1964 a decision was handed down in the case of *Escobedo* v. *Illinois.* This decision, based on a five-to-four majority, held it the constitutional right of an indigent to be provided with legal counsel at the time of police interrogation. In June 1966, again by a five-to-four majority, the Court ruled on the case of *Miranda* v. *Arizona.* The *Miranda* decision has the effect of providing legal counsel during police questioning for persons *suspected* of crime.

Because this and the previous rulings were made on the basis of constitutional rights, law enforcement found itself compelled to regard many of its traditional investigative methods as unconstitutional. This led to a search for alternative approaches. And determination of such approaches is at best difficult when the overall function of the courts is undergoing change, resulting from Supreme Court interpretations of the Constitution. With regard to social change, this trend has the effect of making law enforcement and the criminal courts *part* of the change that law enforcement is attempting to confront.

Although somewhat less dramatic than the major decisions already cited, other Supreme Court decisions continue to have profound influence on the evolution of criminal courts and law enforcement. Decisions that interpret or define the interest of a community as opposed to the interest of an individual frequently obscure, rather than clarify, the dilemma faced by law enforcement—retention of an orderly environment for the purpose of conducting a democratic government, versus extreme restraint to protect the rights of all citizens.

Police tend to cope with the conflicting interests of groups representing themselves as the community, but in any given situation, the Supreme Court may strip law enforcement of its prerogative to perceive a "community," with the Court examining a case on its merits in terms of the rights of individual members of the group. Several decades of complaints regarding the "second-guessing" of police officers faced with emergencies from large groups have done little to improve the plight of law enforcement; a decision in the midst of a riot may be reviewed as though an officer and a civilian were in a kind of personal combat.

Law enforcement has by and large complied with the intended spirit of civil and individual rights, but the evolution of the police function is scarcely complete.

CIVIL RIGHTS AND POWER

Supreme Court decisions since World War II have influenced a number of interesting definitions, particularly in the area of civil rights. The majority of these decisions have contained an implied definition of the individual's interest in political power—a kind of suggestion that every person is entitled to some sort of political power. For indeed, constitutional guarantees have little value unless they provide an opportunity to exert political power. This philosophical point, however, is of little use to law enforcement in its attempt to discriminate between *legal* and *illegal* efforts to gain political power. Voting, some say, affords sufficient political power; but Supreme Court decisions frequently suggest a kind of legitimacy to exceed the guaranteed political power of the vote.

Take, for example, the situation posed by a militant minority opposed to nuclear electric-energy production. If such a group is without sufficient votes to achieve a referendum that would further their goals, they may opt to trespass on land, vandalize property, and disturb the peace and quiet of those they oppose. Lower criminal courts have acquired what appears to be a Supreme Court philosophy of regarding such "crime" as no crime at all—as simply a matter of citizens seeking the political power that their Constitution guarantees. This poses no immediate problem for the arresting officer, who is rarely held liable in any way following the arrest, but it nonetheless dramatizes what many believe is a growing schism between the judicial segment of criminal justice and the enforcement segment—a schism that presumably could provide a major contribution to anarchy.

ANARCHY

In a general discussion of the effect of social problems on law enforcement and constitutional government, many might argue that the term *anarchy* is an excessive concept. Indeed, there is currently little evidence that anarchy is an immediate threat, in spite of the growing evidence that criminal justice, at least as a system, is deteriorating rapidly.[4] Whether or not the term *anarchy* is excessive in such a discussion, it is abundantly clear that ultimately, having one segment of government give legitimacy to law-violating

---

[4] See, for example, Alan R. Coffey and Vernon E. Renner, *Criminal Justice as a System: Readings* (Englewood Cliffs, N.J.: Prentice-Hall, 1975). See also Alan R. Coffey, *Management Systems in Criminal Justice* (Santa Cruz, Calif.: Davis Publishing, 1978).

behavior and another segment attempt to enforce the law encourages an environment that would presumably foster anarchy. The effect of social problems on law enforcement in constitutional government, then, incorporates at least the possibility that unless many problems within the criminal justice system itself are resolved, law enforcement's efforts to retain an orderly environment are in jeopardy.

Summary

Law enforcement was examined in this chapter in terms of the effect on it of social tensions and social problems within a milieu of changing constitutional government, and of some of the government functions claimed to be solutions to social problems.

The limitations of law enforcement within a constitutional government contrast with those in other forms of government in regard to property rights, free speech, and, in particular, the right of dissent. Concerning the right of dissent, alternate methods of affording an orderly environment are being sought — orderly environment being one of the primary responsibilities of government in general, and of law enforcement in particular.

Contradictions and paradoxes surround the attempt to retain an orderly environment while at the same time refraining from interference with private citizens who have not violated specific laws.

In regard to some of the conflicts that emerge from the disparity between the interests or needs of some citizens versus those of others, or of the government versus those of individuals, we have the historical example of student militancy and other forms of militancy that have emerged in the last few decades. The concept of extremism is now viewed by law enforcement in terms of the *degree* to which demands are made, and the effect of such demands on violation of law.

The judicial process in constitutional government is in a continuing trend of handing down decisions that, first, "second-guess" law enforcement practices, and second, rationalize conduct that was once considered criminal because of the law violation but is now accepted on the basis of the individual pursuit of political power. With regard to political power, the traditional prerogative to vote is gradually giving way to other remedies when sufficient votes cannot be generated to bring about the democratic method of governmental change.

Discussion topics

1. Relate the process of governing, as presented in the first part of this chapter, to the concept of enforcement.
2. Distinguish between the constitutional form of government and totalitarian dictatorship in terms of differences in enforcing law.
3. Elaborate on the significance of orderly environment in terms of impact of social problems on law enforcement.
4. Discuss extremism in terms of law enforcement.
5. Elaborate the context in which the subject of anarchy was considered toward the conclusion of this chapter.
6. Discuss the dilemma of law enforcement restraining itself from interference in the lives of citizens who have not violated criminal laws, and the responsibility to provide an orderly environment in which to conduct government.

Annotated references

Coffey, Alan R., *Police Intervention into Family Crisis.* Santa Cruz, Calif.: Davis Publishing, 1975. Chapter 1 elaborates the broad ramifications of family crisis.

——, *Prevention of Crime and Delinquency.* Englewood Cliffs, N.J.: Prentice-Hall, 1977. Chapter 1 provides a comprehensive context for what this chapter discussed as the crime segment of social problems.

Freeman, W., *Society on Trial.* Springfield, Ill.: Chas. C Thomas, 1965. Affords a broad context for relating social problems to criminal justice.

Flocks, R., ed., *Conformity, Resistance, and Self-Determination: The Individual and Authority.* Boston: Little, Brown, 1976. Develops the concept of social problems in a broader format than that used in this chapter.

McDowell, Charles P., *Police in the Community.* Cincinnati, O.: W.H. Adamson, 1975. Affords a good general context for this chapter's discussion of government.

Reasons, C.E., and J.L. Kuykendall, eds., *Race, Crime and Justice.* Pacific Palisades, Calif.: Goodyear, 1972. Elaboration of the societal ramifications of government efforts to control behavior in a free society.

chapter four

Social Change, Community Tension, and Enforcement of Law

Having introduced the concepts of social change and constitutional government in the last chapter, attention will now be directed to the relationship of law enforcement to community tensions that accompany social change. Not all tensions generate police problems, but enough do to justify further consideration.

Human tensions exist in every community. It is axiomatic that human beings dealing with one another generate tensions of some kind—sometimes related to anger or fear, sometimes to competition or envy. Human tension also emerges in relation to biases and prejudices that impinge on one human being's perception of another. But in any case, at least some degree of tension accrues to virtually all human relationships.

It is worth noting that not all tension is "bad." Many tensions are associated with facing and conquering legitimate challenges, and these can presumably be considered "good." Indeed, the tensions experienced by courageous police in the protection of an often indifferent public can be—indeed, should be—thought of as "good." The point is that community tension, like all human tension, can be either "good" or "bad," depending on the orientation and value system of the observer.

This is an important concept in the enforcement of law during social change and the community tensions that accompany it—that community tensions associated with social change may or may not be undesirable. Were police to assume that a problem exists every time there is a perceptible rise in community tension, a great deal of police effort would probably be wasted. Every contested election generates some type of tension in the community. Even a controversial ballot measure generates community tensions that, in most cases, are of little consequence to the enforcement of law. On the other hand, if police were to simply ignore community tension entirely, they might end up with an enormous amount of work that could have been anticipated and dealt with before becoming a major police problem.

Tensions, then, should be evaluated in terms of *potential* problems—particularly problems that carry potential difficulty for law enforcement. This potential, in turn, can often be evaluated in terms of social change.

Social change

Social change does not necessarily create tension. If the change is gradual, there may be no tension in the community, the state, or, indeed, anywhere in the land. But if social change is rapid, a great deal of tension may be created, and created in many different areas.

For police to evaluate the potential problems of tension, then, community tensions resulting from *rapid* social change deserve far more attention than the gradual evolutions in the social structure of our society.

It should be noted that change is not optional. All things are always changing at all times. Aging, for example, proves that change is inevitable. Earthquakes change the earth rapidly and often create enormous problems. Conversely, the more subtle changes in the earth can be discerned only by trained scientists— for example, the fact that the Grand Canyon becomes an inch deeper every year, or that Europe and the United States grow a foot farther apart every year. Social changes, like these changes in the earth, can also be slow and gradual or rapid and dramatic. They have major differences in pace or tempo, in their severity, and in their effects. The interest of police in social change is, of necessity, interest in the *effects* of social change. Because of the variations in social changes, police efforts to cope with problems related to the subsequent social tensions can profit by an understanding of the changes that make up the American culture and its social structure.[1]

American social structure

For the most part, early American culture developed in the rural areas. Farmers in the North depended mainly on the labor of their children, and the growing economy of the South depended on the labor of slaves. The main source of energy was human beings. Of course, inventions in the field of agriculture and the use of tools helped to make human energy more effective, and early rural America enjoyed many labor-saving devices. Nevertheless, the primary source of energy was human effort.

The transition from agriculture to industry, known as the Industrial Revolution, tended to displace both the northern workers and the newly freed southern slaves, forcing them to the cities. These cities, however, were busily replacing human labor with machinery even faster than farms were being mechanized.

One immediate result of the Industrial Revolution was increased leisure for many, since the mechanization of labor reduced the amount of time needed to achieve desired production levels. Another was the advent of more and more farm-oriented people seeking employment in the factories. And the dawn-till-dusk workday continued to give way to the efforts of organized labor and political figures to improve the plight of factory workers.

Ever-increasing leisure has marked virtually all significant social changes in America since its own Revolution.

LEISURE

There is no question but that leisure has a great many positive factors. Inventions of tools, the use of animals, and the discovery of numerous other sources of energy placed prehistoric man on a path ultimately leading to enough free time for the creation of the arts and sciences, neither of which was conceivable until sufficient leisure was available.

In this context, leisure has a favorable connotation, because it

---

[1] Alan R. Coffey, *Police Intervention into Family Crisis* (Santa Cruz, Calif.: Davis Publishing, 1977). The first three chapters elaborate on the family changes that have evolved in American culture.

can be equated with either recreation or productivity. But not all leisure is recreational or productive, and therein lies a source of community tension and of potential concern for police. Among the unemployed and underemployed of the ghetto, leisure may mean idleness, providing more time in which to get into trouble.

At one time, police were concerned also with aspects of the leisure time of those who were *not* in ghettos and *not* unemployed— the American middle class. This happened when entertainment— in both movies and nightclubs, for example—became increasingly permissive. Middle-class men and women became able to spend some of their leisure time in pursuits that in most jurisdictions often generated massive police response. However, the laws restricting what were then considered immoral exhibitions have since been greatly relaxed on the grounds of the First Amendment's guarantee of freedom of expression. Entering the 1980s, middle-class leisure has expanded even further—and in many instances, so has the permissiveness. But it is notable that leisure time did once relate to law enforcement in recreational areas outside the ghetto, when what we now refer to as "X-rated movies" and other then-frowned-upon social conduct of the middle classes were of direct concern to the police.

When American buying habits are examined, it might seem that the increasing leisure of affluence has been dominated by recreation. In the decade from 1940 through 1950, expenditures for sports equipment and toys increased threefold, for musical instruments and sound equipment fivefold. Money spent for operas and legitimate theater doubled, with opera companies increasing in numbers from two to fifteen. In the same decade, twice as much money was spent on books, the amount spent on foreign travel increased nearly nine times, and the number of classical music concerts held outside New York City more than doubled. This trend appears to have continued in the three decades that have followed; the affluence of the American economy has grown to the point that major concern is now expressed in terms of the inflation to which such expenditures contribute.

In and out of recessions, the middle class of the United States has enjoyed an extremely high standard of living, concerns about the recessions and inflation notwithstanding. But not everyone has enjoyed affluence to the same degree, and some not at all. Segments of any affluent community that are deprived of comparable increases in affluence would, on a commonsense basis, appear to be perfect breeding grounds for the kinds of tension with which police should be concerned during periods of social change. And when these segments do have comparable leisure, such negative results of social change can, then, produce heightened tensions and ultimately lead to police problems.

Correction of the tension generated by leisure in this negative setting is by no means easy. It depends on a number of variables relating to the political and economic factors in our society. A key variable, in our increasingly automated society, is educational opportunities.

EDUCATION

It would scarcely be accurate to state that there is a universal "demand" for education. Indeed, an increasingly large number of American young people question whether education—particularly higher education in college and graduate school—is of any value at all in career planning. Nevertheless, education continues to be at least a symbol of the means by which affluence is gained, and perhaps prestige or status. From this perspective, there continues to be a demand for at least the benefits that education can supposedly produce. Whether in the purely academic area, or in the increasingly popular technical areas, learning the skills that give young people advantages in the job market is a factor.

With each discovery of a new source of energy, or development of machinery to replace human labor, there is a corresponding demand for increased sophistication in methods of productivity. Automation, cybernetics, and electronic data processing, with their associated advanced technology, simultaneously provide challenging new jobs for the educated and displace those without the newly needed skills.

Unemployment in America is traditionally considered a blot on our record. The moralistic Puritan ideas that developed many of the American work mores drew heavily on the belief that labor is not only imposed by nature as a punishment for sin, but also an esthetic discipline willed by God.[2] This Puritan heritage has given rise, in parts of the population, to some quite rigid tenets. People who were raised to believe in the necessity for and the value of work are likely to feel that those who are not employed are simply lazy. Such an oversimplification, of course, ignores the vast complexity in the true nature of rapidly changing technology in a highly competitive employment market. Of course, it also reduces the confusion that would be generated by such a sophisticated

---

[2] H. Stein and R. Cloward, *Social Perspectives on Behavior* (New York: Free Press, 1977), p. 273.

analysis, presumably indicating a general preference for oversimplification rather than analysis.

The luxury of oversimplifying is no longer available to law enforcement. Police are increasingly confronted with the violent consequences of oversimplifications of this kind and should, in their own interest, examine the potential result of depriving people of the educational means to compete and survive in a complex job market.

Before examining equality of access to education, let us give some thought to the concept of social change as it relates to education in general. The occupational field of law enforcement itself serves as a model of the lag between the growth of social institutions and the rate of change in modern America. In cities having growing populations, for example, there are fewer police per 10,000 inhabitants than in cities with decreasing populations; this fact has remained relatively constant since it was first put forth in the literature some three decades ago.[3] In like fashion, certain school programs for the disadvantaged child have lagged far behind the growth in numbers of these children in the educational system.[4] This lag has continued in spite of the compulsory school attendance that distinguishes the United States from much of the rest of the world.

Social change that increases leisure brings attention to education in two ways, both of which have indirect significance for police concerned with community tensions. As already noted, an increased demand for technical skill accompanies the discovery of new sources of energy and labor-saving machinery and technology. Here there is, of course, an obvious role for education and training. But social change draws attention to the *length of time* necessary for a student to complete his education—the length of time that the student is at home.

Both the family and the public have traditionally been prepared to support a child's education at least through grade school, and usually through high school. But what about college? And how much college?

Before the so-called knowledge explosion following the technical advances of World War II and the Korean War, college was not a requisite in most people's educational aspirations. But automation, combined with government sponsorship through the G.I. Bill and other subsidized college programs, rapidly focused attention on college training as a crucial part of the educational process.

[3] See, for example, W. Ogburn, "Cultural Lag as Theory," *Sociology and Social Research,* January–February 1957, pp. 167–74.

[4] R. Kerckhoff, "The Problem of the School," *Journal of Marriage and the Family,* 26, No. 4 (November 1964), 435–39.

Even currently, with less emphasis among the young on a college degree, college-level technical courses are in demand. To many, this social change has unveiled vast new horizons of opportunity. But this ever-lengthening educational process has appeared to the disadvantaged to widen even further an already unacceptable gap between affluence and poverty. For, unlike the masses of middle-class families prepared and motivated to support children through an increasingly expensive process of education, poverty-stricken families necessarily consider the child of high school age a potential source of income—or at least potentially capable of supporting him- or herself. Therefore, the relatively small number of college students from poor backgrounds should not be surprising even in view of affirmative-action recruiting.

Community tension has many sources, but none are so influential as those associated with social changes that draw attention to the disparity of opportunity and seem to increase the disparity as they occur. Education is, or could be, a primary ingredient in social problems generating social tensions that in turn become a law enforcement matter.

As an example, then, of tension that may associate itself with social change, education might be considered in terms of the unrest preceding heightened tensions.

SOCIAL UNREST

Many of the numerous causes of community unrest lie beyond the scope of law enforcement or criminal justice. There is, nonetheless, a significant relationship between law enforcement and certain aspects of unrest. As noted, symptoms of unrest frequently foreshadow direct intervention by law enforcement agencies. The growing tensions that underlie the violent forms of protest are almost invariably preceded by periods of general unrest. Moreover, law enforcement may become involved even in certain random aspects of this unrest. Sometimes these involuntary involvements have to do with a particular minority's perceiving police as insensitive to its social problems; the involvement may be less fortuitous when police arrest practices appear to a group to be excessive. In any event, the unrest preceding serious tensions in the community can, and frequently does, involve law enforcement.

In this context, at least part of the community tension can be thought of, first, as a disparity between certain citizens and our society, and second, as a disparity between certain citizens and the authority of police. Police options, obviously, are in the area of their direct relationship with the unrest rather than fairness or lack of fairness in distributing society's affluence.

UNREST WITHOUT VIOLENCE

Law enforcement could not, of course, even determine, let alone correct, all the matters that generate unrest. But to whatever degree law enforcement is able to achieve a system of dealing with people in such a manner that police function does not heighten the unrest, to that same degree it can at least mitigate the tensions that become serious police problems.

The significance of a reduction in the degree to which the police function heightens unrest cannot be overestimated. Such a reduction can make the difference between a minor demonstration and a full-scale riot. Rioters rarely conceive of law enforcement as reasonable, sensible, or fair, and almost never perceive it as sensitive to the social tensions. Police, conversely, taking the stand that they have nothing to do with the social changes that caused this dissension, often bear the brunt of violence erupting out of social protests spawned by unrest that is followed by heightened tensions. It remains a valid area of conjecture that at least the *degree* of violence relates to the attitude of the rioter toward law enforcement.

Regrettably, enforcement systems that satisfy the criterion of making sense while being fair do not *ensure* favorable attitudes toward law enforcement. They nevertheless remain a significant factor in law enforcement's attention to social tensions during social change.

PUBLICITY

One of the lessons learned by many police over the past few decades is that publicity is a significant factor in community tensions that lead to problems for police. In most cases, publicity that does relate to police problems is sensational publicity.

Sensationalism, as it is often called, is the kind of press coverage of police matters that emphasizes the incident more than the causes—the dramatic event more than the rationale. Not surprisingly, such publicity often obscures rather than clarifies the fact that law enforcement is merely coping with rather than causing the problem. With regard to unrest that becomes tension, generating problems for police during social change, a press oriented to sensationalism is frequently as much of the problem as any other factor with which police must deal.

Although police cannot control the often unfavorable effect of sensational publicity, a great deal could be done to foster other forms of publicity that encourage a more positive attitude toward police, and perhaps toward government in general. The calling of press conferences to present progressive programs is one possibility. This may not in itself attract publicity, favorable or otherwise. However, where matters with public appeal are featured, the chance of attracting favorable publicity improves for law enforcement. Consider, for example, the hiring of minority members or women in police service as a feature of some progressive program. As this practice becomes more common, it is less likely to attract the news media; but when such a feature is combined with progress reports and police training information, or similar factors of public interest, public relations becomes easier.

There is no doubt that police in general could improve their general approach to press relations and, in turn, improve the effect that publicity has on the unrest and tensions leading to police problems during social change:

> It is a fact of newspapering that most seasoned police reporters know more about the inner workings of law enforcement agencies than the peace officers know about the principles of journalism. Accordingly, for many reporters of good will, educating the cops is an ongoing ambition. We want police to recognize the public's right to know about their operations. We want them to realize that it is news media's constitutional obligation to fulfill that right.

> In any educating process, it takes two to tango. The police must be willing. If they are, and the learning begins, the eyes of both "sides"—press and police, attempting in their own ways to serve a shared community—are likely to be opened wider. . . .[5]

Sensationalizing problems and the causes of problems tends to exaggerate community tension, not so much through the distortion of facts as through the distortion of perspective. In the many contacts of law enforcement with all segments of the public, some abuses of police power are real, some are fancied; both pose a problem, because both are frequently reported and generate unrest. But when the abuses of power are real, they are newsworthy, because they are not expected.

Sensationalistic press coverage of police brutality may serve two functions, and law enforcement should be aware of both in its struggle for an effective system. First, sensational news is of high commercial value. Second, it is of great attention-gaining value to any group seeking relief for actual or imagined social ills. Virtually any social movement achieves a greater stature if it is "picked on" by police in a democratic society. Realization of this by law enforcement personnel will help them to anticipate sensationalism

---

[5] B. Carter, "A Magna Carta for Media–Police Relations," *The Police Chief*, 37, No. 9 (September 1970), 28.

that may lead to high levels of tension during social change. The result will be better communications between police and the community served.

Although the more violent forms of campus demonstrations are now quiescent, no one can say for certain that the era of the riot has passed. However, a great deal of enforcement effort is now being expended to prevent skyjackings and similar crimes. And police responsibility to understand and deal realistically with social change remains whether or not the times are marked by violence. This responsibility, of course, includes the anticipation and prevention of overwhelming social tensions growing from social change. Community tensions, in large measure, stem from those social changes over which police have no control. But there are many factors, as noted in this chapter, that police do either control or strongly influence. Contact between police and the public is greatly susceptible to efforts to improve the negative effect of social changes—at least insofar as law enforcement is concerned. Because change is inevitable, the obvious methods of meeting the problems it creates, through awareness, increase in importance for law enforcement in a changing community. For criminal justice to remain a value, the manner in which all justice is dispensed must remain as sensitive to unrest and tension as is feasible. The initiative in avoiding gross civil disruption always falls ultimately on the shoulders of law enforcement personnel. Police, far more than the courts and corrections, deal with the root causes of the failure of criminal justice to exert maximum positive influence toward avoiding serious problems resulting from social change.

Accepting the responsibility for such initiative means many things to law enforcement. Above all else, it means developing a systematic and effective organizational approach to the problem. Elsewhere in this volume, some of the more effective approaches to bringing law enforcement influence to bear on community tensions will be explored.

Summary

The effect of community tensions on law enforcement was presented in this chapter in a general context of human tension—tension between human beings undergoing increasingly rapid change in the mores and folkways of the society.

Change itself is an ongoing process subject to neither prevention nor control. The Industrial Revolution was the background for the current technological development of American society that has led to a great increase in leisure time. More leisure carries advantages to those with employable skills, but disadvantages to those who encounter difficulty in gaining meaningful employment. Education is also related to the problems of people with employment difficulties, and underemployment, in turn, is related to community unrest and tensions, leading to problems for police.

It is up to the police to anticipate such problems, particularly by seeking to improve relations with groups perceiving inequities. Law enforcement, more than other segments of criminal justice, carries the responsibility of improving the perception of criminal justice insofar as efforts to reduce community tensions are concerned. The sensationalizing of alleged abuses of police power increases such tensions, so the motivations of those seeking sensational press coverage of police involvement in social movements must be understood.

Discussion topics

1. Review what this chapter presented in terms of human tension as inevitable in human interaction.
2. Relate social change to human tension and unrest.
3. Contrast social change and community tension in the context of problems for law enforcement.
4. Discuss change as a concept.
5. Discuss social change.
6. Discuss the sources of increased leisure time in America.
7. Relate education to social problems.
8. Discuss the effects of sensationalist press coverage of police functions.

Annotated references

Coffey, Alan R., *Police Intervention into Family Crisis.* Santa Cruz, Calif.: Davis Publishing, 1977. Detailed descriptions of the effect of social changes on police activity.

——, *The Prevention of Crime and Delinquency.* Englewood Cliffs, N.J.: Prentice-Hall, 1977. A comprehensive elaboration of relationships between public attitudes and criminal justice.

Kuykendall, J.L., "Police and Minority Groups: Toward a Theory of Negative Contacts," in *Police*. Springfield, Ill.: Chas. C Thomas, 1970. Covers the subject of the title in the general context of this chapter.

McDowell, Charles P., *Police in the Community*. Cincinnati, O.: W.H. Anderson, 1975. Chapter 3 offers a context for social change.

Meissner, H., ed., *Poverty in Affluent Society*. New York: Harper & Row, 1966. A number of articles dealing with influences on the community of poverty evolving over an extended period.

Sarason, Seymour B., *The Psychological Sense of Community: Prospects for Community Psychology*. San Francisco: Jossey-Bass, 1976. Excellent overview of the general context in which the tensions discussed in this chapter evolve.

Smith, A.B., and H. Pollack, *Crime and Justice in a Mass Society*. Lexington, Mass.: Xerox College Publishing, 1972. Provides a broad context for what this chapter discussed as government control.

Stretcher, V.G., *The Environment of Law Enforcement: A Community Relations Guide*. Englewood Cliffs, N.J.: Prentice-Hall, 1971. Elaborates on police reaction to varied levels and kinds of community tensions.

PART TWO

LAW ENFORCEMENT
IN A
DEMOCRATIC SOCIETY

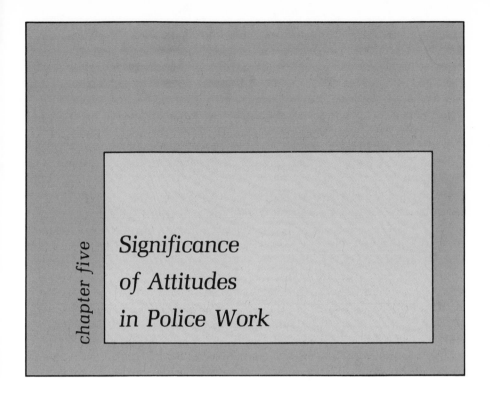

chapter five

Significance
of Attitudes
in Police Work

Hostile attitudes of citizens toward the police are probably as disruptive of order as is police malpractice. And people will probably not get the complete protection their taxes are paying for until they change their viewpoint toward law enforcement officers. In many ways, this presents a paradox, in that the people who display the most animosity toward the police generally need their protection the most. Many minority-group members harbor a resentment against authority and have doubts about American ideals. In view of the history of race relations and of ghetto conditions in the United States, these by-products should be expected.

A report by the federal government expresses this problem most succinctly:

> It is . . . almost . . . a truism that ghetto residents will not obtain the police protection they badly want and need until policemen feel that their presence is welcome and that their problems are understood. However, in the effort to achieve this state of affairs, the duty of taking the initiative clearly devolves on the police, both because they are organized and disciplined and because they are public servants sworn to protect every part of the community.[1]

---

[1] The President's Commission on Law Enforcement and Administration of Justice, *The Challenge of Crime in a Free Society* (Washington, D.C.: U.S. Government Printing Office, 1967), p. 100.

The major problem with the police's taking the initiative is that they must first have some understanding of people's motives and attitudes, how they were formed, and how they can be changed. The rest of this chapter is devoted to providing a basis for this understanding.

Approaches to studying human behavior

The behavior of mankind can be studied from two points of view. The first focuses on the group processes of mankind, the *sociological* approach. The second is the *study of the individual*. This chapter will concern itself with the latter approach.

Obviously, these two methods cannot be completely independent of each other. Because man is a social being as well as an individual, they are interdependent. To better study the behavior of the individual, we will use a framework that views social behavior as being influenced by various factors.

According to one psychologist, there are five major factors that influence social behavior: the nature of the social situation, the norms of the social group, and the personality, transitory condition, and perception of the individual.[2]

The Nature of the Social Situation. An onlooker might cheer for a fighter in the boxing ring but not at a street fight. The two fights are generally considered different social situations.

The Norms of a Social Group. A delinquent gang member and a middle-class teenager react to the police in different ways.

Personality. A person who has an authoritarian personality will tend to act rigidly in social situations. Personality is the result of both heredity and environment.

Transitory Condition. An angry person will probably react to a peace officer in a manner much different from that of one who is not angry. Transitory conditions include various physical and emotional states, such as illness, drunkenness, and so on.

Perception. If a person perceives the police as having a Gestapolike organization, he will react to them much differently than if he perceived them as friends.

Attitudes

When social scientists wish to describe how a person perceives situations and objects and how his or her behavior is affected by

[2] S. S. Sargent, *Social Psychology: An Integrative Interpretation* (New York: Ronald Press, 1950), pp. 242–71.

these perceptions, they do so in terms of attitudes. A definition of *attitude* is *a long-lasting perceptual, motivational, emotional, and adaptive organizational process concerned with a person or object.*[3] Attitudes may be either negative or positive; that is, a person can be either favorably or unfavorably predisposed toward a person or object.

It can be seen that by this definition, prejudice can be regarded as a kind of attitude. Prejudice categorizes persons or objects in a good or bad light—usually bad—without regard to the facts.

Attitudes are regarded as having various dimensions and attributes. As suggested by several different authors, five dimensions appear to be descriptive of most attitudes. In this text, we have modified and adapted them to fit the subject. Briefly described and illustrated, they are as follows:

1. *Direction:* What is the direction of the attitude? Is it for or against the person or object?

2. *Degree:* How positive or negative is the attitude?

3. *Content:* Although different people may dislike the police in the same degree, this does not mean that their attitudes are necessarily the same. Investigation of the content of their attitudes may show that they perceive the police in markedly different ways. The attitude of one may stem from unpleasant personal contacts; of another, the fact that as a child he was taught to dislike them.

4. *Consistency:* Attitudes differ in how they are integrated with and related to other attitudes a person holds. One person, for example, may show enmity toward police because he sees them as enforcers for the power structure he hates. Another may have a dislike for the police that does not fit into his general framework of beliefs and attitudes. Consistency relates to the dimension of strength.

5. *Strength:* Some attitudes continue for a long time despite data that contradict them. These are known as strong attitudes. Weaker attitudes are those that are more easily changed.[4]

It can be seen that attitudes may serve many functions. Generally speaking, a man's ability to react consistently in situations is made possible by his attitudes. These arise from a combination of his many feelings and experiences, creating a meaningful totality.

[3] D. Krech and R. S. Crutchfield, *Elements of Psychology* (New York: Knopf, 1970), p. 692.

[4] O. Klineberg, *Social Psychology* (New York: Holt, Rinehart & Winston, 1954), pp. 489–90; and Krech and Crutchfield, *Elements of Psychology*, pp. 672–73.

How this comes about has been speculated upon by many social scientists. Two theories that we will examine are the *psychoanalytical theory* and the *learning theory*. These have been used considerably more frequently than other theories to explain the development of attitudes by minority-group members and/or ghetto residents.

MINORITY-GROUP ATTITUDES AND THE PSYCHOANALYTICAL THEORY

Psychoanalytical theory is concerned with the development of a person from early childhood, as well as with motivational conflicts that might occur at any time. Basically, development is a kind of unfolding of the sexual impulses, certain transformations being the result. This theory emphasizes changes within a person, with a stronger emphasis on biological maturation than on social and environmental influences. Greatly simplifying the matter, we can say that culture and experience affect sexual impulses, and these in turn affect behavior and attitudes. (In contrast, the *learning theories* suggest that culture and experience directly affect behavior and attitudes.)

One psychoanalytical theory of how attitudes are acquired by minority-group members is set forth using the blacks as an example.[5] According to the authors of this work, everyone in the United States grows up with the idea of white supremacy. Some Americans, furthermore, find that it is a basic part of their nationhood to despise black people. No one who lives in this country can avoid this hatred. Black people are no exception, and they are taught, in essence, to hate themselves.

This theory claims that these attitudes have been rooted in American life since the days of slavery. Black people have been oppressed and treated as inferiors so many times and in so many ways that they themselves are often convinced that they are inferior. Their thinking has been so perverted that they even perceive a connection between high status and fair skin. For instance, the black woman's personality is undermined from girlhood. She regards herself as the antithesis of the American concept of beauty, for her blackness is the opposite of the creamy white skin that seems so desirable in the American culture.

Conversely, the black man occupies a very special sexual role in American society. He tends to be thought of as possessing great

---

[5] W. H. Grier and P. M. Cobbs, *Black Rage* (New York: Basic Books, 1968).

masculine vigor. However, at the same time, he is rendered socially, politically, and economically impotent. Very often, he even lacks the power to fulfill the fundamental role of providing a good living and protection for his family. Consequently, black males' attitudes toward American society and toward law enforcement, the guardian of that society, are often greatly affected by their own self-concepts.

It is obvious that the self-concept of blacks needs to be enhanced, particularly in the educational, economical, and political areas. The slogan, "Black is beautiful," and all that it entails is an attempt to improve this self-concept.

MINORITY–GROUP ATTITUDES
AND THE LEARNING THEORY

Learning theory, in its broadest sense, says that a person is born into a social environment, and his or her personality is shaped as a result of interaction with other human beings in this social environment.

The distinguishing characteristic of a culture is that it contains a body of behavioral patterns such as skills, habits, and activities. Also, certain types of thought patterns may be as much a part of the culture as are behavioral patterns. Thus, it can be seen that attitudes and opinions may well be determined by culture and may in turn reflect that culture and/or subculture.

The subculture of the ghetto tends to be made up of people in a low class, by virtue of their inability to succeed economically. As explained in another chapter, this inability does not appear to be the ghetto resident's fault in most cases. According to one theory, lower-class culture has a set of attitudes that are passed on to each succeeding generation. "A large body of systematic interrelated attitudes, practices, behaviors, and value characteristics of lower-class culture are designed to support and maintain the basis of the lower-class structure."[6]

The lower-class attitude toward the police tends to be hostile. In another study, this hostility is described thus: "A deep-seated distrust of authority figures pervades [lower socioeconomic class] persons from childhood to old age. Suspicion is directed toward police, clergymen, teachers. . . ."[7]

---

[6] See W. B. Miller, "Lower-Class Culture as a Generating Milieu of Gang Delinquency," *Journal of Social Issues*, 14, No. 3 (1958), 5–19.

[7] A. B. Hollingshead and F. C. Redlick, *Social Class and Mental Illness: A Community Study* (New York: John Wiley, 1968), p. 130.

In addition to frequently being a member of the lower class and being thoroughly indoctrinated with the values of that class, the black person has had experiences that have further alienated him or her from law enforcement. By and large, one of the more important contacts the black makes with white society has been through the white police officer. Therefore, the police officer has personified white authority. In the past, the officer enforced not only laws and regulations but also the whole set of social customs associated with the concept of "white supremacy." Historically, law enforcement was on the side of the slavemaster. In more recent times, the so-called Jim Crow laws (found primarily in the South) of separate facilities were stringently enforced by the police, who punished minor transgressions of caste etiquette on an extrajudicial basis.[8]

Studies of attitudes toward the police

Opinions are closely related to attitudes. The term *attitude* implies a preparation to act, whereas *opinion* refers to what we believe is true. Because what we believe to be true affects our readiness to act in a certain way, it can be seen that opinions and attitudes are intertwined. Therefore, we shall be concerned with both attitudes and opinions while reviewing studies of attitudes toward the police.

Another thought to be considered during this review is that it is not yet possible to apply the scientific approach to human behavior with the same degree of certainty that it is applied to the physical sciences. We know, for example, that the mere amassing of data does not necessarily lead to an understanding of human behavior. However, it is not necessary to make exacting evaluations of all the factors that operate in this regard. Rather, from a practical standpoint, we will identify only the major trends of behavior, so that we can understand human behavior and attitudes more fully.

TASK FORCE REPORT: THE POLICE

A great deal of research has been conducted into the public's attitude and opinions regarding the police. The best gathering and reporting of research information, despite its age, is still the 1967

---

[8] A. Rose, *The Negro in America* (Boston: Beacon Press, 1948), pp. 170–88.

Task Force Report: The Police.[9] It drew upon a number of sources for its information, such as a 1966 Harris poll, a 1965 Gallup poll, and a survey conducted by the National Opinion Research Center.

The results of these three surveys were substantially the same. The Harris poll indicated that the public rated local law enforcement as good or excellent 65 percent of the time, state law enforcement as good or excellent 70 percent of the time, and federal law enforcement good or excellent 76 percent of the time. The Gallup poll found that 70 percent of the public had a good deal of respect for the police, 22 percent had some respect, and only 4 percent had hardly any. The National Opinion Research Center, which is affiliated with the University of Chicago, conducted similar studies in 1947 and in 1963. In 1947, 41 percent of those polled indicated that they thought the police has an excellent or a good standing in the community. In 1963, 54 percent were of this opinion. No other occupational group achieved such a striking improvement in its image as did the police during the 16-year period.

The *Task Force Report* cites a number of other studies suggesting that there is no widespread police–community relations problem. However, the report goes on to point out that these surveys show only part of the community's reaction. When a comparison is made between the white and the black communities, an interesting difference of opinion and/or attitude becomes apparent.

The National Opinion Research Center surveys show that nonwhites, particularly blacks, are much more negative than Caucasians in evaluating police efficiency. Nonwhites indicated only half as often as whites that police gave protection to citizens at a very good rate, and nonwhites tended to give a not-so-good rating twice as often as whites. According to the report, these differences are not merely a result of greater poverty among nonwhites; they exist at all income levels, and among both men and women.

The *Task Force Report* says that a bare majority (51 percent) of nonwhites, as recorded in the Louis Harris poll, believed that local law enforcement was doing a good or excellent job. This is 16 percent lower than the rating among Caucasians. A survey by John F. Kraft, cited in the *Report*, indicated that 47 percent of blacks believed the police did an excellent job, and 41 percent thought they were doing a not-so-good or a poor job.[10]

Generally, the information seems to show that approximately two-thirds to three-fourths of the Caucasian community, but only

[9]The President's Commission on Law Enforcement and Administration of Justice, *Task Force Report: The Police* (Washington, D.C.: U.S. Government Printing Office, 1967), pp. 145–49. See also *Public Attitudes About Crime: A National Crime Survey Report*, U.S. Department of Justice (Washington, D.C.: U.S. Government Printing Office, 1981).

[10] President's Commission, *Task Force Report*, p. 146.

half the black community, believe that police deserve more respect and are doing a good job. Percentage differences between what the racial groups think about police performance range from 16 to 25 percent. Obviously, the black population has a much less favorable attitude than the white population toward police.

However, the surveys may not accurately reflect the extent of minority-group dissatisfaction with law enforcement. When an in-depth interview is held with minority-group members, frequently neutral or even favorable statements at the beginning of the interview give way to strong statements of hostility before it is over.

A study by Paul A. Fine reported upon in the *Task Force Report* points up the fact that there is intense hostility toward police in the black community.[11] This hostility is clearly pointed up when the factor of age is included. In most research studies, only adult attitudes are measured. When young minors of an ethnic minority were interviewed, it became apparent that the antipolice attitude is much greater. In one study, it was found that approximately 30 percent of the black people over the age of 45 had antipolice attitudes, whereas about 60 percent of the black males between 15 and 29 thought there was a great deal of police brutality. Furthermore, over half the black males under the age of 35 stated that they had been subjected to insulting remarks by police and to searches without good cause, and many felt that unnecessary force was used by a police officer at the time of an arrest.

REPORT ON CIVIL DISORDERS

In an attempt to measure the attitudes of people in the cities in which riots have taken place, a survey team interviewed 1,200 people immediately after the disorders occurred.[12] This study identified the different types of grievances appearing to be of greatest significance to the black community in each city. Judgments with regard to the severity of a particular grievance were assigned a rank, from 1 to 4—1 being the least severe and 4 the most. The ranks were based on the frequency with which the grievance was mentioned, the relative intensity with which it was discussed, references to incidents that were examples of this grievance, and an estimate of the severity of the grievance. Then the points were added together for each grievance for all the cities to create an intercity ranking. Although grievances varied in importance from

[11] President's Commission, *Task Force Report*, p. 147.

[12] *Report of the National Advisory Commission on Civil Disorders* (Washington, D.C.: U.S. Government Printing Office, 1968), pp. 80–83, 344–45.

city to city, the deepest grievances were ranked in three levels of intensity.

Police practices were a significant grievance in the intercity average as well as in virtually all the cities, often being one of the most serious complaints. Included in this category were complaints about physical or verbal abuse of black citizens by police officers, lack of adequate channels for complaint against law enforcement personnel, discriminatory police employment and/or promotional practices with regard to black officers, a general lack of respect for black people by police officers, and the failure of police departments to provide adequate protection to black people.

A more complete picture of how these grievance categories were ranked in intensity can be seen from further study of the report of the National Advisory Commission on Civil Disorders. The report is concerned with twenty cities. Nineteen of them were found to contain significant grievances against police practices. In fact, grievances concerning police practices were ranked first in eight cities, second in four, third in none, and fourth in two. It should be noted that such grievances were present in five other cities; however, they were not ranked in the first four orders of intensity.

OTHER STUDIES

Another very significant matter in regard to violence is police killing of civilians. It is most consistently expressed as follows:

> No aspect of policing elicits more passionate concern or more divided opinions than the use of deadly force. Many community groups and minority organizations believe police killings of civilians are excessive and often unjustifiable; many police agencies are apprehensive and angry about unprovoked fatal assaults on patrol officers.[13]

The best way to deal with the issue of deadly force is by setting up a strict policy in this regard. First and foremost, one should remember that the police, like all agencies of government, should exist only to serve the people. This principle emphasizes the protection of the rights of the individual. Therefore, a policy controlling the use of deadly force should be short, simple, and easily understood by everyone. The FBI has such a policy; it is that "a police of-

[13] J. Q. Wilson, "Police Use of Deadly Force," *FBI Law Enforcement Bulletin,* 49 (August 1980), 16.

ficer is authorized to use deadly force only in the protection of his/her life or someone else's life."[14]

Another concern, obviously not as dramatic as the deadly-force issue, has to do with how the police view citizens:

> Seemingly, the views of police officers toward most citizens suggests that they are seen as uncooperative at best, or even hostile. They feel that citizens generally do not cooperate with law enforcement and that law enforcement does not have the respect of most citizens. Furthermore, the police tend to feel that people obey the law only because they fear being caught.[15]

This feeling by police seems to be prevalent despite the fact that surveys show it to be not completely true. Wilson suggests that this may be explained in the following manner:

> The average patrolman in a big city is most frequently in contact, not with the "average" citizen, but with a relatively small number of persons who are heavy users of police services (willingly or unwillingly), and his view of citizen attitudes is strongly influenced by this experience. By the nature of his job, the police officer is disproportionately involved with the poor, the black, the young—partly because young males, especially poor ones, are more likely to be involved in criminal activities and breaches of the peace, partly because even the law-abiding poor (who are, after all, the majority of the poor) must rely upon the police for a variety of services that middle-class families do not require (if they do, they obtain them from nonpolice sources). The police, for example, are routinely expected, in poor areas, to deal with family quarrels; in more affluent neighborhoods, such disputes are either less threatening to the participants or are kept by them out of public view.[16]

To better understand the effect on the police officer of constant encounters with other than "average" citizens, the experience of George L. Kirkham should be examined. Kirkham holds a doctorate in criminology and is an assistant professor at Florida State University. Dr. Kirkham, academician, had strong feelings about and correctional experiences in the humane treatment of the offender. After working on the Jacksonville–Duval County police force for six months, he had the following to say about his attitudes:

> The same kinds of daily stresses which affected my fellow officers soon began to take their toll on me. I became sick and tired of being reviled and attacked by criminals who could most usually find a sympathetic audience in judges and jurors eager to understand their side of things and provide

[14] L. P. Brown, "Reducing the Use of Deadly Force: The Atlanta Experience," in B. Levine, *Police Use of Deadly Force; What Police and the Community Can Do about It* (Washington, D.C.: U.S. Government Printing Office, 1978), pp. 20–27.

[15] J. Q. Wilson, "Police Morale, Reform and Citizen Respect: The Chicago Case," in D. J. Bordua, ed. *The Police* (New York: John Wiley, 1967), p. 17.

[16] J. Q. Wilson, "The Police in the Ghetto," in R. F. Steadman, ed., *The Police and the Community* (Baltimore: Johns Hopkins University Press, 1972), p. 61.

them with "another chance." I grew tired of living under the axe of news media and community pressure groups, eager to seize upon the slightest mistake made by myself or a fellow police officer.[17]

Dr. Kirkham goes on regarding his change in attitude:

I would like to take the average clinical psychologist or psychiatrist and invite him to function for just a day in the world of the policeman; to confront people whose problems are both serious and in need of immediate solution. I would invite him to walk, as I have, into a smoke-filled pool room where five or six angry men are swinging cues at one another. I would like the prison counsellor and parole officer to see their client Jones—not calm and composed in an office setting—but as the street cop sees him—beating his small child with a heavy belt buckle, or kicking his pregnant wife. I wish that they, and every judge and juror in our country, could see the ravages of crime as the cop on the beat must; innocent people cut, shot, beaten, raped, robbed, and murdered. It would, I feel certain, give them a different perspective on crime and criminals, just as it has me.[18]

The study of attitudes is important because they affect behavior. Consequently, most behavioral scientists feel that if a police officer has a biased attitude against a particular ethnic minority, he will behave in a biased manner toward that group.

Interestingly enough, in research done in three cities for the President's Commission on Law Enforcement and the Administration of Justice, there were some surprises.[19] Careful records were kept of what more than 600 police officers said and did over a period of time. In regard to what they said, more than three-fourths of the white officers working in black neighborhoods expressed negative attitudes against blacks. In addition, almost 30 percent of the black officers working in black neighborhoods expressed negative attitudes toward blacks. On the other hand, black officers assigned to mixed neighborhoods expressed less prejudice against blacks than those in black neighborhoods. If attitudes lead to behavior, then the possibility of fair treatment for ethnic minorities appeared to be rather poor.

However, observation of actual police behavior and practices did not support this contention. In only about 6 percent of the police–citizen contacts, which numbered over 5,000, could a negative attitude toward a particular ethnic minority be detected. The generalization that can be made from these data is that when a

[17] G. L. Kirkham, "A Professor's 'Street Lessons,'" *FBI Law Enforcement Bulletin*, March 1974, p. 20.

[18] Kirkham, "A Professor's 'Street Lessons,'" p. 17.

[19] D. J. Block and A. J. Reiss, Jr., "Patterns of Behavior in Police Citizen Transactions," in *Studies in Crime and Law Enforcement in Major Metropolitan Areas* (Washington, D.C.: U.S. Government Printing Office, 1967), 2, Sec. 1, 135–36.

citizen is deviant in behavior or disrespectful to an officer, no matter what his ethnic background, police officers are more likely to react in at least a discourteous manner.

Some encouraging implications can be made from this study. The main one is that a police officer may show signs of a prejudicial attitude but can still be taught to behave in a scrupulously fair manner. Consequently, an ethical commitment to fairness on the part of police and police administration is a must. In the attempt to develop a positive image throughout the community, law enforcement officers should reflect an attitude that overtly shows a desire to uphold the rights of all the people who are served.

Of late, much has been said about the changing attitudes of the people of the United States, attributed largely to what have become known as the civil rights movement and the youth revolution. But little has been said about the changing attitudes of law enforcement personnel, and evidence shows such changes in the rank and file of the police as well. During the past decade, a whole new generation of law enforcement officers has entered the field. These men and women tend to be better informed and better educated, as well as more impatient, than their predecessors. Because of this, law enforcement has been changing also:

> Although very few policemen would use the term, they have, in essence, become as much "radicalized" as any other American minority group. In support of this point, one needs only to look at police picket lines around city halls, work slowdowns, "blue flu," job actions, boycotts, press releases to the media, court injunctions procured by their legal counsel, association representatives in state capitals lobbying for and against legislation affecting police, and active campaigning for political candidates. Their actions have generated outraged cries from the establishment—the same establishment that complained about similar efforts of ethnic minorities at various points in our history.[20]

Evidence of this sort indicates that police attitudes, just like all society's attitudes, are changing. But besides this evolutionary change, deliberate efforts are being made to change attitudes. These efforts generally come under the broad heading of education.

Changing attitudes

Changes in attitudes are brought about in various ways. Some stem from a change in an individual situation. An example would be the

---

[20] J. P. Kimble, "Crime Solutions: Bigger Guns or Better Cops?" *Crime and Corrections,* 1 (Fall 1973), 31.

young man who develops a new attitude toward police when his brother becomes a policeman. Change in group membership, too, may cause a shift in attitude, as in the case of a youth who quits his gang to go back to school. This may well change his attitude toward police.

Other changes in attitude are brought about through education. A study done in Los Angeles some years ago, but still applicable, points this out rather well.[21] The study, conducted with third-grade youngsters, shows that social class and ethnic background influence children's perception of the police. The sample was composed of thirty black children from an area of low social and economic stability, thirty Mexican-American children from a neighborhood having average to below-average socioeconomic stability, and thirty Anglo-American Youngsters from an area of high socioeconomic stability.

The research consisted of asking the children to draw pictures of policemen at work. The results were analyzed and assigned into two basic categories, according to whether they showed (1) aggressive police behavior, such as fighting, chasing fugitives, and shooting; or police assistance having negative overtones, such as searching a building, unloading a paddy wagon, driving in a car with prisoners, or giving a traffic ticket; or (2) neutral behavior, such as directing traffic, riding in a car, or walking; or assisting with positive overtones, such as talking with children or giving directions.

Black and Mexican-American youngsters differed significantly from the upper-middle-class Anglos. The minority-group children were much more likely to picture police as aggressive or with negative behavior connotations. On the other hand, Anglo upper-middle-class children tended not to see the policeman's task as aggressive, negative, or hostile, but rather as neutral, nonaggressive, and assisting. There is every reason to believe that these children accurately reflected the attitudes of their parents or other significant persons in their environment.

After the children had been tested, the Los Angeles Police Department, in conjunction with the Los Angeles public schools, exposed them to their "Policeman Bill" program, in which a police officer presents a twenty-minute discussion to first-, second-, and third-grade children. He describes the function of the police, and

---

[21] R. L. Derbyshire, "Children's Perception of the Police: A Comparative Study of Attitude Change," *Journal of Criminal Law, Criminology and Police Science*, 39, No. 2 (June 1968), 183–90. Also see V. J. Derlega, N. K. Eberhardt, B. A. Weaver and J. D. Wiggs, "Officer Friendly—Crime Fighter," *FBI Law Enforcement Bulletin*, October 1980, pp. 8–14. Also see J. Jonikas, "Police and You: A Public Relations Program," *FBI Law Enforcement Bulletin*, July 1980, 18–21.

afterward, the youngsters are taken outside the school building and allowed to sit in a police patrol car, blow the siren, and so on.

When the thirty black children were retested two days after being exposed to the Policeman Bill program, their pictures revealed a somewhat different content. They showed significantly less hostility toward the police after this short contact.

This research seems to confirm the learning-theory assumption that attitudes are learned from one's culture or subculture. The most significant finding for the practicing police officer, however, is that with a little effort, attitudes learned from one's culture can be changed.

From studies of this type, it becomes apparent that leaving to chance the development of children's attitudes toward law enforcement may be rather foolhardy. A child's parent is a significant educator of that child. Therefore, efforts should be made to influence the parent, who in turn will influence the child to develop a positive attitude toward law enforcement.

A second important developer of attitudes in children is the teacher. The results of a study conducted in Los Angeles over 25 years ago are still worth reviewing.[22] They indicated that female schoolteachers and housewives tended to rate the police rather low. Approximately 63 percent of the housewives and 87 percent of the schoolteachers gave the police low ratings. This may indicate that police departments need to direct public relations programs toward housewives and teachers, because they greatly influence the attitudes of children, who are the citizens of the future.

In fact, law enforcement needs to be concerned with education of the public in the broadest sense regarding the police and the police role. Representatives of the police need to meet with and talk to all manner of groups and organizations. An alert, forward-looking police administration will make arrangements to see that education of this sort is carried out.

At the same time, there may also be some room for improvement in police officers' attitudes toward the people they serve. Police officers need to appreciate the fact that the majority of their time is spent not strictly in law enforcement, but rather in what could be broadly called a social role. In all beginning training courses for police, as well as in all retraining courses, this matter should be covered. This concern has been stated quite well:

> Broaden the coverage of subjects pertaining to the policeman's social role in training programs, to include law enforcement, orientation to the behavioral

---

[22] G. D. Gourley, *Public Relations and the Police* (Springfield, Ill.: Chas. C Thomas, 1953), p. 78.

and social sciences, human behavior and civil rights, minority culture patterns, needs, values, family structure, religious philosophies, and individual and group attitudes, concepts of mental health, alcoholism and drug abuse, among others.[23]

This recommendation is being made often, since training in these matters does tend at present to be inadequate. In police academies throughout the United States, courses that come under the heading of "human relations" seem to have the least effect on new patrolmen. Courses that treat arrest, first aid, and the use of weapons are taught by lecture and demonstration; but the management of personal relations in a tense situation is not easily taught in an academic setting. At least one authority in the field of police science feels that training in this area is inadequate:

> It is the universal testimony of the officers that I have interviewed that training room discussions of minority groups and police–community relations have little impact and that such impressions that they do produce quickly evaporate when the officer goes on the street and first encounters hostility or suspicious behavior.[24]

Another authority wrote that, in his opinion, the emphasis in police–community relations classes leaves something to be desired. He feels that policemen need to study themselves more. Most of the present study that policemen devote to themselves consists of a sterile, theoretical picture of what police behavior should be. Police need to learn about themselves as persons and as members of a police group. Obviously, studying oneself is a very difficult task. However, because police are in a very sensitive role in the community, this is an essential part of police training. Police officers must learn to be more in touch with themselves, their own feelings, and their own actions and reactions, so that they can better control those actions.[25]

A person receives education not only through formal schooling but also through interpersonal relationships. This is the kind of education that a police officer can make use of to effect attitude changes. Each member of law enforcement should realize that he or she can have some positive effect on the public's attitudes toward police, and that treating every person as humanely as possible under the circumstances—circumstances that are often quite

---

[23] R. V. Badalamente, C. E. George, P. J. Halterlein, T. T. Jackson, S. A. Moore, and R. Rio, "Training Police for Their Social Role," *Journal of Police Science and Administration*, 1 (December 1973), 453.

[24] Wilson, "The Police in the Ghetto," p. 74.

[25] J. F. Heaphy, "Community Relations Training—An Alternate View," *Journal of Criminal Law, Criminology and Police Science*, 62 (December 1971), 570–73.

trying, to say the least—is the best method of cultivating a positive attitude. This is education of the best sort.

Summary

In this chapter we have discussed the nature of attitudes and their relationship to police-citizen contacts. Attitudes are long-lasting, conceptual, motivational, emotional, and adaptive organizational processes concerned with a person or object. There are five influences on social behavior: social situations, the prevailing social norm, a person's personality, his transitional condition, and the way he perceives and interprets a situation. Most social scientists regard the last factor as equivalent to attitude.

Attitudes have certain dimensions. The five most important are direction, degree, content, consistency, and strength.

Both psychoanalytical and learning theories have been used to explain the acquisition of negative attitudes toward the police by minority groups. Psychoanalytical theory stresses culture and experiences as they affect sexual impulses, which, in turn, influence behavior and attitudes. Learning theory suggests that culture and experience *directly* affect behavior and attitudes. If negative attitudes are learned, some effort can be made to change them into what could be called socially acceptable attitudes.

These theories apply not only to minority-group attitudes toward the police but also to police attitudes toward those they serve.

According to the logic of learning theory, it appears that much can be done to improve attitudes. Generally speaking, education in its broadest sense is the best hope for changing attitudes—education of the police as well as of the public.

Discussion topics

1. Of what concern to the police student is the study of attitudes?
2. What is the difference between attitude and prejudice?
3. Describe very briefly how attitudes may be acquired.
4. What do studies suggest about minority-group attitudes toward the police?

5. What do studies suggest about police attitudes toward minority groups?
6. Discuss the idea that behavior changes may precede attitude changes.
7. What bearing does education have on attitude changes?

Annotated references

Derbyshire, R. L., "Children's Perception of the Police: A Comparative Study of Attitude Change," *Journal of Criminal Law, Criminology and Police Science,* 59 (June 1968), 183–90. This is an interesting report of a study done on children. The study concludes that negative attitudes toward police can be changed with a little effort.

Grier, W. H., and P. M. Cobbs, *Black Rage.* New York: Basic Books, 1968. This book sets forth the psychoanalytical theory of the acquisition of attitudes by black people.

Hollingshead, A. B., and F. C. Redlick, *Social Class and Mental Illness: A Community Study.* New York: John Wiley, 1958. Although this book is primarily concerned with mental illness, it gives a very good picture of attitudes and behavior of the different social classes in the United States.

Kirkham, G. L., "A Professor's 'Street Lessons,'" *FBI Law Enforcement Bulletin,* March 1974, pp. 14–22. An interesting article by a college professor who became a policeman for six months. His experiences suggest that the examination and discussion of police attitudes and actions in the classroom may be quite different from reality.

Krech, D., and R. S. Crutchfield, *Elements of Psychology,* 3rd ed. New York: Knopf, 1970. This text has a good working definition of attitude. It also does a credible job of discussing its dimensions and total concept.

Miller, W. E., "Lower-Class Culture as a Generating Milieu of Gang Delinquency," *Journal of Social Issues,* 14, No. 3 (1958), 5–19. This article is a classic in the field of defining the attitudes of dropouts.

Police Use of Deadly Force; What Police and the Community Can Do about It, Washington, D.C.: U.S. Government Printing Office, 1978. This booklet contains six papers presented at a workshop conducted by the Community Relations Service at the Annual Conference of the National Association of Human Rights Workers, Nashville, Tennessee, in 1978.

chapter six

Police and the Community: Historical and Contemporary Perspectives

Law enforcement and the equal administration of justice have become of major concern in recent years. The rapid growth of the minority population (see Chapter 7)—particularly in our urban areas—with attendant problems in inflation, housing, education, employment, and social welfare services, highlighted by increasing social change, has accentuated these concerns.

The subject of social change has many facets, but its most popular concept is bound to the struggle of minorities to gain equality in all aspects of life. The expectations, excitements, and additional frustrations engendered by the failure of some to understand fully the aspirations and problems of minority groups have compounded the difficulties in law enforcement and administration of justice.

Foremost among these difficulties are the relations among police, minority groups, and the general community. According to the Rand Corporation's Population Research Center, police relations with minorities are compounded by urbanization and there is increasing evidence of deterioration in these relations. The research center found that the number of serious racial incidents (those disputes that could erupt into open violence) totaled 336 between October 1979 and April 1980, an increase of 38 incidents from the same period the year before. There are widespread charges of police brutality and demand for greater assertion of civilian control over police actions. On the other hand, many police officials decry the growing disrespect for law, public apathy, mollycoddling of criminals by the courts, and political influence on the law enforcement process. Some police continue to view civil-rights group members as troublemakers, disruptive of the law and order the police have sworn to uphold. At the same time, some minority-group members hold a stereotyped image of the police officer. All these misconceptions severely hamper cooperative relations.

Social change:
implications for law enforcement

According to population experts, America is undergoing dramatic changes in urban population. This means that reappraisals must be made of most governmental operations. Vast are the implications of these changes for the reorganization of law enforcement agencies and for the redefinition of their functions. Quantitatively, the displacement of booming populations to growing suburban areas and the emergence of the "metropolitan area" have introduced new problems of crime control in general and police–community relations in particular.

Even more elusive and perhaps even more difficult to resolve are the qualitative effects. Population growth has changed central-city concentration little, but the "flight to the suburbs" has drained the inner city of those groups in the population that traditionally were forces for social control and stability. Responsibilities for such control come to rest more and more on government—more specifically, on law enforcement agencies. The city provides decreasing psychological security for its inhabitants just when the crying need for some security characterizes increasing proportions of the population, especially the rapidly growing numbers of minority-group members caught in the difficult transition from folk to urban values.

With constant changes in composition in the population, unceasing reassessment is required. If the dialogue between the community and law enforcement agencies breaks down, reassessment becomes impossible and the potential for constructive action is sharply curtailed.

The people and the police:
potential explosiveness in continuing conflict

A process has taken place in the United States that has afflicted many civilizations in the past and has often been a prelude to their disintegration: People who had traditionally made a living from agriculture were driven from the land by technological changes and poured into metropolitan cities that were not able to absorb them.

In the third century A.D., for example, drastic changes took place in the agriculture of the Roman world. Small farms gave way to the *latifundia*—huge holdings engaged in mass production based on slave labor. The productivity of the land was increased by the use of technology, but when free farmers were driven from the soil, their migration caused chaos in the cities. "The social consequence," wrote Arnold Toynbee in *A Study of History*, "was the depopulization of the countryside and the creation of a parasitic urban proletariat in the cities. . . ."

The parallel with the American dilemma is striking. Technological changes in agriculture—primarily the replacement of men by machines—have uprooted masses of farm workers and driven them to the cities to seek precarious refuge in the slums and ghettos. Thus far, American leaders seem as helpless before the problem as were the Romans.

State legislatures and the U.S. House of Representatives have failed to reapportion themselves sufficiently as a population has moved from farm to town. Still another problem, to be analyzed in the future, concerns the effects of the energy crisis on city dwellers. The mobility of the urban dweller has been acknowledged as a barrier to the complete disintegration that would be caused by a *total lack* of respect and cooperation with agents of the administration of justice. If this mobility is removed, there may be some justification, at least for the activists in our cities, for striking out at the police, since, to some, police are symbolic of all that is wrong in our society.

We are witnessing a breakdown in dialogue. The *relationship* of the police to the people, has been transformed into a *confrontation* with racial and ethnic groups, social-action and civil-rights groups, the adolescent community, and the courts. More than at any other time in our history, the police are estranged from other agencies and from groups within the community. This is the most urgent problem facing our police today. This concern is given greater weight when one considers the U.S. Department of Justice reports that indicate cases of *alleged* use of excessive police force nationwide increased from 24 to 58, up 142 percent over the first half of the fiscal years 1979 and 1980. This increase is considered significant because the bulk of such cases usually are reported in the last half of the fiscal year.

If the emotions of fear and hate characterize the current relationship between the ethnic minority community and the police, the continuation of these conflicts has both an immediate and a long-range effect. An immediate effect is the fact that every contact between a police officer and a minority-group member is tinged with the possibility of violence. Of even greater concern, however, is the long-range effect, the transmission of these attitudes to succeeding generations of young people.

The most serious problems are not with the general community; rather, they are found in the relationships the police have with *youth* and *ethnic minority groups*. In these two portions of the community, it is fair to say that the police have been unable to develop effective means of communication. Although they must continue to try to resolve differences, it is doubtful that even the most imaginative public relation techniques would ever be successful in the case of some ethnic minority groups. These techniques, unfortunately, are viewed by some as "self-serving" and "phony," and immediately become suspect. The hard-to-reach cannot effectively be engaged with anything less than genuine communication, and this involves a desire and a willingness to talk, to listen, to discuss, and to act. Genuine communication includes the willingness to adjust operating procedures (such as harassment, disrespect, discourteous demeanor, and the like) when they appear to be irritating already existing police–community relation problems. It also involves a continuous process of dealing effectively with personal problems in the community.

It is expected that the people deeply involved in confrontations or conflicting viewpoints (such as civil-rights movements or civil-disobedience campaigns) are not going to see things from the same point of view as the police. Bitter complaints are often made about the diversity of viewpoints between demonstrators, minority-group members, civil-rights or civil-disobedience activists, and law enforcement personnel, who consider their actions necessary and proper for preserving public peace and order. The complaints quite often concern the *attitudes* shown by the police as well as the *tactics* used.

The following material illustrates the conflicting viewpoints held by both parties.[1] Let us first examine the complaints against the police.

[1] N. A. Watson, *Police–Community Relations*, (Washington, D.C.: International Association of Chiefs of Police, 1966), pp. 28–37 (summarized). For a more current resource, refer to K. W. Johnson and C. A. Hornung, "Importance of Police Contacts in the Formulation of Youths' Attitudes," *Journal of Criminal Justice*, 6, No. 1 (Spring 1978), 53–67.

Police Brutality.   The most frequently mentioned charge is that the police are brutal in their handling of demonstrators and others, even criminals. Police experience shows that these charges range from vague, nonspecific opinions to cases which do involve excessive use of force contrary to police rules and regulations. What is regarded as brutal depends, of course, on the situation and the individual. Thus, such police actions as restraining individuals in a crowd from proceeding with a march where officers do no more than block the way, especially if they have to shove people back, may be so characterized. Any use of the baton, firing over the heads of the crowd, and use of tear gas, fire hoses, or dogs are tactics often included (at least from the minority group's perspective) under the term *brutality*. There have been instances in which the use of language itself has been called brutal. Objection has been made to verbal abuse. Rough, harsh language, and especially the use of such derogatory terms as "nigger" and even "boy" is interpreted by many as indicative of a brutal attitude. As Bowen pointed out:

> The Negro fight for civil rights has created a climate of mind in which any arrest or prosecution of a Negro takes on, for many Negroes and some whites too, an aspect of discrimination. And it has called down upon the police departments a "brutality" charge that has impaired the morale of policemen and hindered police recruitment.

> To a great extent the "police brutality" cries are directed not against actual instances of brutality but against the police as symbols and agents of a white-dominated society. Over a three-year period ending in mid-1965, a total of 4,755 allegations of "police brutality" involving possible violations of federal law were referred to the FBI. Out of all these, indictments were returned in 41 cases and convictions were secured in ten. The smoke billows forth, apparently, out of all proportion to the fire.[2]

Differential Treatment of Blacks.   Just about as frequent as complaints of police brutality are complaints of differential treatment. This is also at times a rather vague and nonspecific charge. It includes a variety of practices that are regarded as discriminatory. Complainants say, for example, that a black is far more likely to be arrested for a given act than a white man is. And, when arrested, he is more likely to be convicted and sent to jail. Blacks complain that they are more frequently accosted and questioned by police— in other words, suspected—than are white citizens. Police are believed by blacks to be more officious with them, e.g., to order them around. Also, and very important, they feel that police do not pay as much attention to complaints by blacks, that they do not

---

[2] W. Bowen, "Crime in the Cities, An Unnecessary Crisis," *Fortune,* December 1965, p. 141; and Johnson and Hornung, "Importance of Police Contacts."

take as seriously offenses by blacks against blacks as they would if a white person were the victim. In line with the brutality charges, they see the police as more likely to use physical force against them than against whites.

One of the problems here, as seen by blacks and others who are largely in working-class minorities, is policing on the basis of social class. Many lower-class people believe that they get different treatment at the hands of the police than do people of greater means. A black who is an official in a labor union drives a Thunderbird. He says he has been stopped by the police five times in two years merely for questioning. On the occasions when he was well-dressed he was courteously requested to show his driver's license and car registration and permitted to go on. On one occasion, he was working around his house and, roughly dressed, went to a lumber yard for some supplies. That time he was ordered out of the car, spread-eagled against it and searched. Obviously, the officers must have thought that a person dressed as he was must have stolen the car. The man was not charged with a traffic violation at any time.

Another example is that of a white-collar-type businessman who drives a nice-looking automobile that was involved in an accident. He did not stop in time at a traffic light and rammed the car in front. The car he hit was a rattletrap driven by a poorly dressed black. The police came to investigate. The businessman said, "They were 'sir-ing' me all over the place, but were harsh and gruff with the man whose car I hit. I had to remind them that I was the one who was at fault."

Another aspect of this class-based treatment is the use of language or remarks which show disapproval or disparagement, which belittle or discredit the person being contacted. An officer stopped a black woman on the street late one night and asked her what she was doing there. She replied she had just finished work and was on her way home. He asked where she worked and what she did. She told him she worked at the hotel (a high-class place) and that she was a cook. The officer said, "You mean you're a dishwasher?" The woman really was a cook. This is one small example of downgrading by a thoughtless remark. It is a type of carelessness we must guard against in our contacts.

It is important for us to understand that when people think they are being treated differently, they are likely to react differently. Acts which to the officer seem entirely proper and justified may be regarded as highly discriminative. It is not unexpected, therefore, that blacks regard some arrests as maliciously intended. This is often the reaction, too, to actions taken by police when searching for logical suspects in a crime.

"Overpolicing" in Minority Districts.   This complaint is actually another instance of differential treatment, but it bears special mention because of its relationship to one of the basic principles of police administration. The effective allocation of men and selective enforcement are administrative procedures which aim at economical and effective deployment of manpower. Police attempt to concentrate their enforcement resources at those times, places, and events where violations of law are more likely to occur. To do otherwise would result in inefficiency and waste as well as markedly reduced progress toward the objectives for which police are maintained.

It so happens, however, that the concentration of police in black districts is regarded by many as both insulting and threatening. The presence of police obviously does lead to arrests for violations of the law. Arrest statistics together with complaints and offenses otherwise known do tend to show higher crime rates in those districts where there are more officers. Some minority-group leaders have maintained that this concentration of police in itself helps produce comparatively higher crime rates because offenses in other districts are going unnoticed, since the police are not there. The difference here is, in part, a controversy as to which is cause and which is effect.

Another aspect of this complaint is the charge by blacks that police harass them. Harassment, they maintain, involves unnecessary and unjustified questioning, frisking under questionable circumstances, traffic stops and car searches on flimsy suspicions, breaking up of small gatherings where no law is being violated, and other practices. They see as a special kind of harassment what they regard as the harsh and unsympathetic reception given a Negro who lodges a complaint against an officer. Arrests on trumped-up charges, false arrests, are also mentioned as a type of harassment.

An example of the kind of policing involved in this complaint was recounted by a member of a human relations commission. In a certain city there was a honky-tonk district where rowdyism on New Year's Eve was common. This particular New Year's Eve was no exception. A fight broke out and officers on the scene called for help. Some of the persons involved were blacks; most were not. Squad cars were dispatched to the scene. But, curiously, squad cars were also dispatched "on the double" to the "downtown" area of the black section—where there was no trouble. The people there pointed to this circumstance as an indication of the readiness of the police to believe the worst about all blacks. The community did not view the precautionary move by police as preventative. Instead they saw it as a special kind of harassment.

In contrast to the attitude of some blacks relative to the presence of police is the widespread feeling among middle- and upper-class blacks that they want and need police protection. Police experience shows that these citizens are just as concerned about civil disorder and crime as white citizens in similar socioeconomic brackets. Instead of complaining about the presence of police, they request it.

Improper Policing of Demonstrations. Complaints have been made that police are too strict in their supervision of legitimate demonstrations. The conditions laid down by the police, the ground rules, are sometimes regarded as unfairly restrictive. Some complainants allege suppression of legitimate demonstrations. This would involve such practices as refusal to grant parade permits and blocking access to the objective of the demonstration, as, for example, city hall. Some demonstrators have complained about police taking their pictures during a demonstration, a procedure they regard as a threat.

Associated with this charge are additional complaints of police brutality. Demonstrators who refuse to move after proper warning and who have to be bodily carried to police vehicles complain of intentional rough handling. Occasionally, women have complained that officers have taken immoral advantage of this situation or have embarrassed them by careless, "undignified," or "ungraceful" handling.

It is unquestionably true that improper policing of demonstrations can divert the demonstrators from their original target and cause them to focus on the police. Militant leaders can take advantage of inept, incorrect police action to escalate the demonstration and enlist sympathizers. The right to demonstrate peaceably, the right of peaceful protest, is basic to our form of government. The actions of demonstrators and protestors, no matter how peaceful, however, cannot be permitted to prohibit the free exercise of the rights of others. This is one of the reasons police control is required. In our democracy it is not the function of the police to prevent properly conducted demonstrations or protests no matter how distasteful they may be, so long as they do not violate the law. It is the function of the police to protect peaceful demonstrators against interference by rowdies or counterdemonstrators. The police are not in business to maintain the old way of life by preventing social change. In these matters there is a fine line between proper and improper policing. This is one of the reasons a community cannot afford untrained police.

Use of Black Officers. The confusion that exists is well illustrated in charges involving discriminatory assignment of black policemen. On the one hand, several instances were reported in which blacks had expressed displeasure when black officers were assigned to answer their calls; they wanted white policemen. So did some white persons. On the other hand, there are also complaints from blacks that not enough black officers are assigned to duty where they live. Then, too, there are complaints that not enough blacks are employed as policemen and that too few of them are employed in command positions. A few years ago, just seeing blacks as officers was enough, but we have moved on from there, and now blacks want increasingly to see black officers move up the ladder. Blacks also sometimes object that black officers are assigned only to black districts, that they are not permitted to arrest white offenders, that they are discriminated against in promotions, and that when police work in pairs, they are assigned only with other blacks. One chief reported he had been criticized for not seeking to recruit black officers in other cities when he pointed out the lack of qualified applicants at home.

Lack of Confidence in Police. There have been well-publicized charges that police are "on the take," some of which are true. Some complaints have charged that police permit gambling, prostitution, illegal liquor and narcotic activities, fencing operations, and the like because they are being paid off by the criminals. Such beliefs produce a lack of confidence in law enforcement in general. The racial situation as it has developed in the past few years has resulted in increased sensitivity on the part of the populace and the police to those aspects of police operations that impinge on the civil-rights question. Some police executives have noted that complaints about the police seem to relate more directly to bad attitudes, whether fancied or real, on the part of officers than they do to improper actions. This lack of confidence has produced demands for citizens' review boards to review complaints concerning police actions.

A good indication of the problems as seen by police officers is found in the complaints they have made:

1. Assaults on officers.

2. Verbal abuse, provocation, and baiting of police.

3. Defiance and interference with lawful arrests and other police functions.

4. Lack of respect for police authority and the law. In this connection, several respondents remarked that their men have noticed an increasing belligerence and arrogance.

5. Lack of manpower, causing fear of unwarranted attacks by black groups against lone officers when making routine traffic stops or other normal enforcement activities.

6. Black officers complain about abusive language from black demonstrators.

7. False accusations against police. Some have noted that the purpose behind these seems to be harassment of the police. Some have also complained that lack of prosecution for false accusations encourages more of the same. As a sidelight, some police officers have complained about the detailed reports that are required when such complaints are made even though the complaints are patently false. In this connection, a man engaged in police–community relations activities in a large city told the writer of his experience. This man is a black and is not a policeman. He said that in his police–community relations work, he has talked with many blacks who complained about police behavior. Some of the cases, although minor in nature, appeared to be justified, in that the officer probably could have handled himself with greater finesse. On the other side of the coin, he said he had been told by some complainants that they had made the complaint as defensive strategy. They felt that a complaint of brutality would give them some bargaining leverage. In other instances, they admitted that the complaint was made in order to "get back at" the officer for arresting them.

8. Lack of police power to take effective action *before* overt acts of violence occur.

9. Despite the fact that many police departments would gladly employ qualified blacks as police officers, they are sometimes unable to do so because blacks will not apply. Some respondents attribute this to the fact that police are looked upon with such disfavor by the black community that young men who would make good policemen are unwilling to face the disapproval they fear would result. Others say it is mainly because qualified blacks can command higher pay than police departments are able to offer. It should be said here that the reaction of many police chiefs to this situation is not one of complete resignation. Some have taken special steps to find qualified men. The general feeling is that qualifications should not be lowered. Nor should black applicants be hired simply for the sake of having some blacks in uniform. That would not be fair to the public, including blacks.

10. Growing resistance to overtures at friendly communication on police beats in minority areas. Some have complained that even though police officers have tried to establish friendly relationships in the interest of harmony and good police service, they have been unable to do so because the people react to them with coldness and remain aloof, if not actually hostile.

11. Many officers have complained that the law is being applied unequally, with preferential treatment being given to minority groups. They feel that pressure groups have succeeded in preventing police from fully enforcing the law where minority individuals are concerned. Officers complain that they must assume a "kid gloves" attitude in order not to overstep their authority and to avoid criticism against which they have no adequate defense. Many officers feel that no amount of bending over backwards to be fair can satisfy what they regard as the unreasonable expectations of the more militant leaders and, at the same time, allow for effective enforcement of the law.

12. Apathy of the public and lack of backing in enforcing the law. Police sometimes feel that they are being asked to do an impossible job. They are expected to maintain order and to arrest violators and, having done so, find that when the heat is turned on, they are left holding the bag. In this connection, they find particularly discouraging the support given by some public officials to acts of civil disobedience. They see in this a kind of encouragement for lawbreaking, with the official "feathering his political nest" at the expense of respect for law and order. On the other hand, the police are required by law to protect from interference and violence people who are engaging in peaceful protest or demonstration. That is a right guaranteed to any citizen, but many people, sometimes the majority, will turn against the police when they offer that protection.

13. Police often complain about the lenience of the courts and their hesitance to convict when the race issue is raised as a defense.

14. Officers remark that minority-group members seem increasingly ready to complain about minor matters, routine matters, and police actions that are essential and unavoidable in the enforcement of the law. However, we must realize that even routine methods that are legally right and properly used may be regarded as objectionable by people who dislike the police anyway.

15. Some officers feel that undue emphasis is being placed on the racial aspects of many questions affecting police performance at the expense of successful enforcement against criminals.

16. Unfair treatment by the news media. Police complain about the nature of the photographs that are printed in newspapers and the interpretation placed upon them. They often feel that the police are portrayed unfavorably and are being used as whipping boys.

17. Complaints have been registered about inflammatory public statements by religious and other minority-group leaders that stereotype police officers as prejudiced and insensitive.

18. In a few instances, officers have complained that incidents have been set up or maneuvered in such a way as to deliberately place the police in an unfavorable light.[3]

[3] Watson, *Police-Community Relations.*

It can be seen from these complaints that there remains a serious communications gap. The viewpoints regarding situations growing out of racial tensions are certainly widely divergent. As one official remarked, "There appears to be a communications block between law enforcement administrators and police officers on the one hand and minority-group leaders and minority-group 'men on the street' on the other." He expressed the opinion that this block appears to be growing. He said, "The minority-group leaders seem to have an increasing fear of an Uncle Tom label which militant leaders place upon those who do communicate." He feels that the average minority-group citizen is being unduly influenced by what he calls the propaganda of the militant leaders, which labels law enforcement as a tool of the white power structure.

The differences in viewpoint illustrated by the foregoing point out the difficulties involved in impartially and impersonally enforcing the law and the importance of reaching an effective medium of communication. The urgent need for clear understanding of the problems as the people see them requires that we go to them. It is only by listening attentively to their ideas and suggestions—even when these are only implied in complaints—that we can arrive at a productive definition of the problems. Why should we not seek the help of our constituents? In their counsel we may find the answers to frustrating situations.

One Negro leader who had been invited to speak to a police–community relations forum started off by saying, "I am a militant, I am a radical. But I am not a lunatic. My reaction to the invitation to speak to you was first one of amazement. This is the first time in all the years I have been active in this work that the police have ever shown any interest in hearing what I have to say. Second, my reaction is one of gratitude. I am pleased to discuss our problems with you. I don't expect you to like everything I have to say, but I do expect that we will all go away with a better understanding of each other." The rest of his talk and the dialogue that followed did promote better understanding. The police officials in attendance went away enriched in their ability to cope with the kinds of problems that were brought out. It would seem wise to listen to the viewpoints, the gripes, the suggestions of many kinds of people— businessmen, the poor, youths, ethnic-group representatives, civic leaders, and so on.

Although we have discussed attitudes more fully in another chapter, it is appropriate to point out here that the view law enforcement has of demonstrators, civil-disobedience participants, and certain members of minority groups is often a result of the attitudes taken toward law enforcement. Attitudes on both sides must change. If law enforcement programs ignore the conditions that have motivated the behavior of these groups, then police officers will continue to act in ways that invite hostility, anger, and even outright violence.

Violence has long been known to our society. It has been part of the history of the United States, and of other countries, for many centuries. The historical content of such activities will be discussed in the following section, as will the tangle of issues and circumstances—social, economic, political, and psychological—that arise out of the historic pattern of police–community relations in America.

Riots and civil disobedience: historical and contemporary aspects

As we have seen, civil disobedience, racial violence, and riots have been part of the history of the United States. Citizen–police confrontations have, therefore, existed as a law enforcement problem in one form or another for a long time. Perhaps such confrontations are indigenous to our society, which was largely founded by dissenters and was from the beginning dedicated to freedom of expression and conscience.

Curry and King have stated that violence has changed very little through the years.[4] Some of the contemporary disturbances in the United States are similar in many respects to those that have occurred throughout history. Thus, the contemporary literature draws on established elements of both past and contemporary problems: persuasive insecurities, a mounting current of crime, prosperity existing side by side with poverty, and the ironic contrast between the positive aspects of our competitive society and the continued spread of crime.[5]

HISTORICAL ASPECTS

In order to trace the pattern and identify the recurrent themes of political and social unrest and, most important, provide a perspective for protest activities of the present era, let us begin with an outline of citizen demonstrations and a brief account of their devel-

[4] J. E. Curry and G. D. King, *Race, Tension and the Police*, 2nd ed. (New York: John Wiley, 1977).

[5] D. J. Bordua, ed., *The Police: Six Sociological Essays*, 2nd ed. (New York: John Wiley, 1973), p. 3.

opment. *The past has much to tell us about the present.* To comprehend the contemporary police–community relation problems in the United States, it is necessary to examine, evaluate, and derive some understanding of such historical problems.

The following are brief summaries of some of the most serious disturbances in the United States. (For a more extensive examination of such historical disturbances, see Appendix A.) Selected from Thomas J. Fleming's article, "Revolt in America," they represent the types of problems that have led to violence over a broad period of time and in different geographical areas.

Shays' Rebellion: In 1786, Daniel Shays, captain of a regiment during the War of Independence, along with 1,500 farmers, prevented the state's court from convening for the purpose of foreclosure proceedings for debts resulting from a depression in the state of Massachusetts. They blocked all attempts on foreclosures of property for debt. The mob soon got out of control and proceeded to physically abuse officials, loot homes, and make serious threats to burn government buildings.

Shays' "army" soon disintegrated into a handful of fugitives, with Shays himself fleeing to Vermont when the governor of Massachusetts declared the state "in a period of rebellion" and ordered the militia into active status.

Nat Turner's Revolt: This significant rebellion on the part of some of Virginia's 400,000 slaves has been covered by numerous books; one written by William Styron received an excellent response.

Nat Turner launched an insurrection in Southampton County, Virginia in 1831 (Figure 6–1). On the night of August 21, he and a few companions murdered several farmers and their families throughout the countryside. Twenty farms were attacked, and before the rampage was brought to an end by the county militia, at least forty Negroes died in the fighting and twelve were executed. The death toll of the whites totaled approximately 57.

Nat Turner was subsequently hanged, and although his insurrection was neither the first nor the last Negro revolt, its mindless violence was "so appalling, [Turner] silenced all hope of emancipating the Negro by peaceful vote, as Thomas Jefferson and James Madison had for decades pleaded."

The Draft Riots: In 1863, President Abraham Lincoln's administration had decided that the war was going badly and the North was in need of a considerable increase in manpower. Therefore, the draft was initiated as a desperate measure. Unfortunately, Congress, in its efforts to push through the bill, constructed a rather unfair—that is, unfair to the poor—draft law, since a substitute could be hired for $300 to take the place of the drafted person.

FIGURE 6-1. *Nat Turner (1800–1831), American slave leader.*
From a nineteenth century wood engraving. Reproduced with per-
mission of The Granger Collection.

This precipitated the infamous draft riots in New York City on July 13, 1863.

Approximately 800,000 draft eligibles resided in New York City, and about 10,000 people protested the drawing of names for the city's first draft on July 11, 1863. With the assistance, in the opinion of some historians, of Confederate soldiers who had infiltrated the city, the mob surged down Broadway to 29th Street where the Federal Provost Marshal was scheduled to draw more names of those eligible for the draft. Police officers, attempting to control the situation, were severely beaten—some critically. The demonstrators forced the Provost Marshal and his staff to withdraw and devastated the building, eventually setting it on fire.

The riot continued for four days, and on several occasions troops were forced to use point-blank artillery fire, as depicted in Figure 6–2, to disperse howling charges. (Federal authorities had eventually dispatched troops to the embattled city.) On the fourth day, battle-tired regiments from the Army of the Potomac poured into the city, and the draft riot was brought to a halt.

The Great Strike: In 1877, when America was in its fourth year of a terrible depression, the four largest railroads in the country announced that wages were going to be decreased by at least 10 percent. The employees were nonunionized and were being paid

FIGURE 6-2. *The New York City Draft Riots of July 13–16, 1863. Wood engraving from a contemporary German-language American newspaper. Reproduced with permission of The Granger Collection.*

very poor wages (approximately $1.75 per day); but a single railroad, the Pennsylvania, reportedly showed net profits of $25,000,000 a year, so the attempt to slash the workers' pay touched off a national crisis.

Employees of the Baltimore and Ohio, the Pennsylvania, the New York Central, and the Erie refused to work—in essence, they struck. The strikers seized the railroad yards in Baltimore and permitted no trains to move. Freight and buildings were destroyed. And the rioters' numbers grew to an estimated 15,000. President Rutherford B. Hayes responded to the plea from the governor of the state and dispatched 500 federal troops to Baltimore. The disturbance subsided almost immediately upon the show of force.

In Pittsburgh, the strikers followed the same pattern, but there they were far better organized, and their leaders were men with wilder ideas. It was necessary, therefore, to rush 650 state militiamen from Philadelphia. Upon their arrival, they fought a battle with the strikers, killing approximately 25. The rioters forced the Philadelphia militia into the Pennsylvania roundhouse and bombarded them with bricks; in fact, in several instances, the dissenters utilized firearms. Freight cars were burned, and the Philadelphia militia was forced to "fight their way out from the roundhouse and retreat."

Like a contagious disease, the strike moved from city to city; Omaha, San Francisco, and St. Louis felt the sting of the reactionary mob. In New York and Buffalo, the Central yards were seized. Rioters stormed through the streets of Chicago, forcing workers to quit their jobs, shutting down factories, stores, and construction projects, and intimidating officials into signing papers promising to raise wages.

Acting on advice from a Civil War general, President Hayes actually ordered a proclamation prepared declaring that the unruly rioters were "levying war" against the United States. However, before the proclamation was made, the great strike had begun to be brought under control by state militiamen, local policemen, and, on several occasions, federal troops, (Figure 6–3).

Jacob Coxey's "Industrial Army":   In 1894, Jacob Coxey, a reformer, led a group of unemployed in a march on Washington. In order to sustain themselves, his followers stole food as they advanced. However, Coxey soon saw that a majority of the people of the United States were extremely hostile to his "industrial army." He gathered only 1,200 protesters in Washington instead of the 100,000 he had so confidently predicted prior to the march.[6]

The riots, mob disturbances, and all-out rebellion described above (see Appendix A for a more detailed listing of major riots affecting police) certainly do not constitute the entire scope of disturbances that have taken place in the United States. There have been other times when Americans were extremely concerned, fearing that the nation was on the fringe of anarchy. For example, when the Industrial Workers of the World issued a cry for the removal of the system utilized to set wages and called for strikes to sabotage the war effort during World War I, Americans were very apprehensive. The federal government quickly took the union leaders into custody and filed charges of sedition; such tactics eliminated the IWW as a force in American labor. In 1932, 15,000 World War I veterans assembled in Washington in the "Bonus March" to demand from Congress immediate payment on certificates that had been issued for their war service, and that were not legally due until 1945. The majority returned home peacefully when Congress declined to pass the bill they wanted. The president reluctantly ordered the army to expel the 300 who refused to leave the Capitol grounds.

NATURE, SCOPE, AND EXTENT OF CONTEMPORARY POLICE–CITIZEN CONFRONTATIONS

In the 1960s, we witnessed numerous savage urban disorders in American society. It is apparent that attacks upon both representatives of government agencies (police, firemen, National

---

[6] Summarized with the permission of T. J. Fleming from his "Revolt in America," *This Week*, Sept. 1, 1968, pp. 2–8.

FIGURE 6-3. *The Great Railroad Strike of 1877. Wood engraving from a contemporary American newspaper. Reproduced with permission of The Granger Collection.*

Guardsmen, court and correctional personnel) and property are ageless manifestations of social problems. The events that touch off violent mass disturbances are deeply rooted in the neighborhood, the community, the family, the times in which we live and, as we shall see, the administration of the criminal justice system and process (police, courts, and corrections).[7] Some of our contemporary problems have centered on the Vietnam War, the radical transformations in community life of our time, and the transition of urban populations, which involves the wholesale settlement of minority-group members and causes problems of housing, income, and so on. These changes within metropolitan regions, along with the more liberal attitude of college students, have generated problems of crime control that have ultimately resulted in the use of law enforcement personnel.

The following observations were made after a brief examination of urban disorders and police–community relations problems during the past two centuries.[8]

1. Major disorders or riots have occurred frequently in cities of the United States.

2. The causes of riots have been consistently identified as major social issues—for example, labor strikes; wartime conscription; and social, racial, ethnic, religious, and nationalistic prejudice and reactions to it.

3. Major disorders generated by social movements or by the reaction to government and all nonspecific "others" nearly always take the form of police–mob conflicts.

4. In disorders that involve two or more struggling factions, the police invariably become engaged as a third faction in an effort to restore tranquility. Their participation may assist or appear to assist the cause of one of the factions or, barring that, may invite the animosity of both factions, neither of which welcomes the attempt to end the contention.

5. Although riots and poor police–community relations have both frequently been described in histories of the United States, the two phenomena have rarely been joined as cause and effect. Before the present decade, there was no mention of strained police–community relations as a contributing factor to community disorders. On the other hand, there were several depictions of police commanders who, to their later benefit or detriment, established great riot-suppression reputations during major disorders.

6. Following virtually every major disorder, according to contemporary published accounts, the police have been criticized for (a) forbearance in the presence of public disruption and insults to the rule of law, or

---

[7] Much of the information in this section relating to population change was adapted with permission from D. L. Lohman, "Race Tension and Conflict," in N. A. Watson, *Police and the Changing Community* (Washington, D.C.: International Association of Chiefs of Police, 1977); pp. 42–47. See also G. A. Deters, "Changing Attitudes in Police–Community Relations and the Warren Court Effect," *Law and Order*, 26, No. 1 (January 1978), 76–80.

[8] V. G. Strecher, *The Environment of Law Enforcement: A Community Relations Guide* (Englewood Cliffs, N.J.: Prentice-Hall, 1971), pp. 50–51.

(b) use of excessive force in dispersing mobs and restoring order. Additionally, the police have consistently been accused of (a) slowness in the deployment of force against riotous crowds, or (b) a too-quick, provocative use of force, which nourished the full-scale disorder.

7. Riots usually result in the arrest of many people, with varying quality of identification and substantiation of charges. Disposition of the cases, however, has nearly always been discharged without prosecution, even when the number of deaths and serious injuries and the destruction of property have been great. This fact is seldom deplored in contemporary accounts of riots, even in those by police historians. It is as if there is tacit acknowledgment that grave social issues are being worked out.

Miami violence: different from the 1960s

The riot that broke out in May 1980 in the Liberty City section of Miami, Florida differed dramatically from the racial disturbances of the 1960s, a study conducted for the Ford Foundation said.[9]

In a 48-page preliminary report, the anti-white violence in the Miami riot was called "unprecedented in this century." It was the first time since pre-Civil War slave uprisings that blacks had risen spontaneously with the sole purpose of beating or killing whites, the report said.

"It was not within the bounds of our study to speculate whether the 'Miami style' will become the national norm," wrote the authors of the report, Dr. Marvin Dunn, associate professor of psychology at Florida International University, and Bruce Porter, director of the journalism program at Brooklyn College. "What does seem clear is that, compared to Miami, the 1960s riots were merely a warning about the hostility that lay beneath the surface rather than the out-pouring itself."

The Liberty City disturbances began May 17, 1980, shortly after an all-white jury in Tampa acquitted four white police officers of beating to death a black insurance executive. As news of the acquittal spread, angry blacks massed in the main streets of Liberty City, burned and looted white-owned stores and attacked whites driving through the area.

The three-day riot left 18 people dead and destroyed $100 million in property.

In the 1960s riots, the study said, the beatings and killings of whites by blacks "occurred always as a byproduct of the disorder, not as its sole object." In 1,893 individual racial disorders between 1964 and 1969, there was not one report of blacks rising spon-

[9] Marvin Dunn and Bruce Porter, "The Miami Riot Study." Ford Foundation, 1981.

taneously to beat and kill whites as they did in Miami, the study said.

Although "probably as many blacks saved whites from harm as did the harming," the crucial factor was "not in the numbers but in the general air of approval that pervaded the scenes of violence," it said.

Moreover, in their analysis of data gathered by the Dade-Miami Criminal Justice Council about the 855 persons arrested in the riot, Dunn and Porter said that "the riot in Miami seems to have drawn a vastly different class of people than did the eruptions of the 1960s."

In the Watts riot in 1965, and in the Newark riots in 1967, about 74 percent of the adults arrested had prior arrest records. In Miami, the study said, "the figures are almost directly the reverse"—only 32 percent of those arrested had records of prior arrest.

Poverty worsened in Liberty City from 1968 to 1978. Unemployment rose to 17.8 percent from 6 percent, and the number of persons below the poverty line increased to 52 percent from 28 percent. Nonetheless, the study said, "poverty alone does not make people riot."

Pointing to other characteristics that Miami shared with other cities that had riots, the study cited a *lack* of black policemen, a low number of black-owned stores and the election of public officials on an at-large basis, depriving blacks of political representation.

The changing american scene: black inner cities

Basic changes are taking place in the community, and they affect the problems that confront law enforcement officials. One of the most significant problems causing discontent and subsequent intervention of law enforcement personnel has been the emergence of the black inner cities, which developed in the 1950s and 1960s and continued through the 1970s. As a result, cities are becoming the residence of black minority groups, while the whites are moving to the suburbs.

Between 1970 and 1980 (most recent census) the twelve largest cities of the United States lost over $3\frac{1}{2}$ million white residents and gained almost exactly the same number of nonwhite residents. Residents of the older portions of these cities had had social and economic success, and the young people moved on to the widening circle of residential resettlement, the middle-class suburbs. *Three and a half million blacks and hispanics moved into the places evacuated by more than 3 million white residents.*[10] Some of these people came as immigrants to move into the great cities.

It is well known that many of the problems of law and order are concentrated in particular neighborhoods and involve the trials and tribulations of those groups in transition. But the neighborhoods have now burgeoned into entire cities in transition. Vast sections of cities have been occupied by the new immigrant people. In places like Baltimore, Detroit, Cleveland, Chicago, Washington, D.C., and St. Louis, as much as a third of the city is made up of these new immigrant groups. So the transition is a transition of cities rather than of neighborhoods.

The consequence of this trend is a new way of life for many people. Diverse groups with conflicting customs and interests suddenly find themselves side by side. And there have been changes in the relative wealth and power of various groups. From these many changes have come special problems, such as housing, that throw groups into competition with one another and thereby become police problems.[11]

The National Commission on Urban Problems recently released a study reporting that if present trends continue, "America by 1985 would be well on the road toward a society characterized by race classification along racial and economic lines as well as geographic separation."[12]

A projection of population figures by a team of demographers shows that by 1985, central cities will have gained 10 million more nonwhites—a 94 percent increase. This would be an acceleration of the trend begun in 1960 of increasingly black inner cities ringed by burgeoning white suburbs.

Unhappily, the projection vividly portrays the geographic fulfillment of fears expressed by the President's Commission on Civil Disorders—that American society is becoming an apartheid society; that is, divided into two societies, black and white, separate and unequal.

A study by Patricia Leavuy Hodge and Philip Hauser of the University of Chicago points out that although nonwhites are expected to increase numerically in the suburbs to 6.8 million in 1985 (from 2.8 million in 1960), "they will be all but lost in the sea of whites, with the nonwhite suburban population increasing from only 5 to 6 percent of the total." Hodge and Hauser also point out that, because of their high fertility rates, nonwhites will increase at

[10] Lohman, "Race Tension," p. 46.

[11] Lohman, "Race Tension," p. 47.

[12] *The National Commission Report on Urban Problems*, (Washington, D.C.: U.S. Government Printing Office, 1978).

a greater rate throughout the nation than whites, their proportion of the total population rising from 11 percent in 1960 to 14 percent in 1985.

In the central cities, the increase in nonwhites is expected to be even greater by 1985. According to projections, the white population there will have dropped to 69 percent (82 percent in 1960), and the nonwhite population will have increased to 31 percent (18 percent nonwhite in 1960), with many major cities having nonwhite majorities. As an example of this situation (black inner cities), the Newark (New Jersey) Housing Authority estimates that since 1950, some 200,000 whites have moved out of Newark, while 85,000 blacks have moved in. More than half the population of Oakland, California, will be black by 1983 if present trends continue, the President's Commission on Civil Disorders stated in its recent report. Washington, D.C., and Newark, New Jersey, are already at that point, the commission noted, and it listed other cities where blacks would be in a majority in 1984 if the present trend continues: New Orleans; Richmond, Virginia; Baltimore; Jacksonville, Florida; Gary, Indiana; Cleveland, Ohio; St. Louis; Detroit; Philadelphia; and Chicago. In addition, in 1985, these cities will probably have black majorities: Dallas; Buffalo, New York; Cincinnati; Harrisburg, Pennsylvania; Louisville; Indianapolis; Kansas City, Missouri; Hartford, Connecticut; and New Haven, Connecticut.

The majority of black immigrants are deficient in education and job skills. Some of them must be supported by public welfare, and many do not know how to live in cities. Obviously, dialogue and communications are difficult; therefore, these specific features of the discontent and deprivation are separately and together an expression of radical changes in population distribution. The central features of the times that are commonplace in our society make up the context in which we must identify all problems. And if we so identify them, it may be possible that we will see them quite differently. In any event, if there are those who expect groups in our society to act differently from the way they currently do, they should realize that this will happen only if the necessary conditions come about.

Despite the "Great Society" programs of the 1960s, organized to alleviate the underlying causes of riotous conduct, economic and social progress of the nation's blacks and other minorities was to be agonizingly slow:

1. When the national unemployment rate was 7.8 percent, it was 13.9 percent for blacks and other minorities. For nonwhite teenagers, the rate was a staggering 35.2 percent.

2. In California, the nonwhite unemployment rate was 11.9 percent, compared to 5.9 for whites.

3. In 1978, the national median family income for whites was $18,368, compared to $10,879 for blacks and $12,566 for those of Spanish origin.

4. Blacks constitute about 9 percent of California's population, but nearly 20 percent of those living below the poverty level—in the five-county Bay Area, 30 percent.

"We've seen some progress but we've a very, very long way to go to eliminate large racial differences," said Dr. Reynolds Farley, a sociologist with the University of Michigan's Center for Population Studies.

Farley, who studies residential segregation, says society is still largely polarized into black and white areas, even with the migration of blacks into the suburbs, and that such racial isolation is expected to continue through the end of this century.

In the wake of the recent violence in Miami, officials everywhere are trying to assess whether that violence is an indication of what is in store for the nation's cities in the 1980s.

Julian Klugman, regional director of the community-relations arm of the U.S. Department of Justice, says it is "foolish to try to predict whether another riot will happen here or there." But, he said, "Miami is a warning. It says to city officials, 'If you've got problems, you'd better start addressing them now.'"

The question then arises, What is the role of the police in our contemporary society? With the transition of the urban community generating conditions that promote and sustain social problems, the role of law enforcement agencies will expand rapidly.

Social unrest: implications for law enforcement

Police work is a phrase that conjures up in some minds a dramatic conflict between a policeman and a criminal in which the party with the stronger arm or the craftier wit prevails. When a particularly desperate or dangerous criminal must be hunted down and brought to justice, police work has heroic moments, but the situations that most police deal with most of the time are of quite another order. Much of American crime, delinquency, and disorder is associated with a complexity of social conditions: poverty, racial antagonism, family breakdown, or restlessness of young people. During the last twenty years, these conditions have been aggravated by such profound social changes as the technological and civil-rights revolutions and the rapid decay of inner cities into densely packed, turbulent slums and ghettos.

It is in the cities that the conditions of life are the worst, that social tensions are the most acute, that riots occur, that crime rates are the highest, that the fear of crime and the demand for effective action against it are greatest. But crime itself has increased not only in the big cities; it has shown a drastic increase everywhere in the United States. Serious and violent crimes (particularly murder, assaults, and forcible rape) have been soaring throughout the nation, according to nationwide summaries of police statistics gathered by the Federal Bureau of Investigation.

One of the most fully documented facts about crime is that the common, serious crimes that worry people the most—murder, forcible rape, robbery, aggravated assault, and burglary—happen most often in the slums of large cities. Studies of the crime rate in cities and of the conditions most commonly associated with high crime rates have been conducted for well over a century in Europe, and for many years in the United States. In city after city, in all regions of all countries, the variations in the rates for serious crimes have been traced. The findings have been remarkably consistent. Burglary, robbery, and serious assault occur in areas characterized by low income, physical deterioration, dependency, racial and ethnic concentrations, broken homes, working mothers, low levels of education and vocational skills, high unemployment, high proportion of single males, overcrowded and substandard housing, high rates of tuberculosis and infant mortality, low rates of homeownership or of single-family dwellings, and high population density. The offenses, the victims, and the offenders were found most frequently in these areas. Studies that have mapped the relationship of these factors to crime have found them following the same pattern from one area of the city to another.

Crime rates in American cities tend to be highest in the center of the city and to decrease in relation to distance from the center. This pattern has been found to hold fairly well for both offenses and offenders, although it is sometimes broken by unusual features of geography, enclaves of socially well-integrated ethnic groups, irregularities in the distribution of opportunities to commit crime, and unusual concentrations of commercial and industrial establishments in outlying areas. The major irregularity found in the clustering of offenses and offenders beyond city boundaries is caused by the growth of satellite areas that are developing such characteristics of the central city as high population mobility, commercial and industrial concentrations, low economic status, broken families, and other social problems.

The city slum has always exacted its toll from its inhabitants, except where those inhabitants are bound together by an intensive social and cultural solidarity that provides a collective defense against the pressures of slum living. Several slum settlements inhabited by people of Oriental ancestry have shown a capacity in this regard. However, the common experience of the great numbers of immigrants of different racial and ethnic backgrounds who have poured into the poorest areas of our large cities has been quite different.

A historic series of studies by Clifford R. Shaw and Henry D. McKay, of the Institute of Juvenile Research in Chicago, documents the disorganizing effect of slum life on different groups of immigrants as they moved through the slums and struggled to gain an economic and social foothold in the city.[13] Throughout the period of immigration, areas with high delinquency and crime rates kept this high rate, even though members of new nationality groups moved in to displace the older residents. Each nationality group showed high rates of delinquency among its members who were living near the center of the city and lower rates for those living in the better, outlying residential areas. Also, for each nationality group, those living in the poor areas had more of all the other social problems commonly associated with life in the slums.

This same pattern of high crime rates in the slum neighborhoods and low rates in the better districts is true among blacks and other minority groups who have made up the most recent waves of migration to the big cities. (Minority groups and crime will be discussed in another chapter.) Like other groups before them, they have had to crowd into areas where they can afford to live while they search for ways to live better. The disorganizing personal and social experiences of life in the slums are producing the same problems for the new minority-group residents, including high rates of crime and delinquency. As they acquire a stake in urban society and move into better areas in the city, their crime rates and the incidence of other social problems drop to lower levels.

Summary

Racial tensions, civil disobedience, and mob violence are not new phenomena in the United States. Such problems have been a part of our society since its beginning. The rapid growth of

---

[13] C. R. Shaw and H. D. McKay, *Juvenile Delinquency in Urban Areas,* 5th ed. (Chicago: University of Chicago Press, 1971).

the population, particularly in urban areas, with attendant social problems in housing, education, employment, and social welfare services has accentuated social unrest to a degree that has caused law enforcement officers to become the symbols of social ills. They have been placed in the difficult position of attempting to enforce society's laws as well as concerning themselves with a variety of social conditions.

Some of the major historical disturbances in the United States were quite similar to contemporary disorders. Antisocial behavior as it relates to mass disturbances and violence is not in itself the problem; it is instead a product of various social conditions. In fact, people in all societies and in all classes respond to economic, social, and psychological pressures by acting-out behavior.

The social changes that emerged from the displacement of huge populations to suburban areas and the migration of the minorities to the metropolitan areas have had a great effect on law enforcement agencies. Although population growth has changed central-city concentration little, the "flight to the suburbs" has drained the city of those groups that traditionally were forces for social control and stability.

Contemporary society is marked by many demands for change in important areas of national life, controversies produced by these changes, and resistance to them, all of which creates disorganization and deviance, and norms that are cherished by some and rejected by others. The job of policing a society in which there are so many complex crosscurrents of social change is a very difficult one.

Social unrest carries great implications for police work, since it increases enormously the amount of crime generated, or aggravated, by profound social changes—such as the technological and civil-rights revolutions and the rapid decay of the inner cities into densely packed, turbulent slums and ghettos. Deviant behavior is usually generated by the unhealthy social conditions found in such slums.

Discussion topics

1. Discuss the major riots throughout United States history, utilizing Appendix A as well as material in this chapter.
2. Discuss the effect of social unrest on law enforcement.
3. Why is it so important that policemen gain historic and contemporary perspectives of societal disorder?

Annotated references

Bayley, D. H., and H. Mendelson, "The Policeman's World," in Charles E. Reasons and J. L. Kuykendall, eds., *Race, Crime and Justice*, 2nd ed. Ventura, Calif.: Goodyear, 1977. Contains an excellent chapter discussing the occupation of law enforcement and the necessity to understand the world as it is for better police–community relations.

Brown, C., *Manchild in a Promised Land*, 3rd ed. New York: Macmillan, 1975. An excellent work, discussing the black's psychological problems in American society.

Byrd, R. C., "Police Brutality or Public Brutality," *The Police Chief*, 33, No. 2 (February 1966), 8–10. The author discusses the lack of public support for the police officer in the United States, taking a hard line with those he feels are attacking the laws of our nation and making such laws impotent. The author's lack of sympathy toward these people might be of some interest to the reader who may overidentify with such groups.

Clark, R. S., *Police and the Community*. New York: Franklyn Watts/New Viewpoints, 1979. This book analyzes the literature and case histories on, and the current status of, police–community relations.

Keiley, J. A., and T. W. O'Rourke, "An Appraisal of the Attitudes of Police Officers toward the Concept of Police–Community Relations," *Journal of Police Science and Administration*, 1, No. 2 (June 1973), 224–31. An assessment of police personnel attitudes toward the concept of police–community relations prior to their participation in a police–community relations program under the auspices of the University of Illinois Police Training Institute. See also C. E. Pope, "Race and Crime Revisited," *Crime and Delinquency*, 25, No. 3 (July 1979), 347–57.

Skolnick, J., ed., *The Politics of Protest*, Task Force Report, National Commission on the Causes and Prevention of Violence. New York: Simon & Schuster, 1969. A collection of contributions dealing with the facets of protest and politics.

Strecher, V. G., *The Environment of Law Enforcement: A Community Relations Guide*. Englewood Cliffs, N.J.: Prentice-Hall, Essentials of Law Enforcement Series, 1971. An excellent discussion of the environment within which police officers operate. Focuses on the police officer who works in a variety of settings—territorial, social, and organizational. A highly recommended paperback, in nontechnical language—a must for a police library.

Whitehouse, J. E., "Historical Perspectives of the Police–Community Service Function," *Journal of Police Science and Administration*, 1, No. 1 (March 1973), 87–92. This article ties in nicely with the historical and contemporary aspects of police–community relations discussed in this chapter.

chapter seven

Police–Community Relations

One of the major characteristics of our society is the presence of groups in conflict with each other. Nowhere is this conflict more evident than between the police and the community. In these times of social upheaval and strife, the law enforcement agencies come under much criticism from the community because of the way the police are perceived to be resolving problems not of the community's making. John Herber of *The New York Times* puts the dilemma into proper perspective:

> The tension between the police and minority groups, a factor in the race riots in Miami, has intensified in a number of cities around the country this spring, according to a number of community and national leaders.
>
> In a series of interviews after the outbreak of violence in Florida, the leaders said that unrest resulting from uncertain economic conditions and a decline in sensitivity training for new police officers that was instituted after the violence of a decade ago, were among the causes of what they called deteriorating police–community relations.
>
> In almost every city examined there were reports of a renewed antagonism and belief among members of minorities that the police had different stan-

dards for them than for whites. In many cities this feeling has been reinforced by recent police actions that members of the minority communities
viewed as unjust.[1]

The police, on the other hand, see the community as making
their job much more difficult by lack of support and cooperation.
Thus, each group attempts to place the responsibility for social
problems on the other. This antagonistic situation is vividly portrayed in a study by Joseph D. Lohman and Gordon E. Misner, who
describe the situation as a "basic police failure, i.e., the failure to
communicate effectively with certain members of the minority
community."

> The description of a rookie policeman . . . expecting to find a majority of in-
> habitants to have criminal tendencies and to be antagonistic to law and
> order is not an uncommon observation. . . . There is repeated reference to
> the lack of communication which might be initiated by the police officer on
> patrol. There is constant referral to his unwillingness to learn the language
> of the people . . . to appreciate their culture and motivations. According to
> this belief, a policeman sets himself up as one who is not to be questioned,
> whose actions are not to be attacked; to question him means to attack him.
> There is a built-in barrier to communication which underlies distrust of him
> and what he represents. Thus, there is fashioned an image which may be pre-
> destined to give negative flavor to the contact that arises when a police of-
> ficer confronts a citizen. . . . The police contact with the man in the com-
> munity should be of primary importance in assuaging the tensions which
> may underlie the attitudes of community members; if this contact generates
> tension rather than assuaging it, then an essential aspect of the police pur-
> pose has been lost.[2]

Deterioration in the police/minority-group relationship is increasingly evident. During the last decade, we have seen a great
deal of publicity relating to charges of police brutality and
demands for greater civilian control over police actions. In a bleak
report a group of black leaders stated that the potential for racial
violence in the nation's cities is greater than in the 1960s because
blacks, especially young blacks, are losing hope. The report, issued
March 17, 1981, by the Grassroot Network, which is composed of
black storefront organizations and the National Black Police Association, painted a scene more desperate than even black community leaders expected.

According to the report the riots of the summer of 1980 were

---

[1] John Herber, *The New York Times*, June 7, 1980. © 1980 by The New York Times Company. Reprinted by permission.

[2] J. D. Lohman and G. Misner, *The Police and the Community: The Dynamics of Their Relationship in a Changing Community* (Washington, D.C.: U.S. Government Printing Office,
1966) 1, 14.

"led by the young, and the violence has shifted to youths of younger and younger age."

While Miami cooled after riots, and before Chattanooga, Tennessee, erupted, the Network began campaigning for new police policies, better child welfare services and altered juvenile justice programs.

"Black and minority people do not start riots," the Network said. "They only become participants. They usually are catalyzed by a police incident, which may range from a perception of police misconduct to the actual use of deadly force."

Ironically, the first test of the Network's recommendations came in Philadelphia, its home base, where the shooting of a black youth by a white policeman a week after the report was released caused three days of sporadic violence.

Police/minority-group relations:
a distorted image

Relationships between the police and the ethnic minority groups appear to be conditioned by many factors, among which are *the police view and attitude toward ethnic minority groups, the customs and the traditions of the police service, and a built-in resistance to outside pressure.* Consequently, the relations are almost inevitably negative.

The police officer is provided with an automobile which provides mobility but also isolation from contact with the public. The mission is to enforce the law, particularly in those locations where statistics prove that violations of it occur with predictable regularity. Because of the workload, the officer has few opportunities to relate in any other fashion to the residents of the community. The only long-term persistent association that is formed with these people is the one that has been assigned—a negative enforcement relationship.

Consequently, bad stereotypes form that create filters in the perceptual screens of each group, distorting images and information about each other. At a time when clear communication is most important between groups, it tends to decrease; neither group wants to listen to the other, but hears only information that supports its own position. Each group is focused only on the differences, obscuring the similarities or common goals they might share. When solutions are offered, each group feels committed to defend its own proposals rather than considering the merits of the other group's solutions. Mutual distrust and defensiveness prevent most attempts to get together to resolve differences and to work cooperatively on community problems.

The conflict between the police and the community interferes seriously with public confidence in the police and consequently with the ability of the police to deal effectively with the crime problem. Without doubt, the community's hostility toward and lack of confidence in the police interfere with police recruiting, morale, day-to-day operations, and safety of the individual officer. This obviously has an adverse effect on total community stability. Hostility toward the police is often so intense that even routine police procedures antagonize ordinarily law-abiding residents. Because, for many members of minority groups, the police symbolize all that is hated and feared in the dominant society, the policeman receives hostility that actually has very little to do with him. It is a hostility generated by social conditions such as inadequate housing and underemployment. Actual police misconduct, as documented by four authoritative national commissions,[3] further intensifies hostility toward the police.

Thus we have two groups in conflict, each perceiving the other as the enemy and each feeling that it has to defend its own position. Bayley and Mendelsohn point out that, considering the expectations that most policemen have about the reception they will receive from members of a minority group:

> . . . it seem plausible to expect that they might build up an enormous amount of resentment against them. The middle-class and upper-class dominant community, constituting the majority of people in the city, are seen by policemen as being cooperative, making straightforward demands involving little risk to the officer, and frequently requiring no enforcement at all. At the same time, these people are familiar with avenues of redress and not unwilling to challenge the officer whom they believe presumes too far. Nevertheless, since their demands are generally not exorbitant from the point of view of the officer, policemen may not mind becoming unassuming, informal, polite, and even deferential in their presence. Minorities, on the other hand, especially Negroes, in the eyes of police personnel, demand the most, raise the greatest amount of anxiety about personal safety, pose the greatest criminal threat, are the most hostile, and on top of it all are as likely to be truculent in their appeals against officers as prosperous Dominants. . . . One can understand why policemen often show a sense of being aggrieved, mistreated, and put-upon by minorities. Minorities react in an exactly similar fashion against members of the majority community. *There seems to be a reciprocating engine of resentment at work in relations between police and minorities, an engine which is fueled with demands each side makes on the other and the expectations each entertains about the other.* If police–commu-

---

[3] "Report on Lawlessness, 1931"; "To Secure the Rights, 1947"; "The Fifty State Report, 1961"; *Report of the National Advisory Commission on Civil Disorders* (Washington, D.C.: U.S. Government Printing Office, 1968).

nity relations are to be improved, the nature of this relationship—and especially of the structural basis for it—must be understood and studied in great detail.[4]

The situation confronting the law enforcement officer is undoubtedly far from ideal, but he or she is still responsible for the maintenance of an orderly society. The laws of the United States, of course, continue to include the minimum obligations imposed on any free society: to provide in an *impartial manner* both *personal safety* and *property security*.

In a fundamental context, all regulated behavior—from some family activities to vehicle speed—are law enforcement functions. And as the complexities of maintaining order through law enforcement multiply, there is an every-increasing responsibility placed on those who enforce the law. This responsibility is to learn to *anticipate* and *prevent* the destruction of an orderly society.

People who don't even know you[5]

Transactions made by those in police uniform occur between *roles,* not between human beings, although the human carriers of the roles do not escape the consequences of the action. This is merely a very strong and quite strange way of making the point that while on duty a policeman is rarely able to function as a person. His identity as an officer easily overwhelms his personal characteristics and his identity as an individual human being. This phenomenon results in stereotyping, prejudice, stigmatization, and also fulfills a form of social efficiency demanded in everyday life. There is, of course, a vital difference between an efficient designation of the police role as it relates to function and a stereotyped inference of unpleasant characteristics. The first is a form of social shorthand which gives us useful concepts such as "waiter," "scientist," "child," and "mother"; the latter, which would have us believe in uniformity within huge populations of human beings, gives us "kike" and "nigger," "flatfoot," "fuzz," and "pig." Citizen perception of the police role ranges from the generally useful connotations through prejudiced interpretations. Sometimes these perceptions result from personal experiences with the police, but

[4] D. H. Bayley and H. Mendelsohn, *Minorities and the Police: Confrontation in America* (New York: Free Press, 1971), pp. 107–8. (Italics added.)

[5] The material beginning here and running through the subsection, "The Shock of Culture," was taken from V. C. Strecher, *The Environment of Law Enforcement: A Community Relations Guide* (Englewood Cliffs, N.J.: Prentice-Hall, 1971), pp. 67–87. (By permission of the publisher.)

often they are related more directly to the citizen's own role in the community, and especially his membership in one of the several *subcultures* which make up our large, pluralistic social system. By "subculture" we refer to a part of the population which subscribes to the broad outlines of our way of life but whose concepts, beliefs, habits, art, apparel, dwellings, institutions, or implements differ markedly from what is customarily found in the majority population. A subculture also has the characteristic of persistence: It continues through time by renewing its membership in each generation, in effect, by reproducing itself.

SUBCULTURES AND LAW ENFORCEMENT

In pluralistic societies subcultures have always presented an interesting challenge to the forces of social control. In a large community if there is a dominant or conventional set of values, customs, and artifacts which closely determine how its members look and behave and which establish the limits of appropriateness, then a smaller group within the community which differs markedly in custom, dress, or behavior immediately demands a decision of the larger group. The *decision is whether social control will be predicated rigidly upon the dominant cultural norms or upon some other abstract standard.* This dilemma inherent in our open society has consumed much time, thought, and energy, and has been at the center of the law-morality relationship controversy for several generations.

Because it is not the kind of issue which can be decided precisely and equitably, working it out continues while we go on living and working and making difficult judgments about human conduct within the guidelines which have thus far flowed out of this continuous process.

Confronted with the need for performing his duties routinely, the police officer occupies the cutting edge of both social *change* and social *difference.* He works in all neighborhoods including those which do not resemble conventional ones, and when changing values, customs, or ways of behaving antagonize the more conventionally oriented residents of the community, the policeman is called. But, for some reason, even social change appears easier to accept than the unconventionality of subcultures within the community. The policeman is often called upon to mediate disputes at points of contact. And he works *within* the subcultures as well.

Included among the subcultural communities served by the American police officer are those of the lower-class Negroes, lower-class whites, Chicanos (Mexican-Americans), Puerto Ricans,

Chinese-Americans, Japanese-Americans, American Indians, and many smaller groups. It must also be mentioned that the superrich, the "old money," constitute a nonconventional subculture, which at times presents law enforcement with problems few in number but of considerable perplexity.

Although it is often complained that police–community relations issues are reduced to race relations, it must be said that the everyday pressures of work make this tight focus inevitable. In the urban centers of the United States, with a few notable exceptions, the police–community relations issue *is* bound up with black-white interactions. However, the narrow focus need not be maintained. Police-community relations will be discussed in this chapter. The discussion will be carried on within a framework of subcultural relations which applies to all the minority populations living in the United States, even though much of the subcultural behavior dealt with is that of slum-dwelling Negroes.

The concepts of *subcultural behavior, culture shock, culture fatigue,* and *social change,* when considered from the perspectives of history and personal experience, can provide a fresh and more accurate insight into one's individual, personal position in the total scheme of things. It helps also in the making of judgments which lead to fewer, rather than more, tensions and difficulties on the job.

POLICEMEN AND BLACK PEOPLE

Relations between the police and lower-class Negro residents of large urban areas of the northern and western United States have become increasingly and more visibly discordant in recent years. [See Figure 7–1.] Ironically, this has occurred during a period of growing technical competence in law enforcement and greater police sensitivity to community reactions. But it has occurred also during a "revolution of rising expectations" among the urban poor, and curiously, the discord has been more pronounced and is most often found in the best cities of the country.

Police–community relations programs have achieved considerable popularity in recent years, but to many members of the community they seem to be "preaching to the converted," because of their limited reach. Even while Negroes and police officers meet to discuss large-scale problems, the individual police officer and the individual black man on the street find little improvement—more often a worsening—in their encounters.

These individual encounters obviously provide the medium in which the negative relationship is acted out, but consider for a mo-

FIGURE 7-1. *Often when police-black relations are at their lowest ebb, the mere sight of a police vehicle can trigger a melee. Courtesy of Berkeley (Calif.) Police Dept.*

ment that the factors that really underlie these harsh confrontations were probably operating long before the officer and black man came together. Unfortunately, most police–Negro encounters are predisposed to mutual hostility before they take place. This is *not* to suggest that the outcome of every contact must be inevitably negative; it is *not* to say that all of us—policemen and citizens—are trapped in a crystallized system of behavior within which we merely react in ways that are predetermined. However, it is clear to any policeman or observer of police work that each police–citizen encounter begins with a lot of history behind it, that neither the officer nor the citizen enters the situation with a totally objective, assumption-free state of mind. Both are likely to carry into the meeting their personal quotas of "cultural baggage," those complex networks of knowledge, attitudes, and social awareness which are indispensable to everyday living. And to further complicate the conditions of the encounter, there are the personalities of the officer and the citizen, and the immediate conditions that brought them together.

It becomes increasingly apparent, however, that the factors of personality, individual intentions, and the conditions of meeting have less to do with the outcome of the encounter than the so-called cultural baggage of those involved. The forces of personality, intention, and immediate situation are overpowered by cultural forces which thrust upon the officer and the black man certain roles which become mutually antagonistic. Again, it must be said that unconscious behavior in response to social forces is not inevitable. However, unconscious reaction to those cultural urgings *is* exceedingly likely if the cultural urgings are not brought to the surface of the mind, clearly understood, and made part of the individual's total perspective of the conditions surrounding him. A number of factors have come together to complicate the everyday experiences of police officers and city residents. They include the internal migration patterns of the United States, which have formed the nation's cities; the historical relationships between Negroes and whites; the previously mentioned revolution of rising expectations among slum dwellers; and the values and patterns of behavior dominant in two distinct segments of the larger American culture. These segments can properly be called *lower-class Negro subculture* and the *police occupational subculture.*

The quality of life for in-migrants in cities

In 1939 Edward I. Thorndike published the results of a three years' study of 310 American cities. It was based upon the notion that "... the cities of the United States do differ enormously in many, and widely in almost all, of the features of qualities which are important for human living."[6] Thorndike analyzed differences in life-style among these several hundred cities in terms of factors relating to health, public educational opportunities, public recreation, economic well-being, creature comforts, literacy, and similar indicators of good conditions. The 310 cities of 30,000 or more population (in 1930) scored from 330 to 1110 points on a scale of 9 to 1541. Recently these "goodness of life" scores from the 1930s were compared with the rates of nonwhite in-migration for those same cities for the 1950–60 decade. The correlation coefficient was .81, indicating a very strong relationship between the quality of life in cities and their influx of southern rural black people.

So the Negro migrants went to the good cities; but there they discovered that northern and western cities did not dispense their "goodness of life" equally or randomly. "Social vacancies" existed—largely at the bottom of the socioeconomic scale—just as

[6] E. L. Thorndike, *Your City* (New York: Harcourt Brace Jovanovich, 1939), p. 5.

they had generations previously for the Irish, Germans, Italians, Poles, and other immigrant populations. There is clear evidence that Negroes fare better in earning power and education in the Thorndike high-score cities.[7] It is equally clear, however, that large numbers of unskilled, poorly educated in-migrants from the rural South, ignorant of city life, become the neighbors of settled second- and third-generation Negro residents who have done relatively well. One result of this is that the poorer, less capable in-migrants who came to the city expecting much—the expectations were reinforced by the relative success of established black residents—have been extremely frustrated by falling so short of their aspirations. Another result, given the nature of residential segregation in large cities, is that the long-time Negro residents have felt the full impact of the flood of socially unskilled migrants. Also, they are most often the victims of the crimes committed by the in-migrants, and as the established black populations push outward, seeking adequate living space, they are confronted on the one hand by white hostility to their expansion, and on the other by undesirable living conditions among the undereducated, socially different new-comers. This condition appears to be similar to the "lace curtain" and "shanty" Irish division of past generations. But the stigma of having black skin continues to block social assimilation, and it was social assimilation that eventually resolved the European immigrant crisis during the past 100 years.

The lower-class negro subculture

Culture has been defined by Oscar Lewis, a well-known social scientist and author, as a ". . . design for living which is passed down from generation to generation."[8] This intergenerational design for living consists of behavior, goals, values, attitudes, personality patterns, and achievement levels, and it is a direct consequence of patterns of child-rearing and family life-style.[9]

The idea that a "culture of poverty" exists has been with us since 1961, when Oscar Lewis used the phrase.[10] Another expert, Catherine Chilman, feels that ". . . it would probably be more accurate to talk about the subcultures of poverty . . . because most of

[7] V. G. Strecher, "Police–Community Relations, Urban Riots, and the Quality of Life in Cities," doctor's thesis, Washington University, St. Louis, Mo., 1968, pp. 106–7.

[8] C. S. Chilman, *Growing Up Poor*, (Washington, D.C.: U.S. Department of Health, Education and Welfare, 1966), p. 5.

[9] Ibid., p. 5.

[10] Ibid.

our poor would seem to subscribe to the 'middle-class American way' as . . . a cultural ideal which most would accept, in theory and fantasy,"[11] This last point—that the poor subscribe to middle-class norms, but behave in some other way—has been discussed by Lee Rainwater,[12] who suggests that a valid interpretation is found in Hyman Rodman's concept of a "lower-class value stretch," which permits the member of the lower class to scale down a set of values to an operable level without abandoning the conventional middle-class values of society.[13] Rainwater credits Rodman with avoiding:

> . . . the pitfall of making lower class persons out as "conceptual boobs" by not implying that (1) they are ignorant of or indifferent to conventional norms and values, or that (2) they persist in maintaining full-fledged allegiance to conventional norms despite their inability to achieve satisfactorily in terms of them.[14]

"It is now generally recognized that lower-class and middle-class families tend to raise their children and conduct their family relationships in quite different styles."[15] These different styles of child-rearing and family relationships do much to maintain behavior differing from conventional norms, behavior which is sufficiently distinctive to be called *subcultural*. Just what are the differences of behavior, goals, values, attitudes, personality patterns, and achievement levels of the lower-class Negro subculture?

Frazier calls attention to the pattern of family desertion by Negro men and estimates that women head the households in 10 to 30 percent of northern urban Negro families.[16] He calls this pattern an "inevitable consequence of the impact of urban life on the simple family organization and folk culture which the Negro has evolved in the rural South."[17]

Rainwater explores the view that in the lower-class subculture, scaled-down values and norms constitute "legitimate cultural alternatives" to conventional norms. His analysis centers on the heterosexual behavior—particularly premarital sexual intercourse, extramarital intercourse, and illegitimacy—of lower-class

---

[11] Chilman, *Growing Up Poor*, p. 6.

[12] L. Rainwater, "The Problems of Lower Class Culture," Pruitt-Igoe Occasional Paper No. 8, Washington University, St. Louis, Mo., 1966, p. 5.

[13] H. Rodman, "The Lower Class Value Stretch," in *Planning for a Nation of Cities*, ed. S. B. Warner, Jr. (Cambridge, Mass.: The M.I.T. Press, 1965).

[14] Rainwater, "Problems of Lower Class Culture," p. 5.

[15] Chilman, *Growing Up Poor*, p. 5.

[16] E. F. Frazier, *Negro Family in the United States* (Chicago: University of Chicago Press, 1966), p. 246.

[17] *Ibid.*, p. 255.

Negroes. He compares the *normative* expressions of housing project residents—"how things ought to be"—with their *existential* views—"how things are." Rainwater summarizes his findings in this way:

> Lifelong marriage is the only really desirable way of living. . . . Children should be born only in marriage relationships . . . any kind of sexual relationship outside of marriage is a dangerous thing. . . . Sexual and procreative events outside of . . . marriage are not normative and they do involve costs . . . [however] reality makes it extremely difficult to live up to these norms. . . . The more impersonal socioeconomic forces and the intimate interpersonal forces of the community militate against living up to these norms and the majority of the population does not indeed live up to them.[18]

The result is that over a period of time, a set of more or less institutionalized alternatives has developed for adapting to the actual pressures under which men and women live. But these adaptations are not really satisfactory to those who make use of them, both because these people realize they have somehow fallen short of full moral status and feel themselves open to criticism, and because of the pains, frustrations, and tensions built into their way of living.

Boone Hammond has described "a 'contest system' which serves as a survival technique in the Negro lower-class subculture."[19] This system is one of nonphysical competition; in it the actors seek, through strategies of manipulation, to obtain the scarce goods of others. It is described as a "zero-sum" game because one person gains only that which another loses. In this system the two prime scarce objects are money and women, although women often represent another means of getting more money. "The ideal male type in this culture is the pimp or procurer who lives off the proceeds of seven or eight women, and never has to engage in the manual labor. . . ."[20] Hammond's major findings are that (1) the contest system causes an overriding atmosphere of skepticism and distrust, where an act of friendliness is construed as a prelude to one's being used or manipulated; (2) the methods of the contestants are at variance with conventional social norms; (3) the contest system pervades every phase of life and prevents the development of stable interpersonal relations; and (4) inevitably intrudes between husbands and wives. "Deferred gratifications are not seen to be of any utility. . . . In a culture where dreams never come true and

---

[18] Rainwater, "Problems of Lower Class Culture," pp. 26–31.

[19] B. E. Hammond, "The Contest System: A Survival Technique," unpublished essay, Department of Sociology, Washington University, St. Louis, Mo., 1965, p. 1.

[20] *Ibid.*, pp. 17–18.

middle-class-oriented goals are seldom achieved, a man's thoughts do not go too far into the future."[21]

The city as cauldron: relative deprivation

The urban disorders of recent years were followed by extensive studies of their causes. Among other things, these studies explored aspects of Negro life in cities which had been neglected until then. Separately and independently, several research groups uncovered substantial support for the theory of *relative deprivation*.[22] Although the researchers rarely called this phenomenon by name, they described a condition lucidly explained in the following passage:

> . . . people's attitudes, aspirations and grievances largely depend on the frame of reference within which they are conceived. . . . A person's satisfactions, even at the most trivial level, are conditioned by his expectations, and the proverbial way to make oneself conscious of one's advantages is to contrast one's situation with that of others worse off than oneself. The frame of reference can work in either of two ways. . . . Although at first sight a paradox, it has become a commonplace that steady poverty is the best guarantee of conservatism; if people have no reason to expect or hope for more than they can achieve, they will be less discontented with what they have, or even grateful simply to be able to hold on to it. But if, on the other hand, they have been led to see as a possible goal the relative prosperity of some more fortunate community with which they can directly compare themselves, then they will remain discontented with their lot until they have succeeded in catching up. It is this natural reaction which underlies the so-called "revolution of rising expectations."[23]

Ghetto Negroes are said to compare their lot with the affluent life-styles of whites, and of Negroes who have been able to leave the ghetto. In a sense they are forced into this comparison because, "Through television . . . and the other media of mass communications, this affluence has been endlessly flaunted before the eyes of the Negro poor. . . ."[24]

Urbanologist Daniel P. Moynihan and the members of the McCone Commission view the riots, not as a simple consequence of poverty, but less directly, as a correlate of *perceived deprivation*.

---

[21] *Ibid.*, pp. 11–13.

[22] This term was first used in *The American Soldier: Adjustment during Army Life*, by Samuel A. Stouffer et al., (Princeton, N.J.: Princeton University Press, 1949).

[23] W. G. Runciman, *Relative Deprivation and Social Justice* (London: Routledge & Kegan Paul Ltd., 1966), p. 6.

[24] *National Advisory Commission on Civil Disorders Report* (New York: New York Times Company, 1963), p. 204.

In introducing data from a 1964 statistical portrait of American cities prepared by the Urban League, the McCone Commission report posed the question, "Why Los Angeles?" The data established Los Angeles as first among 68 cities in quality of housing, employment, income, and seven other important factors affecting the quality of life for Negroes. The report states:

> The opportunity to succeed is probably unequaled in any other American city. . . . Yet the riot did happen here, and there are special circumstances here which explain in part why it did. . . . In the last quarter century . . . the Negro population has increased almost tenfold, from 75,000 in 1940 to 650,000 in 1965. Much of the increase came through migration from southern states and many arrived with the anticipation that this dynamic city would spell the end of life's endless problems. To those who have come with high hopes and great expectations and see the success of others so close at hand, failure brings a special measure of frustration and disillusionment.[25]

In a series of widely published articles, Moynihan discussed the overwillingness of government bureaucrats and "liberals" to accept the "pathetically underfinanced programs which have normally emerged from Congress, and then to oversell them both to ourselves and to those they are designed to aid. . . . We have tended to avoid evidence of poor results, and in particular have paid too little heed to the limited capacities of government bureaucracies to bring about social changes."[26] Writing from a vantage point of personal involvement in the Kennedy administration, Moynihan discussed government-planned social action as follows:

> . . . our programs might have had far greater impact if only they had been of sufficient size, but they were not. . . . Anyone who was involved with the establishment of the War on Poverty knows that it was put together by fiscal mirrors; scarcely a driblet of new money was involved. . . . Huge-sounding bills were passed, but mini-appropriations followed . . . liberals both within and without the administration gave in to an orgy of tub thumping such as would have given pause to P.T. Barnum. . . . It does not follow that we raised hopes out of all proportion to our capacity to deliver on our promises, but if we did, and we must have, we have only ourselves to blame—ourselves and the federal bureaucracy.

> Somehow liberals have been unable to acquire from life what conservatives seem to be endowed with at birth, namely a healthy skepticism of the powers of government agencies to do good. . . . As an instrument for providing services, especially to urban lower-class Negroes, it [the federal government] is a highly unreliable device.[27]

---

[25] Governor's Commission on the Los Angeles Riots, *Violence in the City—An End or a Beginning?* (Los Angeles: State of California, December 2, 1965), pp. 3–4.

[26] D. P. Moynihan, "Liberals Advised to Look into Sources of Failures That Led to Race Rioting," *St. Louis Post-Dispatch*, August 7, 1967.

[27] D. P. Moynihan, "Negro Poverty Deepening," *St. Louis Post-Dispatch*, August 9, 1967.

Although the subject at hand is not urban disorders, there is clear relevance of these reports to our discussion of lower-class Negro behavior in large cities, and for their customary reaction to police uniforms.

The police subculture

A great majority of policemen are Caucasians, who have been reared in working-class or middle-class families. And unfortunately, the generalized pattern of residential segregation makes it likely that at the time of recruitment to police service, most of these young men know little more about the lower-class Negro subculture than they know about foreign cultures. Military service has afforded many young men a generous exposure to foreign cultures, but life in American cities normally provides few encounters with Negro communities. Relatively few white police recruits have been on social visits to Negro homes, and still fewer have had persisting friendships with black contemporaries. The point being stressed here is the *degree of separation* between the dominant conventional culture from which most policemen emerge and the black culture—particularly the lower-class or poverty-level Negro subculture. This almost complete separation of cultures, from birth through maturity, is powerfully significant for the officer's reactions when he first encounters Negro living patterns; this matter of personal reactions as it affects police work will be considered in detail later.

In addition to childhood and adolescent socialization into the conventional culture, the police recruit undergoes a process of occupational socialization, through which he becomes identified—by himself and his associates—as a policeman, and he begins to share all the perspectives relevant to the police role. Some years ago, a book entitled *Boys in White* presented a model of an occupational subculture, medicine.[28] This model fits law enforcement equally well. Much of the following section is adapted from that model.

The police subculture refers, first of all, to a set of group assumptions among policemen—assumptions about their work and their roles as officers. Secondly, there is "coherence and consistency" among the police perspectives, and those perspectives are related to the officer's role in the police organization. Responsibilities, duties, rights, and privileges are also part of the subcultural setting. "Because they all occupy the same institutional position, they tend to face the same kinds of problems, and these are the

[28] H. S. Becker et al., *Boys in White* (Chicago: University of Chicago Press, 1961), p. 47.

problems which arise out of the character of the position. . . . The opportunities and disabilities of the [*police*] *role* are decisive in shaping the perspectives [policemen] hold."[29] The concept of the police subculture emphasizes that policemen proceed beyond those perspectives learned during all the previous years before they entered law enforcement work. The press of new problems related to their work is far more decisive in shaping new outlooks than prior experiences, even though backgrounds may influence individual adjustments to the new police role. We use "police subculture," then, as a kind of shorthand term for the organized sum of *police perspectives*, relevant to the *police role*.[30]

Boys in White describes a number of perspectives of medical students toward medical practice and patients, drawn from medical culture. A few of these perspectives are given here, followed by transformation to make them appropriate to policemen. These perspectives provide considerable insight into the dimensions and texture of the occupational subculture.

> . . . the concept of medical responsibility pictures a world in which patients may be in danger of losing their lives and identifies the true work of the physician as saving those endangered lives. Further, where the physician's work does not afford (at least in some symbolic sense) the possibility of saving a life or restoring health through skillful practice . . . the physician himself lacks some of the essence of physicianhood.[31]

Transformed for applicability to the police occupation, this passage [including the succeeding paragraph] reads:

> . . . *the concept of police responsibility pictures a world in which the acts and intended acts of criminals threaten the lives or well-being of victims and the security of their property. The true work of the police officer is the protection of life and property by the intervention in, and solution of, criminal acts. Further, where the policeman's work does not afford (at least in some symbolic sense) the possibility of protecting life or property by intervening in criminal acts, the police officer himself lacks some of the essence of police identity.*
>
> Those patients who can be cured are better than those who cannot. *Those cases which can be solved are better than those which cannot.* Students worry about the dangers to their own health involved in seeing a steady stream of unscreened patients, some of whom may have dangerous communicable diseases. *Policemen are concerned about personal hazards involved in approaching a steady stream of unknown persons, some of whom are wanted criminals, some of whom may have serious behavioral problems, and some possibly having intentions of causing them injury or even death because of circumstances unknown to the policeman.*

[29] *Ibid.*, pp. 46–47.

[30] *Ibid.*, pp. 4–7.

[31] *Ibid.*, pp. 310–20.

The most interesting and applicable medical perspective—one that resounds in the police world—is the following: "Perhaps the most difficult scenes come about when patients have no respect for the doctor's authority. Physicians resent this immensely."[32] The transformation is left to you.

THE PROFESSIONALISM VALUE
IN THE POLICE SUBCULTURE

Much of the present content of the police subculture has derived from the move to professionalize law enforcement. One of the consequences of the Spoils Era (1829–1883)[33] was a strong desire to eliminate the influence of politicians over the internal management of police departments. Political interference in police matters which had brought on this strong and enduring reaction included the manipulation of personnel, a practice which often resulted in promoting compliant, incompetent officers to executive rank. It also resulted in a dictation of enforcement policies; policemen were frequently required to overlook gambling and prostitution in establishments whose owners were heavy contributors to the political party controlling the executive or legislative unit of government.

Such experiences led to a powerful drive toward *autonomy* for the police, in the sense that the medical and legal professions are self-regulating, or autonomous. Unfortunately, this laudable effort to elevate the ethical standards of the police service depended to a large extent on a model of autonomy which does not fit in with the American philosophy of government. The idea of each individual practitioner's being responsible for his own conduct, and that there would be review by an organization of practitioners, is incompatible with the organizational structures and systems within which policemen work. There are civil administrative laws regulating conduct; executive-branch public policies; police departmental policies, procedures, rules and regulations, supervision, command, and inspection; there is judicial review. Thus professional autonomy is not only not available to the patrolman, but neither is it available to the supervisor, commander, or executive.

Beyond these immediate concerns for improved ethical standards, there was a tendency to isolate the factor of coldly efficient, technical competence as a major criterion of professionalism, and

---

[32] *Ibid.,* pp. 320–21.

[33] A. C. Germann, F. D. Day, and R. J. Gallati, *Introduction to Law Enforcement* (Springfield, Ill.: Chas. C Thomas, 1967), p. 68.

to judge police policy, action, and process on this basis. In this respect, several highly regarded law enforcement executives of the past generation were models of police professionalism and led in the movement for it. Theirs was a response to the problems of administering police services in a pluralistic society; such problems seemed to demand scrupulous attention to legal and administrative objectivity. It was also a response to the history of politics in law enforcement, and the professionalizers were justified in associating politics with corruption, incompetence, and maladministration. Thus, professionalism demanded responsiveness largely to the abstract criteria of ethics and technical competence. This in turn resulted in an occupational fixation upon *process* or *technique* to the exclusion of *function* or *goal orientation.* One of the most discernible trends in law enforcement has been the outright rejection of functions that are clearly aspects of community protection, and these functions have been rejected merely because the process or technique involved was not a traditional police method. Conversely, the police have taken on the most outlandish functions because they could be accomplished by means of traditional police procedures or because they required field forces such as the police could allocate to them.

SUBCULTURAL PERSPECTIVES
OF POLICEMEN

Several of the police subcultural perspectives which are relevant to dealing with Negro-slum dwellers are the following:

1. The officer is responsible for *maintaining order* in his patrol territory. There is supervisory, departmental, and general community pressure for orderliness and tranquility.

2. The policeman must be *respected.*

3. In every encounter, the policeman must gain *control* of, in the sense of initiating and orienting, each part of the situation and maintain that control; he must encounter and prevail; psychological and strategic advantages must be maintained.

4. Incongruous activities or conditions must be investigated to determine whether the law is being violated. *Curiosity* and *suspiciousness* are valued traits in the police service; they are considered indispensable to craftsmanship; they shape the appropriate frame of mind for the officer as he goes about his work.

5. A general sense of social *appropriateness* is as much a part of the policeman's frame of reference as is the criminal law. From the earliest days of policing, the broad charge to the police to protect life and property and to preserve the peace has included maintenance of community order as conventionally defined. Public displays of certain human activities are to be curtailed: quarrels, drinking, sexual petting, loitering in large groups, loud conversations, boisterous joke telling, sitting on sidewalks, and dozens of other miscellaneous activities which offend the conventional sense of propriety.

6. Policemen share a general assumption that the amount of illegal activity, the harm to human beings, the loss of property, and the amount of disorderly activity far exceed what comes to their attention. Part of their function is to seek out and deal with *elusive crime and criminals.*

There are, of course, numerous other elements in the total police perspective; however, these few will serve to highlight the particular occupation-oriented pressures on policemen in parts of the community which do not strongly hold middle-class or working-class values. These areas include the neighborhoods of lower-class Negroes and whites and also the habitat of the wealthy and superwealthy, especially the "old money."

Whenever a policeman works in a social setting greatly different from the one in which he was born and reared, he faces many of the same tensions and complexities as those encountered by foreign-service personnel working for the first time in a strange country.

THE SHOCK OF CULTURE

In every society, people learn the behavior that is appropriate to them and that they may expect from others in an infinite number of situations in which they may find themselves. Differing perceptions of role behavior frequently cause difficulties in intercultural settings because the members of each group are faced with unexpected behavior or with behavior that they feel is not appropriate to the setting. They are also handicapped by being unsure as to what is expected of them.[34]

For consideration of what happens to the policeman who is assigned to a neighborhood socially different from his own, the preceding paragraph can set the framework. It may be tentatively stated that police officers suffer *culture shock* during their early exposure to the lower-class Negro subculture. Culture shock has been defined as "an occupational disease of people who have been sud-

---

[34] G. M. Foster, *Traditional Cultures and the Impact of Technological Change* (New York: Harper & Row, 1962), p. 130.

denly transplanted abroad."[35] The term has rarely been applied to police work, but there is a precise correspondence between the experiences of policemen and foreign-service personnel under similar conditions.[36]

> Culture shock is set in motion by the anxiety that results from losing all one's familiar cues. These cues include the thousand and one ways in which we orient ourselves to the situations of daily life: when to shake hands and what to say when we meet people, when and how much to tip, how to give orders to servants, how to make purchases, when to accept and when to refuse invitations, when to take statements seriously, and when not to. Cues to behavior (which may be words, gestures, facial expressions, or customs) are acquired in the course of growing up and are as much a part of our culture as the language we speak. All of us depend for our peace of mind and our efficiency on hundreds of cues, most of which we do not carry on a level of conscious awareness.[37]

For the policeman, personal disorientation through the loss of familiar cues is due to unprecedented working problems as well as to the cultural strangeness and resulting communications problems. But more about that later. At this point it is useful to recognize the stages and symptoms for officers serving for the first time in urban slums. "Immunity to culture shock does not come from being broadminded and full of good will. These are highly important characteristics . . . and they may aid in recovery, but they can no more prevent the illness than grim determination can prevent a cold. Individuals differ greatly in the degree to which culture shock affects them. A few people prove completely unable to make the necessary adjustments . . . [but most people recover fully]. . . ."[38]

There are four discernible stages in the culture-shock syndrome.[39] The first is a kind of honeymoon period, lasting anywhere from a few days to several months, depending on circumstances. During this time the individual is fascinated by the novelty of the strange culture. He remains polite, friendly, and perhaps a bit self-effacing. The second state begins when the individual settles down to a long-run confrontation with the real conditions of life in the strange culture, and he realizes fully that he needs to function effectively there. He becomes hostile and aggressive toward the

[35] K. Oberg, quoted in Foster, *Traditional Cultures*, p. 187.

[36] This application of the culture-shock concept was first established in Victor G. Strecher, "When Subcultures Meet: Police-Negro Relations," in *Law Enforcement Science and Technology*, ed. Sheldon Yefsky (Washington, D.C.: Thompson Book Co., 1962), pp. 701–7.

[37] Foster, *Traditional Cultures*, p. 188.

[38] *Ibid.*, p. 189.

[39] Adapted from Foster, *Traditional Cultures*, pp. 189–92.

culture and its people. He criticizes their way of life and attributes his difficulties to deliberate trouble making on their part; he seeks out others suffering from culture shock and, with them, endlessly belabors the customs and "shortcomings" of the local people. This is the critical period. Some never do adjust to the strange culture; they either leave the environment—voluntarily or involuntarily—or suffer debilitating emotional problems and, consequently, become ineffective in their relations with the local population. In the third stage the individual is beginning to open a way into the new cultural environment. He may take a superior attitude to the local people, but he will joke about their behavior rather than bitterly criticize it. He is on his way to recovery. In the fourth stage the individual's adjustment is about as complete as it can get. He accepts the customs of the other culture as just another way of living.

Of course, this description of culture-shock phases does not apply directly to law enforcement officers, because with them the third and fourth stages do not always follow the first two. Foreign-service agencies recognize, expect, and prepare for culture shock; they assume that it is a form of sociopsy (often informal). They expect that those affected will make the transition to satisfactory adjustment and effective cross-cultural relationships. This however, is not the experience in police departments, as will be discussed later in this chapter.

It should be stressed that the problems which lead the policeman into culture shock are real, not imagined. There is nothing quite so disruptive as a set of experiences which challenge one's working assumptions about the nature of the world and the people in it. Nor does the personal difficulty caused by the initial subcultural contact end the officer's problems of adjustment if he weathers the attack of culture shock. Recent experience indicates that later, more enduring intercultural tensions often follow the strains of early adjustment.[40]

> A second major complex of reactions . . . can be summed up by the term "culture fatigue." This term refers to a phenomenon different from the "culture shock" experienced by many Americans immediately after they enter a new culture. . . . Culture fatigue is the physical and emotional exhaustion that almost invariably results from the infinite series of minute adjustments required for long-term survival in an alien culture. Living and working overseas generally requires that one must supply his automatic evaluations and judgments; that he must supply new interpretations to seemingly familiar behavior; and that he must demand of himself constant alterations in the style and content of his authority. Whether this process is conscious or

[40] R. B. Texter, *Cultural Frontiers of the Peace Corps* (Cambridge, Mass.: The M.I.T. Press, 1966), pp. 98–99.

unconscious, successful or unsuccessful, it consumes an enormous amount of energy, leaving the individual decidedly fatigued.

One effect of culture fatigue, a tendency toward negative interpretations of all foreign culture, has led American business and government personnel in one nation to regard close family ties as "clannishness," personal sensitivity as "sulkiness," avoiding unpleasant subjects as "dishonesty," and lavish hospitality as "wastefulness."[41]

A new police officer quickly learns these reponses through his associations with more seasoned officers. The fact that a response is routine does not mean that it is satisfactory. To the contrary, many routine responses are applied on the basis of indefensible and improper criteria. But once developed, they generally are immune to critical reevaluation unless a crisis situation arises. Because of their informal character, such responses tend not to be influenced by developments in police training. And, because they consist of the accumulated experience of front-line officers, they tend to take on vitality that continues even without the active support of the higher echelon of police administration.

Unique situations do arise, usually where the frequency of a given kind of incident is small, for which there is no routine response. Unless time permits him to confer with his sergeant, the individual officer is left to respond without any form of guidance. Under such circumstances, the decision of the individual officer will reflect his own personal values and opinions about people and about group behavior.

Improvement in the capacity of law enforcement agencies to perform the essential and highly sensitive functions that comprise the total police task requires a willingness on the part of the public and the police to take several bold steps. There must, in the first place, be a more widespread recognition on the part of the citizenry and the police of both the range and the complexity of the problems which the police confront. Secondly, there must be a willingness on the part of the police to respond to these problems by the careful development and articulation of policies and practices which are subject to continuing reevaluation in the light of changing social conditions.

The problems in police–community relations

Undoubtedly, one of the major problems in law enforcement in the United States is concerned with community acceptance and support of law enforcement and its agents. Let it be noted at the outset

[41] *Ibid.*, p. 49.

that this, like many issues in the area of police–community relations, is not strictly a racial problem; the negative public attitudes toward police work in general are common to all citizens.

Unlike the police force in Great Britain, which generally enjoys not only a considerable degree of public confidence but also a measure of real popularity, police officers in the United States have been accorded a second-class position in society. They are frequently the object of attack by press and pulpit, bench and bar, civic and commercial associations, labor leaders, professional politicians, ambitious office seekers, reformers, and criminals. Police work by its very nature is not calculated to be totally successful; that is, it can never succeed in completely preventing the occurrence of crime or apprehending everyone who commits a criminal act. It is obvious, however, to all law-abiding citizens, that a healthy society owes its agents of law enforcement a profound respect, for a good police department is a bulwark against a sea of disorder. The general attitude in the community today, however, toward those agents is frequently one of apathetic indifference, if not social antagonism—neither of which is beneficial in effecting vigorous enforcement of the law.

Also, the American law enforcement tradition appears to be influenced by the major differences in the backgrounds of those making up the population of the cities—black, Puerto Rican, Italian, Mexican, white, Oriental, and so on. What these various peoples seek in terms of law and order no doubt varies, as do the methods of those providing the enforcement.

To get an idea of the variation, consider a mythical western sheriff attempting to bring his antirustling skills to bear on the violence of San Francisco's early Chinatown, or New York's 1844 immigration riots, or interstate prostitution.[42] The frustrations of this imaginary sheriff would probably be no greater than those experienced by many contemporary police officers confronted with civil disobedience, sit-ins, protest demonstrations, riots, and unfounded charges of brutality—all occurring in the most affluent society the world has ever known. Indeed, on a comparative basis, the sheriff might well be envied for his firm and uncomplicated belief that people were either good or bad, with the bad ones placed in jail, where they learned to be good. Uncomplicated beliefs of this nature would permit the ever-increasing forces of social change to be interpreted simply. But they are not simple; neither is the tremendous task of understanding and programming effective community relations.

[42] E. Eldefonso, A. Coffey, and R. C. Grace, *Principles of Law Enforcement: Overview of the Justice System* 3rd ed. (New York: John Wiley, 1981), pp. 165–75.

Through evolution, society's enforcing of behavior regulation has moved beyond the point of uncomplicated answers for law enforcement agencies. Now police teams, chemicals, and noise generators are steadily supplementing the performance of individual police in the control of violent demonstrations. And the causes of these demonstrations—the various community tensions—have become a legitimate law enforcement concern.

In our grossly complicated, urbanized society, the philosophy of enforcing law must continue to expand. In the matter of *personal safety* and *property security,* law enforcement must include positive efforts to anticipate and redirect those social forces that jeopardize people's personal safety and property security. Discharge of this responsibility must necessarily become a matter of community relations.

COMMUNITY AND HUMAN RELATIONS

If society is to survive, at least in a civilized manner, it is imperative that laws be enforced.[43] Because the observance of law is so vital, society cannot depend on simple persuasion for its accomplishment; rather it must rely in part on force. The term *enforcement*—and indeed, the very nature of man—implies a possible use of force. This potential to wield force, then, is necessarily part of the police image. The manner in which the potential is viewed by the public often determines whether the police image is good or bad. And, because a good police image tends to affect favorably a person's willingness to observe the law voluntarily, police retain a rightful interest in having a good image. The police officer embodies the law so visibly and directly that neither the officer nor the public finds it easy to differentiate between the law and the enforcement of it. The public is confused and unable to recognize the broad concept of the police officer. As the late Bruce Smith pointed out:

> Relatively few citizens recall ever having seen a judge; fewer still, a prosecutor, coroner, sheriff, probation officer or prison warden. The patrolman is thoroughly familiar to all. His uniform picks him out from the crowd so distinctly that he becomes a living symbol of the law—not always of its majesty, but certainly of its power. Whether the police like it or not, they are forever marked men.[44]

As will be expanded upon in Chapter 8, any officer of the law is partly a symbol, and law enforcement work consists to some ex-

---

[43] Eldefonso et al., *Principles of Law Enforcement,* pp. 35–49.

[44] Bruce Smith, "Municipal Police Administration," *Annals of the American Academy of Police and Social Science,* 40, No. 5 (September 1971), 22.

tent in creating impressions based on symbolic attributes. Thus, an unoccupied police vehicle can slow down turnpike traffic or motivate drivers to stop at designated intersections, and the presence of half a dozen officers can control a large crowd.[45]

The uniform of the police officer is viewed as a symbolic license to judge and punish. That is, it not only represents the right to arrest but also connotes the role of a disciplinarian. Unfortunately, it is for this reason that many parents try to make small children behave by pointed references to policemen. Needless to say, this "punishing role" does not lend itself to the promotion of any social role other than that of an enforcer.[46]

Police interest in a good image is vital for a number of reasons. One that is singularly practical is that the greater the voluntary law observance, the less the need for forceful enforcement. So the question becomes, What can be done to promote the standing of the police officer and of social influences to encourage voluntary law observance?

The various theories presented in the literature make clear the lack of agreement among biologists, anthropologists, criminologists, sociologists, and psychologists and psychiatrists concerning the causes of crime. Yet these behavioral scientists generally agree that societal influences both encourage and discourage crime. As it relates to criminal behavior, such influence is merely a power to affect human willingness to conform to law. And so the question of influence becomes a consideration of those forces having enough power to encourage voluntary law observance.

The manner in which the public views a police method of enforcement is considered one such force. Another, perhaps more fundamental force relates to the manner in which children are raised. The old saying, "As the twig is bent, so grows the tree," has particular significance in every society. The citizen who holds little respect for law enforcement goals may merely reflect the values he or she learned as a child. Racial tensions, economic conditions, and various physical and emotional deprivations have probably helped shape that attitude. But it is likely that the major contributing factor was early and unfortunate experiences with police. The detrimental and sometimes lasting effects of such negative encounters will be discussed in later chapters. For now, mention of experiences of this nature serves to introduce the subject of human relations—a matter of increasing concern to police, as evidenced,

[45] H. H. Toch, "Psychological Consequences of the Police Role," *Police*, Vol. 10, No. 1 (September–October 1965), 22.

[46] Toch, "Psychological Consequences." See also T. J. Crawford, "Police Overperception of Ghetto Hostility," *Journal of Police Science and Administration*, 1, No. 2 (1973), 168–74.

for example, by the great number of courses devoted to this subject at most police academies and colleges throughout the United States.

HUMAN RELATIONS DEFINED

More and more, the literature reflects an implied definition of human relations in terms of "avoiding police brutality."[47] A further definition includes police discretion or decision in terms of "police attitudes."[48] Going beyond these rather narrow considerations, a definition of law enforcement human relations might be: *police participation in any activity that seeks law observance through respect and acceptance of enforcement of laws in a positive manner.*

Regardless of how the term *human relations* is defined, however, police interest in the subject should be related in some way to the causes of crime. It has been noted already that behavioral scientists fail to agree on these. A cause or a group of causes can be isolated—such as alcoholism, poverty, broken homes, and parental neglect—that seem to turn one person but not another to crime, even though both may be subject to precisely the same influences. Even such an extensive catalog of human characteristics as the Yale University Human Relations File (originally the Cross-Cultural Survey) fails to clarify how cultural causes affect different people in different ways.

But despite the behavioral scientists' lack of agreement on crime causes, law enforcement practitioners tend to agree that there appears to be a relationship between at least some kinds of crime and certain community influences. These influences, more often than not, relate to combinations of problems such as poverty, racial tensions, and parental inadequacies. An additional influence that has already been indicated is the police image held by the community, a topic that will be thoroughly discussed in another chapter.

Because the community's attitude toward police (or the police image) is one of the influences that carries enough force to encour-

[47] See, for example, J. T. Duncan, R. N. Brenner, and M. Kravitz, eds., *Police Stress: A Selected Bibliography* (Washington, D.C.: National Criminal Justice Reference Service, U.S. Department of Justice, 1979); C. E. Pope, "Race and Crime Revisited," *Crime and Delinquency*, Vol. 25, No. 3 (July 1979); P. D. Mayhall and D. P. Geary, eds., *Community Relations and Administration of Justice* (New York: John Wiley, 1979); and R. N. Brenner and M. Kravitz, eds., "Community Concern: Police Use of Deadly Force," (Washington, D.C.: National Criminal Justice Reference Service, U.S. Department of Justice, 1979).

[48] J. H. Skolnick, *Justice Without Trial: Law Enforcement in Democratic Society* (New York: John Wiley, 1976).

age voluntary law observance, it is of primary concern to law enforcement. The citizen who is convinced that police are brutal will probably find it difficult to respect police goals, particularly if the brutality is believed to be directed only toward certain minorities. And, as a practical matter, the *validity* of the belief matters less than the *strength* of the belief. A person usually functions on the basis of what he or she believes, regardless of the validity of those beliefs.

Law enforcement in a period of uncertainty

Currently, law enforcement agencies are caught in a period of unusual uncertainty that can be primarily attributed to two separate but relatively interdependent developments. The first, elaborated upon in another chapter, is directly related to the U.S. Supreme Court. The Court has made a series of decisions relative to the protection of personal liberties of those accused of crimes. In 1963, the Supreme Court ruling on the appeal case of *Gideon v. Wainwright* had the effect that a new trial could be demanded by anyone convicted of crime who did not have legal counsel. Moving closer to the field of law enforcement, the 1964 decision handed down in the case of *Escobedo v. Illinois* protected the constitutional right of an indigent to be provided with legal counsel at the time of interrogation. Then, in June 1966, the ruling in *Miranda v. Arizona* provided for legal counsel as soon as the interrogated person is considered a suspect in an investigation.

The mixed feelings regarding Supreme Court decisions was the subject of a Task Force study in San Diego, California.[49] The study showed that the judges and lawyers in San Diego generally support the recent Supreme Court decisions regarding police interrogation. Most emphasize, however, that it is a complex issue and that the decisions have mixed benefits. The tone of many of the comments is that these decisions were necessary, to counteract past police abuses. As one explained, police departments "have no one to blame but themselves." He noted:

> Cases have been coming up to the Supreme Court for decades showing abuses by police forces and policemen across the country—third degree, prisoners being beaten, confessions that were extorted out of individuals. There was a wide variety of abuses of individuals' rights to due process. ... The Supreme Court in all those years was reluctant to get involved in this squabble, except in a few minor areas. ... [50]

[49] Lohman and Misner, *Police and the Community*, p. 15.
[50] Lohman and Misner, *Police and the Community*.

A lawyer stated that he was very much in favor of the decisions, for they curb practices that have long needed control. Another lawyer expressed support but explained some of his reservations in this manner:

> The decisions indicate an imbalance. The problem is to give the accused full protection of his rights yet give society its protection against criminal elements. I take full cognizance of the fact that there is a good deal of crime on the streets. The difficulty is that police officers were abusing the rights of the accused and I would prefer to see some system by which it was possible to hit the police officer directly. I feel that the Supreme Court has taken really the only practical course available to it—namely, that the evidence that the police obtained would have to be held inadmissible in court and thereby discourage officers from abusing the rights of the accused. I still resent the fact that this has to be done, for it impairs the right of society generally to be secure itself.[51]

Several judges commented that they did not think the decisions would hinder law enforcement. Federal agencies, for example, which have high-caliber personnel, have worked within these restrictions for a long time. Some judges did express the opinion that the decisions would "hamstring" local police departments, but they did not elaborate further. Some said that not all police departments would be able to afford the competent police officers needed for effective conformity with the court rulings. Those who stated that they were aware of investigative procedures of the San Diego Police Department did not believe that that department would need to make any changes.

A number of judges and lawyers criticized police departments for "bellyaching" about the Supreme Court decisions; they thought police should stop complaining, accept the rulings, and do their job. "Some in the legal community support the need for the changes required by the *Dorado* decision but think that *Miranda* goes too far."[52]

These decisions have elicited a great deal of debate—hot debate—and have been attacked as placing a great deal of restraint on the police by "coddling" the law violator. Furthermore, according to the dissenters, the police are placed in the position of having to fight by "Marquis of Queensberry rules," whereas criminals are not bound by such rules. On the other hand, these decisions have been received as evidence that the Supreme Court has finally become more concerned with human liberty than with the protection of property rights.

The second development creating uncertainty, which is just as

---

[51] Lohman and Misner, *Police and the Community.*

[52] Lohman and Misner, *Police and the Community.*

important as the first, is the current series of civil disturbances associated with a wide range of efforts to upgrade minority groups to the full citizenship and socioeconomic privileges guaranteed by the U.S. Constitution. The strategies and nonviolent techniques of civil-rights groups are creating unusual problems for law enforcement agencies, because exploiting excessive use of police coercion is one of their major weapons. This nonviolent method involves the explicit and knowing violation of a particular law by people who are quite ready to accept, without resistance, the retribution attached to that violation. By utilizing the nonviolent-resistance method, minority groups dramatize certain laws as unjust. Furthermore, the use of police coercion is invited—and welcomed—as an opportunity to identify peace officers as the "intimidators" or "aggressors" against peaceful demonstrators. It is not unusual to use children, women, ministers, and other people who have a favorable image as "victims" for police "aggression." Needless to say, the resulting arrests play havoc with the judiciary machinery.

Nonviolent resistance has its ideological genesis in the values of Christian morality and humanitarianism through the premise that minority groups have a moral obligation *not* to cooperate with the "forces of evil."

> In essence, the nonviolent resistance is a form of passive aggression, in that it frustrates its opponents by enveloping them in a cloud of "Christian love" for one's enemies. The established power structure of the community is to be forced into the role of "bad guys," whereas the Negroes assume the mantle of Christian heroes. Noncompliance with carefully selected laws creates a community crisis, but, by refraining from violent resistance, the law violators make application of police coercion an opportunity to present social protest as consistent with the highly prized values of humanitarianism and concern for the underdog.[53]

A noted author and professor in the fields of criminology and law enforcement has made this explicit point:

> Another area of current dispute is "control of conduct" or "maintenance of the peace." This nation is currently beseiged by acts of violence, civil disobedience and riot. On the one hand, there is a cry for "law and order," and on the other hand, some espouse a policy of "absolute permissiveness." The police are presently scapegoats of this dichotomy, therefore it is imperative that standards be established that will protect us from anarchy, and at the same time, allow for reasonable dissent.[54]

[53] E. H. Johnson, "A Sociological Interpretation of Police Reaction and Responsibility to Civil Disobedience," *Journal of Criminal Law, Criminology and Police Science* 58, No. 3 (September 1967), 407.

[54] H. W. More, Jr., *Critical Issues in Law Enforcement*, 2nd ed. (Cincinnati, O.: W. H. Anderson Co., 1977), p. 7.

DISSENT AND CIVIL DISOBEDIENCE

In the United States, the question is not, "May I dissent?"; that right is guaranteed by both the Constitution and the courts. The question is *how* the dissent shall be carried out. The First Amendment confers "the right of the people peaceably to assemble, and to petition the Government for a redress of grievances"—but there are limitations to the right. And contrary to popular belief, freedom of speech does not guarantee a person's right to offer a false statement about someone else (there is a possibility of a civil suit, or tort). Nor does it permit a person to state what is on his or her mind anytime, anywhere. According to Justice Oliver Wendell Holmes, one may not shout "Fire!" in a crowded theater when fully aware that such a warning is untrue. Regardless of how positive one's motive may be—such as dissatisfaction with inadequate fire regulations—actions that will injure others cannot be excused.

Abe Fortas, former justice of the Supreme Court, stated that the term *civil disobedience*, which has been applied to the refusal to obey a law believed to be immoral or unconstitutional, has in recent years been misapplied. Civil disobedience does not apply to attempts to overthrow or seize control of the government by force, or to the use of violence in order to compel the government to grant a measure of autonomy to a segment of its population. Such programs advocate revolution, and the term *civil disobedience* is not appropriately used in this context.

> Some propagandists seem to think that people who violate the laws of public order ought not to be punished if their violation has protest as its purpose. By calling criminal acts "civil disobedience," they seek to persuade us that offenses against public and private security should be immune from punishment and even commended. They seek to excuse physical attacks upon police; assaults upon recruiters for munitions firms and for the armed services; breaking windows in the Pentagon and in homes; robbing stores; trespassing on private premises; occupying academic offices, and even looting, burning and promiscuous violence.[55]

The First Amendment freedoms are not a sanction for riotous behavior; freedom of speech, of the press, and of assembly do not correlate with looting, burning, assault, and physical abuse. The U.S. Supreme Court has stated explicitly that the First Amendment protects the right to *assemble* and to *petition*, but it requires that these rights be peacefully executed.[56]

The police department is recognized as the strongest and most

---

[55] A. Fortas, *Concerning Dissent and Disobedience*, 2nd. ed. (New York: The New American Library, 1973), p. 10.

[56] Fortas, *Concerning Dissent.*

sensitive arm of the local government; therefore, it is the normal agent for promoting a community-relations problem. The identification is not founded in political essence but is an offspring of social values. As mentioned in this chapter and elaborated on in chapters to follow, the ills of a community are most apt to be directed toward the symbolic wielder of the community's authority, and the police agency is the normal objective of the scorn of the oppressed.

In the final analysis, effective law enforcement depends upon the full participation of all members of our society in the legislative and administrative process. In this period of dynamic social change and the movement toward full integration of hitherto excluded minorities into the decision-making structure, there will continue to be difficulties, tensions, and crises that spring from the dissatisfaction and despair fostered by social, economic, and political patterns of discrimination against minority groups.

Summary

Among the problems relating to police–community relations are the conflicts between minority groups and police agencies. When clear communication is most important between minorities and policemen, it actually tends to decrease, thus obscuring the similarities or common goals they might share. This conflict interferes seriously with public confidence in police and consequently with the ability of the police to deal effectively with the crime problem.

American law enforcement tradition appears to have been influenced by major differences in the ethnic background of those making up the city's population. Society's enforcement of behavior regulations has moved beyond the point of simple, uncomplicated answers, and law enforcement in urbanized societies increasingly needs positive efforts to anticipate and redirect those social forces that tend to jeopardize personal safety and property security. Discharge of this police responsibility therefore must become a matter of community relations.

Law enforcement human relations is defined in this chapter as "police participation in an activity that seeks law observance through respect rather than enforcement." But this is hindered by the absence of adequate resources, training, and guidance for police officers, as well as the concurrent tendency of individual officers to depend largely on improvisation. Other problems associated with enforcement of laws during the last decade have been related to (1) recent decisions made by the Supreme Court, and (2) the series of civil disturbances associated with efforts to upgrade the status of minority groups.

Civil disobedience is not the correct term for violent and destructive behavior, but applies instead to peaceful demonstration against laws believed to be unjust or immoral.

Discussion topics

1. Discuss the problem of police–community relations.
2. Define *human relations.*
3. Why is law enforcement undergoing a period of uncertainty?
4. Discuss the misapplication of the term *civil disobedience.*

Annotated references

Bayley, D. H., and H. Mendelsohn, *Minorities and the Police: Confrontation in America,* 2nd ed. New York: Free Press, 1972. The authors explore the "texture of relations between the police and the community, especially minority groups." In this study, completed in Denver, Colorado, the authors show how police and minorities perceive their relationship and also attempt to show what factors cause them to view each other in a particular way. An excellent study, relating quite significantly to the subject matter in Chapter 7.

Bouma, D., *Kids and Cops: A Study in Mutual Hostility,* 2nd ed. Grand Rapids, Mich.: William B. Erdmans, 1977. This volume concerns itself with police relations with youth. It discusses the opinions held by young people relating to the police, and vice versa, according to a study of 10,000 students in ten Michigan cities, and more than 300 police officers in three cities. Robert L. Derbyshire's article, "Children's Perceptions of the Police," in the *Journal of Criminal Law, Criminology and Police Science,* June 1968, covers the same topic, with emphasis on the younger child. See also R. Portune, *Changing Adolescent Attitudes toward Police.* Cincinnati, O.: W.H. Anderson Co., 1971. Portune's book treats the same subject but much more extensively.

Brenner, R. N., and M. Kravitz, *Community Concern: Police Use of Deadly Force.* Washington, D.C.: National Criminal Justice Service, 1979. The authors discuss hostility, danger, anxiety, distrust, and hatred inherent in police/minority-group contacts. They also examine the dynamics of the negative contact situations. The authors give a vivid picture of the existing strains in black–white relations.

Manning, P. E., and Van J. MacNew, *Policing: A View From the Street.* Ventura, Calif.: Goodyear, 1978. An excellent, concise study of the title subject. The authors pay particular attention to street-level encounters between police and public.

chapter eight

The Problem
of Police Image
in a Changing Community

It is not the intention of this chapter to address itself to police-community relations *programs;* this is a major topic of another chapter in this text. Instead, emphasis will be on the effect of a negative police image and the problems confronting law enforcement agencies in developing and maintaining a positive police image. As indicated in an earlier chapter, a good police image tends to affect favorably the individual's willingness to observe the law voluntarily. Therefore, police retain a vital interest in projecting a good image.

In the nation's large cities and in many small cities and towns as well, the need for strengthening police–community relations is critical today; Minority groups are taking action to acquire rights and services that have historically been denied them. As the most visible representative of the society from which these groups are demanding fair treatment and equal opportunity, law enforcement agencies are faced with unprecedented situations, which require that they develop policies and practices governing their actions when dealing with minority groups and other citizens.

Even if fair treatment of minority groups were the sole consid-

eration, police departments would have an obligation to attempt to achieve and maintain a positive police image and good police–community relations. In fact, however, much more is at stake. For police–community relations have a direct bearing on the character of life in the cities and on the community's ability to maintain stability and solve its problems. At the same time, the police department's capacity to deal with crime depends to a large extent upon its relations with the citizenry. Indeed, no improvement in law enforcement is likely in this country unless police–community relations are substantially improved.

The last decade has seen a great deal of criticism toward police. As a result of such criticism, some of which has been without validity, thousands of loyal, capable, and professional officers throughout the nation are extremely perplexed and apprehensive of the future. The complexity of contemporary law enforcement in conjunction with the rapidly growing problems of traffic control alone has demanded frequent contact, not only with the criminal element but also with the law-abiding citizen. Thus, because of the closer, more personal contact, there is a greater need to present a positive police image.

Police–community relations cannot be viewed as an isolated problem, one confronting only those agents who have a vested interest in administration of the criminal justice system and process. When we discuss the problems of police–community relations, police image, and human relations in general, we really have many things in mind. Because practitioners in the field of community justice are primarily concerned with working with people—every one of them an individual in his or her own right—it is vital for police personnel, as well as those associated with the judicial and correctional process, to understand that there is a common denominator, a sharing of one very important feature. This common feature is *the awareness that every human being has his or her own aspirations, hopes, and standards of behavior.*

The community and the police: controversy over the police role

A great deal of controversy exists today over the role police should play in our contemporary society. The responsibility of the police officer is basically to protect the life and property, regulate the conduct, and minister to the needs of people from all classes of life, all of whom are equally entitled to the services of law enforcement agencies. Other duties have fallen within the purview of law enforcement, but all of them are within the scope of those basic responsibilities.

The primary police–citizen contacts are, contrary to popular belief, with those members of our society who request assistance and protection. These people turn to the police officer for assistance with problems that are extremely difficult and important, at least to them. In analyzing the number and character of contacts the police officer has with members of the public during a tour of duty, we see that he or she spends very little time chasing criminals or locking people up. Let us examine the role—or roles—of the urban police officer.

The urban police officer

VARIETY OF ROLES

It may well be that the public image of "public safety" reduces to some kind of oversimplified stereotypes of the urban firefighter and police officer. But the image of the firefighter may be simpler than the police image because, although both perform far more roles than is generally recognized, the police officer is playing so very many roles. There appears to be little doubt that police roles are more varied, if for no other reason than that their responsibilities go beyond public safety—police deal with "morals," and with "peace and quiet," as well.

The multiplicity of police roles is worthy of consideration for many reasons. Among the more significant is to make certain that evaluations of police performance are related to the proper roles. For example, an assessment of a police officer's public-relations role might not be appropriate to the performance of the officer's role in the arrest of a resisting felon.

More pertinent to the present discussion, some understanding of the variety of police roles is necessary for the overall understanding of law enforcement—that is law enforcement in its context of dealing with the public as *humanly* as possible. With this in mind, let us consider two broad enforcement roles—the *keeping of peace,* and the *enforcement of law.*

At first glance, it might appear that these two roles are the same thing—keeping the peace might appear to *be* law enforcement. But on closer examination, it turns out that many, perhaps most, peace-keeping functions do not relate to actual law violation, and usually do not lead to arrest or prosecution, whereas the enforcement of law generally does.

It becomes obvious that police officers must be able to first recognize the difference in the two roles, and then to adjust the performance of their duties accordingly. Theoretically, police officers are recruited and trained on the basis of their ability to make such adjustments in their performance. Indeed, beyond these two relatively simple distinctions between peace keeping and enforcement, police have numerous roles that must be performed in virtually all jurisdictions, from family counseling to aiding the fire-fighting function.

It has been noted that between peace keeping, or maintaining order, and law enforcement, one of these two roles can be more dominant than the other.[1] Indeed, some students of law enforcement contend that the role of maintaining order does, in fact, dominate the overall police role—even to the point of subordinating the law enforcement role.[2] In any given police jurisdiction, observations might be made that seem to support this contention. Nevertheless, police do, or at least should, perform many roles, even if one can be shown to dominate.

Consider, for example, the effect on the peace-keeping role if there were *no* enforcement role. In such a circumstance, any refusal of citizens to comply with police efforts to keep peace would be in the same category as their refusing to obey their clergymen, or their neighbors, or their relatives. The *availability* of the enforcement role is the strongest enhancement of the peace-keeping role, even when the peace-keeping role is dominant. In its most negative sense, the fear of arrest, even when arrest is not threatened, is one of the strongest influences in the peace-keeping role. Ideally, police officers are recruited and trained in a manner that stresses reliance on communication rather than arrest. But when communication fails, something else is required if the community is to remain reasonably assured that order will prevail. That something else must of necessity be the potential for enforcing the law.

Deceptive to some is the apparent lack of threatened enforcement when skilled police officers keep the peace. That is, there are those who would argue that enforcement has nothing to do with peace keeping because police keep the peace without arrest, or force of any kind, in the majority of situations. Valid though such a contention might appear at first glance, one need only remove the police officers' authority to arrest to discern how very dependent effective peace keeping is upon the potential to enforce law. In-

[1] Charles P. McDowell, *Police in the Community* (Cincinnati, O.: W. H. Anderson, 1975), p. 41. See also E. Eldefonso, A. R. Coffey, and R. G. Grace, *Principles of Law Enforcement: Overview of Justice,* 3rd ed. (New York: John Wiley, 1981), Chapter 9.

[2] Ibid.

deed, it is conceivable that many officers apparently able to maintain order through simple communication skills might become assault victims were they stripped of their enforcement authority.

MUTUAL DEPENDENCE OF ROLES

In much the same manner that the enforcement role complements and secures the peace-keeping role, many other police roles are mutually dependent. The police officer called upon to deliver a baby in an emergency is in a role that depends for success on the overall role of public service. Officers attempting to prevent juvenile delinquency are in a role that may depend nearly entirely on the skills needed to perform the role of arbitrator in serious family disputes. Suicide rescues, hostage negotiations, and mob control are also related by common skills in communication, applied to different police roles.

As noted earlier, the prime requisite is the police officer's ability to recognize the varied situations, and to draw on the appropriate skills for the particular role required. Underpinning all police roles, however, remains the authority role of law enforcement. The more skilled the officer, the less visible the authority role—but authority to enforce the law remains primary.

Police "power"

How a police officer handles the inherent police "power" is often a factor in the public's view of law enforcement in the community. Law must be enforced if civilized man is to survive. Society cannot depend completely upon simple persuasion to induce law observance, and therefore it must require enforcement of law. This enforcement, then, is necessarily a part of the police role. But the manner in which it is viewed by the public often determines whether the police image is good or bad. Neither the police officer nor the public finds it easy to differentiate between the law and its enforcement.[3] Bruce Smith said, "[The patrolman's] uniform picks him out from the crowd so distinctly that he becomes a living symbol of the law—not always of its majesty, but certainly of its power. Whether police like it or not, they are forever marked men."[4]

[3] D. L. Kooken, Ethics in Police Service, 3rd ed. (Springfield, Ill.: Chas. C Thomas, 1967), p. 21.
[4] Bruce Smith, "Municipal Police Administration," Annals of the American Academy of Police and Social Science, 40, No. 5 (1972), 22.

Police are engaged in a traditional occupation that is being loaded down with new requirements because of the changes and social unrest in our society:

> Nothing is tougher than being a policeman in a free society. For one thing, the U.S. Constitution guarantees as much individual liberty as public safety will allow. To uphold that elusive ideal, the policeman is supposed to mediate family disputes that would tax a Supreme Court justice, soothe angry Negroes despite his scant knowledge of psychology, enforce hundreds of petty laws without discrimination, and use only necessary force to bring violators before the courts. The job demands extraordinary skill, restraint, and character—qualities not usually understood either by cop-hating leftists who sound as if they want to exterminate all policemen, or by dissent-hating conservatives who seem to want policemen to run the U.S. in a paroxysm of punitive "law and order."
>
> The U.S. policeman is forbidden to act as judge and jury—for that way lies the police state. Yet, he also has enormous discretion to keep the peace by enforcing some laws and by overlooking others. How does he exercise that discretion? Largely on the basis of common sense and common mores, plus his own private attitudes. Unfortunately, he faces an era of drastically changing mores that challenges his most cherished creeds and preconceptions.[5]

This essay from *Time* magazine continues by noting that the American public is confused in its expectations of the role of law enforcement officers in the United States:

> We ask our officers to be a combination of Bat Masterson, Sherlock Holmes, Sigmund Freud, King Solomon, Hercules, and Diogenes. . . . Indeed, the U.S. often seems lucky to have any cops at all. Plato envisioned the policeman's lofty forebear as the "guardian" of law and order and placed very near the top of his ideal society, endowing him with special wisdom, strength and patience. The U.S. has put its guardians near the bottom. In most places, the pay for experienced policemen is less than $13,000 a year, forcing many cops to moonlight and some to take bribes. Fear and loneliness are routine hazards.[6]

The article concludes its analysis of the basic police problem by commenting that the average cop feels he is unappreciated or even actively disliked by the public he serves. Very often, he is right—and thus he is all the more apt to confine his entire social as well as professional life to his fellow cops, a group that all too often sees the world as divided into "we" and "they."

[5] "Time Essay: The Police Need Help," *Time*, October 8, 1968, p. 26.
[6] "Time Essay."

But the problem involves more than lack of understanding regarding police activities in our free society. There is increasing evidence that Americans of all races, creeds, and income groups have reservations about the police. Some of these are for obvious reasons. Most people tend to come in direct contact with police only under rather unhappy circumstances—when they have parked the car "just a little bit illegally," when caught driving faster than the posted speed limit, or when involved in some "innocent" horseplay that misfired. Coupled with this is belief in the old adage, "When you need a policeman, he's never there." Either way, the police image comes out scarred.

According to a noted author, H. H. Toch, it is the broader connotations of police actions rather than their direct effects that may promote most of the antagonism on the part of society.[7] Although these connotations can probably be ameliorated through stronger emphasis on police courtesy and public relations, they can hardly be completely eradicated. Ultimately, the social and psychological control role of law enforcement is one of essentially one-way communication against a backdrop of latent power.[8]

If it is limited to this type of contact, the police officer's role as a controlling agent within the community will be damaged. Furthermore, according to Toch, such one-way contact will ultimately prove psychologically harmful to the police as well as to the public. The police officer too often exaggerates the prevalence of apathy and projects hostility even where there is none, interpreting public antagonism as an indication of the inevitable separation of the police from the mainstream of the community.[9]

Police as symbol of social problems

There is no doubt that the police officer is the symbol of authority and middle-class values. With the standard equipment of the uniform, the gun, the insignia of rank, and the baton, officers on occasion tend to think of themselves as part of a paramilitary unit, which is certainly not too far from the truth. However, unlike the military, the police have a requirement to keep good relations between themselves and the community. Law enforcement is more

[7] H. H. Toch, "Psychological Consequences of the Police Role," *Police,* 10, No. 1 (September–October 1965), 22.

[8] Ibid.

[9] Toch, "Psychological Consequences."

dependent upon public support than is any single branch of government or any other profession. The average police officer is likely to come from a middle-class community in which he or she lives a well-regulated life according to middle-class standards of ethics and morality. But these officers work at law enforcement in an area populated by people who are largely alien to them. They find the language, customs, and emotions of minority groups strange, hostile, and aggravating. Professionalism has not resolved this problem. Identification with fellow officers is reinforced, "forging a social bond . . . at the same time it generates a great deal of mutual suspicion."[10]

Statistics indicate that there is a definite increase taking place in assaults against police officers. Thus, confronted with hostility and fearing physical injury, the officer is constantly on guard. This contributes to the feeling of isolation and the view of the community, in which the officer sees:

> . . . everything taking place around him as a configuration of events designed to attack him. His natural reaction is to strike first. The idea of the symbolic assailant illustrates one of the two principal variables which make up the working personality of the police officer—reaction to danger. The other is his reaction to authority. . . . His natural suspicion, plus his natural conception of his work as a way of life, reinforce the tendencies previously noted, and draw him further away from the public he intends to serve and protect.
>
> . . . This is especially so in lower-class areas where the cop is seen as standing for the interests and prejudices of dominant [white] society in the role of the oppressor, and where each party sees the other as a misfit.[11]

It may be paradoxical that the people who are the most victimized by crime are also the most hostile to the police, but it is not remarkable, because the policeman is the symbol of middle-class society and values.

In a fundamental sense, it is wrong to define the problem solely as hostility to police. In many ways, the police symbolize much deeper problems. Responsibility for apathy or for disrespect for law enforcement agencies would be more appropriately attributed to:

> . . . a social system that permits inequities and irregularities in law, stimulates poverty and inhibits initiative and motivation of the poor, and regulates low social and economic status to the police while concomitantly giving them more extraneous non-police duties than can actively be performed.[12]

[10] D. J. Dodd, "Police Mentality and Behavior," Issues in Criminology, 3, No. 1 (Summer 1967), 56–57.

[11] Dodd, "Police Mentality."

[12] R. L. Derbyshire, "The Social Control Role of the Police in Changing Urban Communities," Excerpta Criminologica, 6, No. 3 (1966), 315–16.

The ongoing daily affairs of the people of the community are the result of an interplay of social, economic, psychological, and biological forces that influence the behavior of all citizens, whether clerics or criminals, educators or demonstrators, merchants or police. Police problems are not unrelated to welfare problems. Dropouts are obviously not solely the problem of school administrators. Unemployment, bad housing, discrimination, improper family structures, illegitimacy, and disease produce results that directly aggravate those problems more generally regarded as police matters—crime, violence, and the like. Moreover, to the extent that people living under these conditions see themselves as victims of social oppression, the police can expect much of the rebellion to be focused against them.

Everyone certainly agrees that the police cannot be expected to solve all the ills of the community. Many do not realize, however, how directly involved the police are with the problems these ills generate. It is easy enough to see how the police are involved when there is a demonstration, riot, or minor or major disorder, but the less spectacular day-by-day accumulation of social costs and police involvement, although not so dramatic, is nonetheless enormous. When disorders break out, everyone assumes that the role of the police is to stop them; but what is not generally understood is that in their daily performance, the police, along with other government structures, inevitably tend to view things in terms of community mores. People in general go about their daily lives in a sort of unverbalized understanding that "this is the custom; this is the way things are." And for most people in most facets of their daily existence, it is comfortable to be able to rely on things being "the way they are." The police realize this—perhaps more so than most, because they are so close to the conflict potential that accompanies pressures for change. The fact that the police do not take the initiative to change things is not just a case of not wanting to "rock the boat." The police alone are not in a position to change community mores even if they wanted to and knew how.

To a considerable extent, then, the police are the victims of community problems that are not of their making. The police officer, as a symbol not only of law but of the entire system of law enforcement and criminal justice, becomes the tangible target for grievances against shortcomings throughout the system. When a suspect is held for a long period in jail because of having no money to pay a fine, when the jail or prison is physically dilapidated or its personnel brutal or incompetent, when the probation or parole officer has little time to give a prisoner, or when a prisoner is given inadequate counsel from a public defender system that is very often understaffed and overworked, the police are blamed.

Here is a description of a familiar courtroom process that exemplifies this situation:

[The] lawyer goes through row after row of spectators and defendants in the courtroom, calling out his client's name. The chances are that he has seen the client only once in his life before—months ago, when the client's case was in the arraignment stage. Today is the trial date and he keeps calling out his man's name, looking over the rows of faces. "Williams? Harry Williams?" he calls, and finally a man stands up, shrugs his shoulders to get the tension out of them and says, "Yeah." "Just wanted to see you were here," says the lawyer, and tells the client to sit down again and reassures him that he will return shortly. He glances at the wad of papers in his hand, arrest warrants, arraignment records, writs, and all the paper foundations of justice. Then he heads out of the courtroom, where a melee of policemen are moving about, chatting and joking, talking to lawyers, waiting for cases to be called.

The lawyer finds the name of the officer who made the arrest and, because he is familiar with these small type criminal cases, he soon spots him in the crowd. "You got Williams today?" he asks. The officer nods.

The two then set about a bargaining session. Let's say Williams, the defendant, has been arrested perhaps a year before, the way court calendars go today, for carrying a pistol. It was found in a shakedown as he was coming home one night under a "stop-and-frisk" ordinance. He was hurrying because he was late coming from his job, and a hurrying black man is a suspicious person to many police officers. He offered no resistance and the officers made a search for weapons. The gun was found and he was charged with a felony, one which might carry a prison term of several years.

"Can we do business?" the lawyer asks in the crowded courtroom. And the policeman has to think. In most states, stop-and-frisk laws also provide that the officer have "reason to believe" that a felony has been committed or was about to be. In this case, the officer might be letting himself in for trouble. "Did the suspect show the gun?" the judge might ask. "How was he acting suspiciously?" The officer wants to avoid this, and agrees that a better charge might be a misdemeanor such as failure to register a firearm or some such, depending on the state law.

Soon he suggests a lesser charge, the lawyer nods and the two go—more often than not—to stand in line to wait to talk to whichever prosecutor will be handling the case. When they see the prosecutor, he looks at whatever reports he has and generally agrees to allowing a guilty plea on the lesser charge.

The lawyer goes back to Williams, assures him that if he is willing to "cop out" he will receive probably a maximum of 90 days in the county jail, whereas if he pleads innocent to the other more serious charge, he could, if convicted, go to prison for several years. Williams, confused, and afraid of prison, accepts the lesser of two evils.

The practice, roughly akin to buying a rug in an Oriental bazaar, is called "plea bargaining," and it goes on day after day, year after year.[13]

---

[13] David Murray, *America's Crisis in Authority* (Chicago: Claretian Publications, 1972), by permission of the publisher.

Once again, at the risk of repetition, remember that when such situations exist, the police officer who arrested the citizen and started the process will probably be given a large share of the blame.

The police officer assigned to the ghetto is a symbol of increasingly bitter social debate over law enforcement. Several years ago, the Commission on Civil Disorders noted that one group—still present today—disturbed and perplexed by sharp rises in crime and urban violence, demanded that what police need to maintain law and order is better and more sophisticated equipment. These people perceive the police role as seeing that the law is strictly enforced. Those who transgress are to be dealt with, with dispatch and without pampering. Those who hold this view exert a great deal of pressure on police for tougher law enforcement. But another group, blaming police as agents of repression, tends toward defiance and believes that order is maintained at the expense of justice.

Complaints of harassment and brutality as they affect the police image

Many members of nonwhite minority groups believe strongly that they get rougher treatment at the hands of the police than whites do.[14] A report by the U.S. Civil Rights Commission declared that although "most police officers never resort to brutal practices," the victims of police abuse, when it does occur, are almost always those "whose economic and social status afford little or no protective armor—the poor and racial minorities." In other words, if police brutality or harassment does occur, such incidents are directed at the poor and minority groups—including blacks, Mexicans, Puerto Ricans, Indians, and others.

The subject of physical police brutality is one that continues to be surrounded by controversy. Police spokesmen have protested angrily against such charges. Quinn Tamm, former executive director of the International Association of Chiefs of Police, declared that he "knew of no period in recent history when the police have been the subject of so many unjustified charges of brutality, harassment, and ineptness." Tamm contended, "Never have we been singled out so mercilessly and so wrongfully as the whipping boys for demonstrators for so-called sociological evolution and by out-and-out hoodlums who have abandoned the banner of civil rights to engage in senseless insurrection."

---

[14] This belief is dispelled somewhat in a study by Albert J. Reiss, "Police Brutality," *Transaction*, July–August 1968.

Yet many believe that all the denials and explanations will not dispel the deep-seated suspicion that police sometimes practice a double standard in dealing with certain members of the community. In fact, the more intimate a person's knowledge of the ghetto, the stronger his or her feeling that brutality is a fact; and the converse is equally true. The consensus among authorities in the field of race relations is that, although there may be some cases of brutality with racial overtones, brutality, if it does occur, does not generally have such overtones. It is, however, often related to socioeconomic groups.

Press reports of police dispersals and arrests of civil-rights demonstrators—particularly but by no means exclusively in the South—are said to have reinforced in many people a view of the police officer as a defender of the in group and the oppressor of protesting minorities. Many civil-rights leaders remain unconvinced, to put it mildly, that the police always act in the strict line of duty in racial cases. As a result, hostility toward the police has become an increasing problem in neighborhoods having large minority populations.

Harassment or discourtesy by police officers may not be the result of malicious or discriminatory intent. Many officers simply fail to understand the effects of their actions because of their limited knowledge of the black community. Calling a black man by his first name may cause resentment because many whites still refuse to extend to adult blacks the courtesy of the title "Mister." A patrolman's taking the arm of a person he is leading to the police car is more likely to be resented by blacks than whites because the action implies that they are on the verge of flight and may degrade them in the eyes of friends or onlookers.

There is no doubt that most officers handle their rigorous work with considerable coolness and with no pronounced racial pattern in their behavior. However, in the words of the late O. W. Wilson:

> . . . the officer must remember that there is no law against making a policeman angry and he cannot charge a man with offending him. Until the citizen acts overtly in violation of the law, he should take no action against him, least of all lower himself to the level of the citizen by berating and demeaning him in a loud and angry voice. The officer who withstands angry verbal assaults builds his own character and raises the standards of the department.[15]

These views are accepted by all responsible police officials. Although all departments have written regulations setting stan-

[15] O. W. Wilson, *Police Administration,* 4th ed. (New York: McGraw-Hill, 1976), p. 73.

dards of behavior, in many departments these are too generalized. Where standards are violated, there should be a thorough investigation of complaints and prompt, visible disciplinary action where justified.

Threats and challenges in police work

In many everyday situations on the street, police officers find themselves threatened or challenged.[16] How many times has an officer encountered a traffic offender who, as a "friend" of the chief or the mayor, threatens to have him transferred or fired? How many times has an officer found himself facing a man with a gun? Not infrequently, a suspect makes threatening moves and remarks when being arrested. In riots, police are under the serious threat of being injured or killed. Police generally regard the attitudes and behavior of the Black Panthers and certain other organizations of black youths as threatening. Some of the behavior of campus protesters is challenging to the police, and some of it is threatening. The deliberate provocation and insults of the New Left on the campuses are seen by some as challenges.

For the purposes of improving our understanding of human relations, it may be useful to describe various levels or kinds of threats:

Verbal Emotional Release. Some people become upset under pressure, and they blow off steam by becoming verbally abusive and threatening. They have little possibility of actually doing what they are threatening to do and no real intention of trying it. It is often apparent that the chatter is just so much "hot air." The officer calmly proceeds to write the ticket or to hold the prisoner for the paddy wagon without getting involved in a verbal free-for-all. He knows the best procedure is simply to let the person talk, in the meantime maintaining his composure and his control of the situation.

Real Threats. Some people are not "badmouthing" just to relieve the tensions; they mean it, and eventually they will try to follow through. This is not always easy to ascertain, however. But if a suspect pulls a gun, action should be immediate and decisive. This it not the time to wait to find out whether or not he really means it.

---

[16] This section is adapted from N. A. Watson, *Issues in Human Relations: Threats and Challenges* (Washington, D.C.: International Association of Chiefs of Police, 1969), pp. 97–113. (Courtesy of the publisher.)

Threats Intended as Offensive Weapons.   Some threats are made in a calculated manner, the intention being to provoke the officer into a response. In a sense, these threats are challenges. There really is no intention to follow through if the officer does not take the bait. The challenge is issued to goad the officer into injudicious and unprofessional conduct that can then be used as a basis for charges of abuse or brutality. Strict adherence to professional standards is the best defense against this type.

Latent Symbolic Threats.   The three types of threats just described occur on a face-to-face basis during interpersonal contacts. This fourth type, which is as important as the others, does not necessarily involve face-to-face matters. It is based upon certain kinds of beliefs. A person may come to believe, either as a result of personal experience or because of things he has been told, that certain objects, situations, or people are potentially dangerous. We call such threats *latent* because, like attitudes, they are always there, just below the conscious level, ready to spring into action when the symbol with which they are associated is perceived. We call them *symbolic* because the thing that activates them is possibly only a representative of a general class of things—in other words, a symbol.

To clarify, let us take an example. Suppose a hoodlum has been arrested on several occasions for robbery, assault, and carrying a concealed weapon. He has been convicted of robbery and has served time. Under the stop-and-frisk law, he has been questioned a number of times, resulting in arrest and conviction for carrying a concealed weapon. To him, anyone wearing a uniform and a badge is a latent symbolic threat. His perception of the police as a threat is activated when he is planning a "hit" and every time he sees an officer or a patrol car. Both the uniform and the patrol car are symbols in which the essence of the threat is concentrated.

This is a human-relations mechanism to which we must be alert in our own work. As human beings, police officers are as much subject to this psychological process as anyone else. If we are not knowledgeable about such things, we may well be misled by latent symbolic threats. For example, one could make the mistake of regarding all college students who wear beards, sandals, and "odd" clothing as being antipolice. The same is true of young Negro males, all of whom may come to be regarded as potentially dangerous and criminal.

Situational Threats.   These are the obvious or the most subtle threats we face. They operate unilaterally on an intrapersonal basis. They are implicit in many of the situations and circumstances commonly encountered in our daily lives. They often operate without our realizing it. The subtlety in these threats results from the fact that, even though they influence our behavior much like any threat, we do not think of them as threats. Moreover, they are deeply personal and do not affect everyone the same way. What any person does about them depends heavily upon his or her social conditioning, sense of values, aspirations, and many other personal characteristics. These situational threats are steeped in tradition and culture and very important in governing our conduct.

Some examples of situational threats may be helpful here. For instance, it is generally accepted that a male police officer is supposed to be thoroughly masculine. Without even realizing it, he may be careful to act in speech and deed the way he thinks a man should act. He dares not run the risk (expose himself to the threat) of being thought weak. This leads some officers to act *unnecessarily tough.*

Another example: Say you are a policeman hoping for promotion to sergeant. Your lieutenant, an opinionated person who insists that things be done by the book, will be the person who prepares your performance rating. A situation arises in which you must take action. In your opinion, it seems clear in this case that the best procedure, both for the department and for the person involved, is to make an exception to regulations. However, if you do this, you might incur the wrath of the lieutenant, causing him to give you a lower rating. The threat to your ambition to be promoted is very real.

Threats to police officers are more often implied than overt. The officer is regarded by most people as a powerful person, and an open threat is deemed to be rather risky. Most people would, therefore, threaten by implication. This puts the officer in the position of *assuming* the making of a threat. Because officers are assaulted or perhaps verbally abused rather often, it is often easy to assume that a person is threatening when he really is not. When a person shows an attitude of hostility, he may or may not be dangerous. The same may be said for attitudes of fear, anger, or unusual excitement. In other words, these attitudes do not always produce dangerous behavior. It must be admitted, however, that they do often enough to warrant caution and preparedness.

Much the same might be said about challenges. A new, young officer assigned to patrol on foot in a slum area may meet an implied challenge from members of a gang. These youths are going to test the officer. One way or another, he has to meet the challenge or he will not be able to continue patrolling there. This does not necessarily mean that he must resort to physical combat, although that may be what the gang members have in mind. Finding a way to handle the challenge without physical violence is preferable.

The process of communication is seriously curtailed because of people's reaction to latent symbolic threats and situational threats. An important factor in both types is that these threats often involve the perception of other people as "different" and therefore unfriendly—maybe even dangerous. Many people have a tendency to suspect and dislike people who are unlike themselves. People who are "different" may be perceived as the embodiment of latent symbolic and situational threats. This would produce a negative position on the pleasant-unpleasant dimension.

One of the several elements of the culture of youth has been called the "conspiracy of secrecy." Youths sense the embodiment of latent symbolic and situational threats in their elders (and vice versa, by the way). This makes them wary and interferes with effective communication.

Police often complain that blacks are uncooperative in criminal cases, in that they withold information that might lead to a solution. This is the conspiracy of secrecy in another setting. The circumstances are familiar to police officers everywhere. A detective looking for a suspect questions people in the neighborhood, all of whom claim they never heard of the man even though the officer knows the suspect has lived there for years. The detective is convinced they are not telling the truth and are, in fact, protecting the suspect. It must be admitted that this can be a result of antipathies between the police and some people. Clearly, to the extent that this feeling exists, the resulting "conspiracy of secrecy" works to the disadvantage of society.

The same mechanism is at the bottom of demands for police review boards. Charges have been made that police themselves engage in a protective "conspiracy of silence." The idea is that no policeman is going to tell the whole truth about a case in which a fellow officer is accused of harassment, abuse, or brutality toward a complainant. The natural follow-up to this belief is that any investigation conducted *by* police *of* police will turn out to be a whitewash. The so-called conspiracy of silence and the conspiracy of secrecy run head on into each other. As a result, some people believe it is futile to complain about police abuse and feel they must take matters into their own hands, outside the law.

The reduction of the threat potential in these latent symbolic and situational types would undoubtedly relieve the tensions associated with them. A more productive level of communication would result, and the entire atmosphere would be improved.

THE PROFESSIONAL APPROACH

What happens in many cases in which an officer is challenged is that the challenger is trying to get the officer to step out of the professional role. It is as though he were saying, "Look, Buster! You wouldn't be such a big shot if you didn't have that gun and badge." As the wielder of public power and authority, the officer is the dispenser of public discipline. In this capacity, he is required by law to exercise his authority according to rules. The rules do not provide for the administration of punishment by the police. Vindictiveness or harassment by an officer is as much against the rules as are criminal actions.

A police officer is not an ordinary person but a professional; therefore, the officer's conduct must conform to the rules. It is offensive to be called a pig, but no retaliation can be permitted in violation of the rules, because this would threaten destruction of the system the officer is sworn to defend. Moreover, to abandon the professional prescriptions for conduct is to walk into a trap, and this is the objective of the challenger.

The widely held concept of the police role contains an overemphasis on the police–violator relationship. Seldom is a police officer thought of as a helper, even though a large part of his or her time is spent in rendering various kinds of service. The common concept of the role of a firefighter, to the contrary, emphasizes the helper notion. Unfortunately, it is unrealistic to expect that anytime soon we are going to be able to persuade people that the police officer is a helping person, despite the fact that each time a violator is brought to justice, the public good is promoted.

Adopting the professional role as a model for conduct and conforming to it in the face of provocation, frustration, and temptation is not only correct and commendable, it is also a source of great strength for the police. It tilts the balance of power in their favor. Officers who are consistently professional in conduct and bearing are in an advantageous position. They are clearly demonstrating their superiority, and as a result, people give them the respect and admiration their profesional behavior has earned. When an officer weakens and abandons this professional posture, the conduct that results may assume several forms, all of which are seen by the public as deserving of condemnation. Depending upon the circumstances, nonprofessional conduct may consist of anything from vulgar language and petty abuse, to unwarranted physical punishment and harassment, up to outright criminality. Those who seriously challenge the police want them to shed their professional armament and be reduced to their level. The best way to handle such people is to adhere steadfastly to the professional code.

Needless to say, officers should not make threats they cannot or do not intend to carry through. To do so weakens their position and leaves a residue of animosity that will plague them and other officers in the future.

GROUP REACTIONS AND POLICE-COMMUNITY RELATIONS

One of the most important aspects of human relations involving threats and challenges, especially the former, concerns the expectations held by the parties to the encounter. There are many references in police literature to the effect that black slum or ghetto residents, Puerto Ricans, Mexican-Americans, and other minority persons *expect* to be treated rudely or abusively by police. For their part, many police officers expect to meet with hostility and resistance or even violence from these same people. These very expectations come to be regarded as threats, and inevitably they produce behavioral reactions. The reactions are then taken by the other group as evidence of the existence of the threat, and we have a "self-fulfilling prophecy." It is a vicious circle, and if the tensions and hostility are to be reduced, we must find a way to break it.

Probably all experienced officers have encountered people who think the world is against them. Such people are not necessarily psychotic. Some of them may have gotten off to a bad start right from birth. People like this expect others to be cruel, or at least indifferent. Because they expect to be hurt, they often reject others in advance in order to keep from being rejected by them. As a matter of fact, sometimes these people even reject themselves. For them, police may be especially significant. Police have been chosen as the representatives of all those hostile others who have been cruel or indifferent and who wish to keep them down. Therefore, in the police they see concentrated the threats of the hostile world.

People who believe themselves unfairly disadvantaged may react by becoming aggressively militant. Some minority groups, for example, convinced that their troubles stem from white racism, agitate aggressively for change and may even riot. They may physically attack whites or, if none are available, they may attack their property—"Burn, baby, burn!" Of course, because the police, most of whom are white, are always there, they are natural targets for the militants. The militance may take other forms, such as writings, speeches, marches, or picketing. Not all militance is undesirable. A strike by a labor union is a form of militance. It is entirely legitimate for people to be militant in order to advance themselves, as long as they remain within the law. Aggression can be a legitimate way to meet threats and challenges.

There is an opposite kind of reaction. Instead of attacking the source of threat or frustration, people may elect to move away from it. They may withdraw into a world of their own, give up, or perhaps deny that there is a problem and try to ignore it. The withdrawal can take a variety of forms. People who withdraw can take solace in all kinds of substitute adjustments. Among the havens often used are hobbies, religion, and even antisocial or abnormal activities such as crime, drug addiction, and neurotic or psychotic personality disorders.

It is interesting and disturbing to note that some people claim to see similar kinds of behavior on the part of some policemen. It has been said that the police are themselves a minority group and as such are subject to certain disadvantages and discriminations. Some police have been charged with what amounts to aggressive militance in their behavior toward certain groups, such as campus demonstrators, hippies, and black people. Some claim that the police, in giving expression to their militance, have been violent, that they have used unnecessary force, that they have been bigoted and intolerant, and that they have overstepped the bounds of their authority. Frequently this alleged behavior is attributed to the recruitment of the police chiefly from the lower classes, where physical aggression is more often a reaction to frustration. Low pay, little education, inadequate training, and low social status are also said to contribute to the problem.

It should be obvious that among a group of 400,000 people—an estimate of the number of police officers in the nation—there will be all kinds of personalities. It is to be expected that some police officers will meet their problems aggressively, just as people in other occupations do. It is also expected that some will withdraw, just as other people do. The important point is that the best approach by the police to their problems is reliance on the professional code. Although it may be all right for the average citizen to follow his or her personal inclinations, it is not so for a police officer.

The police in many places have taken constructive steps toward dealing with threats and challenges of those who dislike and/or fear them. This is one of the objectives of police–community relations programs. Training programs in human relations for police have been offered. Efforts have been made to reach out to the people through Boys' Clubs, block parent plans, crime-check or crime-stop programs, juvenile recreation programs (see Figures 8–1 through 8–3), storefront operations to bring police service closer to the locality, and similar activities.

Often in police meetings and training schools, the officers say, in effect, "We're willing, but what about them? Who's telling them? There has to be some give on both sides; it can't be a one-way street." They are so right! There must be a change of attitude on both sides. In fact, a large part of the problem lies in the widespread and unquestioned acceptance of the existence of "sides." The vast majority of the people and the police should be allied in the fight on crime and the pursuit of justice and order.

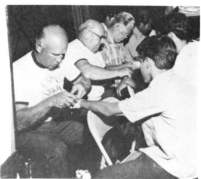

FIGURE 8-1.

FIGURE 8-3.

FIGURE 8-2.

The hard and practical fact that we must accept is that it is the police who have to tell "them." In some cases, the police themselves go directly to the people. In others, the "telling" is done by community organizations with which the police work. Obviously, not everyone can be reached, and despite our best efforts, there will always be a lot of residual hatred and hostility. But a well-conceived, realistic approach to the human-relations problems in police–citizen contacts must be an indispensable part of the daily activities of every police officer before real progress can be made.

Overcoming mistrust and hostility, as far as the police function in the community is concerned, is a *police* problem. Overcoming mistrust and hostility as far as the broad social problems of our time are concerned is a problem for all people, toward which public and private effort must be directed. There is no question but that some of the problems the police face result from the failures of society at large. And in this sense, it must be understood that there are no community problems that are not to some extent police problems, because of the "fallout" resulting in crime and disorder.

The police mission per se, however, must be carried on both at the police level and by each individual officer in the daily performance of duty.

Large numbers of people who now see the policeman as a threat must be convinced through good human-relations practices by officers that they and the police are seeking the same goals and that, therefore, law enforcement people are not a threat. The only ones for whom police should be threatening are criminals and those who seriously abridge the rights of others. The relations between the police officer and the ordinary citizen of any race, creed, or political persuasion should be characterized by mutual respect and goodwill. This becomes very important when making contacts with the public. Police officers must always strive to make other people feel that they are doing their best to see justice done.

MINIMIZING THE EFFECTS
OF THE THREATENING POLICE IMAGE

Every officer should be aware that he or she is symbolically threatening to many people. The police are regarded as disciplinarians, wielders of power, people to be feared. Their very presence constitutes a threat to many people, even those who are not doing anything wrong. It is a common experience for people to slow down when they see a patrol car, even though they are not exceeding the speed limit. Undoubtedly, a lot of people immediately make a behavioral inventory ("Am I doing anything wrong?") and become wary when they see a police officer approaching. This apprehension is part of the aura of threat with which the police are surrounded.

The fact that many people see the police as a threat has some undesirable consequences. The tendency to avoid them is one. Another is refusal or unwillingness to cooperate. Still another is the belief that the police are enemies; this often produces overt aggressive behavior. It has been suggested that if we disarm the police, they would not seem to be so threatening. We are not willing to go along with that suggestion. It would certainly be wonderful as an ideal, but in the harsh realities of today's urban jungles, it would be foolhardy.

The fact that police are regarded as threatening by law violators is legitimate; they should be a threat to such people. But law-abiding citizens and police should be pulling together in a common cause: the prevention of crime and the promotion of justice and order.

What can police officers do about problems growing out of

human relations in which threats or challenges are significant issues? There are some human-relations techniques that the police can cultivate with good effect. Learning how to be an effective person is essentially a matter of developing skill in relating to others. Following are some guidelines to help improve human-relations skills:

1. Don't be trapped into unprofessional conduct by a threat or a challenge.

2. Make sure everything you do is calculated to enhance your reputation as a good officer—one who is firm, but fair and just.

3. When you are faced with a threat and you can't tell how serious it is, try to "buy time" in which to size up the situation by engaging the person in conversation. Make a comment or ask a question to divert attention if possible.

4. Don't show hostility even if the other person does. Often a calm and reasonable manner will cause hostility to evaporate, or at least to simmer down.

5. Reduce your "threat" potential. Avoid a grim or expressionless countenance. Be an approachable human being. Too many officers habitually appear gruff and forbidding.

6. Cultivate a pleasant, friendly manner when making nonadversary contacts. Be ready with a smile, a pleasant word, a humorous comment when appropriate.

7. Let your general demeanor, and especially your facial expression and tone of voice, indicate that you respect the other person as a human being.

8. Let other people know by your reception of them that you don't expect trouble from them and that you don't consider them a nuisance. (Maybe you do, but don't let it show.)

9. Show an interest in the other person's problem. Maybe you can't do anything about it, but often it is a great help just to be a good listener.

10. Go out of your way to improve police–community relations. Even though your department may have a unit that specializes in community relations, never forget that you are the real key. The essence of good working relations between the people and the police is to be found in the way you handle yourself.

11. Always leave the people you deal with feeling that they have been treated fairly. When you render a service or react to a request, show some interest and give some explanation. This will promote good feelings, which, if carried on consistently by the

entire force, will have a cumulative effect resulting in vastly improved human relations.

12. Try in every way you can to encourage people to work with the police for their own protection. Let the average citizen know that, far from being a threat, you are interested in being a help. Drive home the point that the citizen is threatened by crime and disorder, not by the police.

In conclusion, it seems wise to caution readers to be realistic about the threats and challenges posed by others. Remember that some threats are real. Don't let your guard down while trying to be reasonable and decent. At the same time, do not assume that everyone is out to get you. Do conduct yourself according to the best professional standards and traditions. Keep calm and try to get threateners and challengers to see reason. But don't hesitate to use legitimate force to protect yourself from physical harm.

Summary

The roles of police officers are many and varied, as are the problems of the police relationship to the community, including the lack of respect for law enforcement. By its very nature, police work can lead to both private and public resentment, a certain amount of which is natural and must be expected.

Police officers, then, must be realistic—they must realize that the people they serve will not universally like or respect them, particularly since they are symbolically threatening to many people. Thus they must utilize practices that will minimize the effects of such a threatening image. For this, the police officer must realize that it is his or her own attitude that is most important in bringing about goodwill and respect. Also, the proper training and educational procedures are instrumental in helping individual officers maintain a professional demeanor.

However, police should realize that some threats are authentic and must be dealt with realistically. Professional standards and traditions relating to arrest, search and seizure, handling of demonstrators, threatening mobs, and the like must be implemented at all times.

Law enforcement officers confront an "uphill fight" in their attempts to improve their image. In the investigation of complaints of harassment and brutality, it was observed that there are many kinds of abuse that cause hostility of citizens to police. Respect for and understanding of other human beings is a primary need of all law enforcement officers to counter the hostility of the community.

In order to promote and maintain a good police image, it is of great importance that law enforcement personnel thoroughly understand minority groups—their reason for being, their methods of dealing with their world, their desires, and their tactics. The police must be tolerant under all conditions—even in the face of intense provocation. In this respect, they must (1) use techniques that will maintain order by means of legitimate goals, (2) uphold the law by steadfastly using the law, and (3) be able to isolate and arrest those guilty of illegal acts without indiscriminate attacks on the innocent.

Discussion topics

1. Discuss the roles of the police officer in our modern democratic society.

2. Discuss the social and psychological control of law enforcement as presented by H. H. Toch.

3. List the guidelines, as presented by N. A. Watson, in ameliorating the threatening image of the police to many people.

4. What is suggested by the statement, "The police officer symbolizes much deeper social problems"?

Annotated references

Becker, H. K., and J. E. Whitehouse, *Police of America: A Personal View, Introduction and Commentary*. Springfield, Ill.: Chas. C Thomas, 1979. The material on formation of citizen crime commissions, enhancing citizen involvement in law enforcement and gaining feedback from the community, falls into Chapter 8's commentary on the *police:"we"* and *community:"they"* psychology of police work.

Beel, G. B., "Responses of the Justice Department," *American Bar Association Journal*, 64 (January 1978), 53–59. The Justice Department's study on causes of dissatisfaction with the administration of justice are summarized.

Deters, G. A., "Changing Attitudes in Police–Community Relations and the Warren Court Effect," *Law and Order*, 26, No. 1 (January 1978), 76–80. A concise discussion of the evolution of the relationship between police and the courts, and the changing expectations of the public with regard to the proper function of the police. For similar information refer to E. Eldefonso, A. R. Coffey, and R. C. Grace, *Principles of Law Enforcement: Overview of the Justice System*. New York: John Wiley, 1981, Chapter 9.

Manning, P. K., and J. Van MacNew, *Policing: A View from the Street.* Santa Monica, Calif.: Goodyear, 1978. This collection of articles notes the essence of police work is located on the street level. Particular attention is paid to street-level encounters between police and the public.

Reasons, C. E., and J. L. Kuykendall, eds., *Race, Crime and Justice.* Pacific Palisades, Calif.: Goodyear, 1972. This reader incorporates interdisciplinary writings that assess both historical and contemporary ramifications of a dual system of justice. It also probes the dense convoluted relationship between the American legal structure and racial minorities.

Rusenko, W. T., K. W. Johnson, and C. A. Hornung, *Importance of Police Contact in the Formulation of Youth's Attitude toward Police.* Washington, D.C.: U.S. Government Printing Office, 1980. The significance of positive and negative contacts between police and juveniles as determinants of juveniles' attitudes.

Watson, N. A., *Issues in Human Relations.* Washington, D.C.: International Association of Chiefs of Police, 1973. In reviewing the need for public support of police goals, this book deals with the attitude and procedures of police agencies in the context of community-relations programming.

Wrobesley, M., and K. M. Hess, *Introduction to Law Enforcement and Criminal Justice.* St. Paul, Minn.: West Publishing Co., 1979. The authors' discussion of the basic roles of the police officer and factors influencing the public image of the police (and the relationship between communities and police agencies) relates to material covered in Chapter 8.

PART THREE

POLICE AND
SOCIAL UNREST

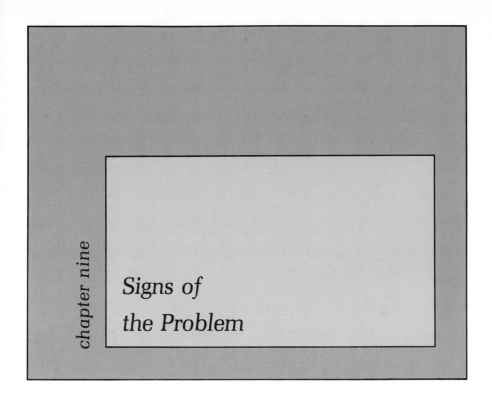

chapter nine

Signs of
the Problem

It has become commonplace among behavioral scientists to state that there are many signs of change in social structures throughout the world. The evidence they point to is the great social unrest found in many geographic areas of the globe.

The three main branches of behavioral sciences, anthropology, sociology, and psychology, each check on changes in social structure in their own manner. The *anthropologist* is concerned with any significant alteration in cultural patterns. Changes in technology, architecture, food, clothing, or art form, as well as in values, costumes, and social relationships, are the concern of the cultural anthropologist. The *sociologist* studies cultural change primarily through the alteration of the nonmaterialistic culture—such things as values, mores, institutions, and social behavior. The sociologist usually finds a pattern of social changes following technological advances. People's attitudes following technological advances are a concern of the *psychologist,* primarily the social psychologist. The psychologist feels that these attitudes either retard social change or allow it to progress at a rapid pace.

Attitudes seem to have been changing more rapidly in the last twenty to thirty years than previously. This is probably due to the advanced technology of communications; now, more people can and do express their views than in the past. Nevertheless, recorded history indicates that a certain proportion of the population in any particular place at any given time have been dissatisfied with their lot. To control the overt expression of this discontent has been one of the responsibilities of government. And because of philosophical commitments, various forms of government tend to control or allow it in a different manner.

Built into each philosophy of government are certain concepts that bear on how dissatisfaction can be voiced. For example, in the philosophy of democracy are the cornerstone concepts of freedom of speech and freedom of assembly. These freedoms create a set of circumstances for the keepers of the peace in a democracy that are different from those present in a nation governed in a different manner. Let us examine the practical implications of these freedoms as they effect law enforcement.

Demonstrations

In a democracy, the prudent person sees riots as threatening, irrational, and senseless behavior. On the other hand, in a democracy, the prudent person feels that he or she has a legitimate right to protest unfair situations through the use of oral and written language and through peaceful assembly.

The practical implications for law enforcement regarding a citizenry that can assemble and demonstrate peacefully are quite significant. This is especially true when the demonstrators run the gamut from affluent college students to the poorly educated, economically depressed minorities of the ghetto.

UNRULY COLLEGE STUDENTS

The involvement of college students in politically motivated mass public disorder is a rather new phenomenon on the American scene. True, there were disorders at American colleges and universities before the decade of the 1960s. During the early nineteenth century, colleges saw a number of incidents of disorder, and even riots. But these incidents could usually be traced to inadequate living conditions, poor food, or harsh rules. Even today, complaints about campus living conditions are the basis of more campus disorders than is generally realized. However, nineteenth-century disorders in American colleges, unlike those in European colleges, were largely apolitical.[1]

Of course, there were exceptions. The following is a statement regarding earlier political activities in American colleges:

> During the 1920s, there were campus protests against ROTC, denunciation of the curriculum for its alleged support of the established system, and attacks on America's "imperialistic" foreign policy. During the depression, there was still greater student discontent. Polls taken during the 1930s showed that one-quarter of college students were sympathetic to socialism and that almost 40 percent said that they would refuse to take part in war. There were many student strikes against war, a few disruptions, and some expulsions.
>
> Thus, it is not so much the unrest of the last half-dozen years that is exceptional as it is the quiet of the 20 years which preceded them. From the early 1940s to the early 1960s, American colleges and universities were uncharacteristically calm, radical student movements were almost nonexistent, and disruptions were rare. The existence of this "silent generation" was in part a reflection of the cold war. But as the tension of the cold war lessened, students felt less obliged to defend Western democracy and more free to take a critical look at their own society. Once again the American campus became a center of protest.[2]

When disorders take place on a college campus, the college's only option may be to call law enforcement officers to preserve and restore order. Under the best of circumstances, the presence of a large contingent of law enforcement officers on a campus tends to be troublesome and troubling. It is troubling because it indicates that an institution in which reason should prevail has had a breakdown. It is troublesome because any campus occupied by police or troops is a spectacle that is abhorrent to the American public.

Furthermore, American colleges and universities are not enclaves from which police are barred, as is true in some South American universities. Police are duty bound to enforce the laws on campuses as well as elsewhere within their jurisdiction. Whenever there is serious property damage or personal injury on the college campus, police must enforce the criminal law.[3]

On June 13, 1970, after a number of incidents of violence on college campuses in the San Francisco Bay Area, New York City, New Haven, Kent State, and Jackson, Mississippi, the president established a commission to investigate campus unrest. The commis-

---

[1] *Report of the President's Commission on Campus Unrest* (Washington, D.C.: U.S. Government Printing Office, 1970), p. 20.

[2] *Report of the President's Commission*, pp. 20–21.

[3] *Report to the National Commission on the Causes and Prevention of Violence: Shut It Down! A College in Crisis* (Washington, D.C.: U.S. Government Printing Office, 1969), p. 154.

sion found that the subject was a difficult one to deal with, inasmuch as "campus unrest" means many things to many people. In fact, the term has become so generalized that it is used to describe the intellectual ferment that should exist in the university as well as peaceful and other types of protests. The term was found to be so broad in its meaning that the distinction was obscured between activities that university and society should engage in or must tolerate and those they should seek to prevent. The report goes on:

> As a result of the muddling of the term "unrest," the university and law enforcement agencies find themselves under pressure to stifle even peaceful and legitimate forms of unrest and to condone its violence and illegitimate forms. Pressures of this sort can lead only to confusion and injustice. Throughout [the Report it is] stressed that campus unrest is in fact a complex phenomenon that is manifested in many kinds of protest activities. Many protests, even today, are entirely peaceful and orderly manifestations of dissent, such as holding meetings, picketing, vigils, demonstrations, and marches—all of which are protected by the First Amendment.

> Other protests are disorderly; that is, disruptive, violent, or terroristic. Campus unrest has taken each of these forms. Protest is disruptive when it interferes with the normal activities of the university, or the right of others to carry on their affairs. Obstructive sit-ins, interference with classroom teaching, blockading recruiters and preventing others from speaking or hearing speakers are further examples of disruptive protest.

> Violent protest involves physical injury to people, ranging from bloody noses and cracked heads to actual death. It involves the willful destruction of property by vandalism, burning and bombing.[4]

At the present time, there are more than 7 million college students in the United States. Of these, only a handful have ever practiced terrorism. In fact, some of the violence for which students have been blamed was perpetrated by nonstudents. But despite their small numbers, the students who adopted violence as a tactic caused much destruction and evoked considerable sympathy from other students as well as a number of other people in the American society. Recommendations on how best to handle campus unrest have been set forth as follows:

- Most student protestors are neither violent nor extremist. But a small minority of politically extreme students and faculty members and a small group of dedicated agitators are bent on destruction of the university through violence in order to gain their own political ends. Perpetrators of violence must be identified, removed from the university as swiftly as possible, and prosecuted vigorously by the appropriate agencies of law enforcement.

[4] *Report of the President's Commission,* pp. ix and x.

- Dissent and peaceful protest are a valued part of this nation's way of governing itself. Violence and disorder are the antithesis of democratic processes and cannot be tolerated either on the nation's campuses or anywhere else.

- The roots of student activism lie in unresolved conflicts in our national life, but the many defects of the universities have also fueled campus unrest. Universities have not adequately prepared themselves to respond to disruption. They have been without suitable plans, rules, or sanctions. Some administrators and faculty members have responded irresolutely. Frequently, announced sanctions have not been applied. Even more frequently, the lack of appropriate organization within the university has rendered its response ineffective. The university's own house must be placed in order.

- Too many students have acted irresponsibly and even dangerously in pursuing their stated goals and expressing their dissent. Too many law enforcement officers have responded with unwarranted harshness and force in seeking to control disorder.

- Actions—and inactions—of government at all levels have contributed to campus unrest. The words of some political leaders have helped to inflame it. Law enforcement officers have too often reacted unethically or overreacted. At times, their response has degenerated into uncontrolled violence.

- The nation has been slow to resolve the issues of war and race which exacerbate divisions within American society and which have contributed to the escalation of student protest and disorder.

- All of us must act to prevent violence, to create understanding, and to reduce the bitterness and hostility that divide both the campus and the country. We must establish respect for the process of law and tolerance for the exercise of dissent on our campuses and in the nation.[5]

Through the medium of television, student unrest and the response to it are often under scrutiny. Images made by TV cameras are relayed to millions of living rooms across the country. How law enforcement tries to handle demonstrations of all sorts must be considered for a fuller understanding of the problem.

PEACEFUL PROTESTS BY MINORITIES

How effectively law enforcement agencies handle organized protests from the minorities of the ghetto may well make the difference between a peaceful demonstration and violence. As has been

[5] *Report of the President's Commission,* pp. 7–8.

noted, members of minorities often view police with a great deal of resentment and hostility. Any police act that might be construed as imprudent could well trigger the eruption of pent-up feelings into violent behavior. The many marches inspired and directed by the late Dr. Martin Luther King are examples of peaceful protests by minority groups.[6] However, these protest marches remained nonviolent certainly as much through Dr. King's influence as through good handling by the police. The important point is that imprudent treatment of peaceful minority protesters by law enforcement agencies might well cause a large segment of society to revolt against constituted authority, or at least to lose confidence in it.

Related to peaceful protests, which are guaranteed by First Amendment rights, are protests that are nonviolent yet disobedient of the law. These are generally attempts at changing laws that are felt to be unfair. How these nonviolent protestors are handled by law enforcement agencies is critical.

It is risky for a society to tolerate the concept of civil disobedience. Yet, despite the compelling logic of opposition to civil disobedience, history will continue to note circumstances when it is not immoral even though it may be illegal. A good deal of the progress of the black people in the United States in the past thirty years can be traced to civil disobedience.

A caution regarding the use of civil disobedience as an approach to bringing about social change: Participants must willingly accept any penalty the law provides for. On the other hand, law enforcement officers should handle these acts of nonviolent disobedience in a positive professional manner. They must make legitimate arrests and they must do so without causing any incidents that may lead to grievances.

Civil disobedience, when handled poorly by law enforcement, tends to support the most militant elements and consequently can lead to full-scale riots. In fact, those who engage in group violence as part of a political tactic advance the following logic:

1. Militants argue that the creation of turmoil and disorder can stimulate otherwise quiescent groups to take more forceful action in their own ways. Liberals may come to support radicals while opposing their tactics; extreme tactics may shock moderates into self-examination.

2. Militants point out that direct action is not intended to win particular reforms or to influence decision makers, but rather to bring out a repressive response from the authorities—a response

---

[6] See nonviolent philosophy set forth in M. L. King, Jr., *Why We Can't Wait* (New York: Signet Books, 1964), pp. 25–26.

rarely seen by most white Americans. When confrontation brings violent response, uncommitted elements of the public see for themselves the true nature of the "system." Confrontation, therefore, is a means of political education.

3. Militants believe that if the movement really seriously threatens the power of the political authorities, efforts to repress the movement through police-state measures are inevitable. The development of resistant attitudes and action toward the police at the present time is a necessary preparation for more serious resistance in the future.

4. Militants state that educated, middle-class, nonviolent styles of protest are poorly understood by working-class youth, black youth, and other "dropouts." Contact with these other sectors of the youth population is essential and depends upon the adoption of a tough and aggressive stance to win respect from such youth.

5. Militants recognize that most middle-class [people] are shocked by aggressive or violent behavior. In the militant view, this cultural fear of violence is psychologically damaging and may be politically inhibiting. To be a serious revolutionary, they say, one must reject middle-class values, particularly deference toward authority. Militant confrontation gives resisters the experience of physically opposing institutional power, and it may force [some people] to choose between "respectable" intellectual radicalism and serious commitment to revolution, violence, or otherwise.

6. Militants respond to those who point to the possibility of repression as a reaction to the confrontation tactics by accusing them of wishing to compromise demands and principles and dilute radicalism. Militants believe that repression will come in any case, and to diminish one's effectiveness in anticipation is to give up the game before it starts.[7]

YOUTHFUL EXUBERANCE

Handling youthful exuberance can pose problems for law enforcement agencies. The high-spirited enthusiasm found at teen-age dances and high school and college athletic events, if misdirected and mismanaged by police, can become a serious problem that can on occasion turn into outright rebellion.

When large crowds of young people assemble in one place, their vivacious, uninhibited behavior can be easily transformed.

[7] J. Skolnick, *Task Force on Violent Aspects of Protest and Confrontation: The Politics of Protest* (Washington, D.C.: U.S. Government Printing Office, 1969), pp. 81–82.

Incidents of this nature have occurred at Ft. Lauderdale, Florida; Seaside, Oregon; and Hamilton Beach, New Hampshire, among other places.[8] And large gatherings of youths attending rock music concerts have also degenerated into disorderly gatherings that have become quite violent in nature.

Controlling exuberant youths can be difficult for several reasons. Young people are often in the process of developing an identity separate from parents and adult authority. Because of this striving for individual identity, they are often rather hostile toward authority per se. Consequently, the slightest mishandling of them in the group situation may precipitate serious civil disorders.

By and large, these disorders tend to be called issueless riots.[9] Although many riots center around a generalized belief, in the issueless riot no such belief is present; these riots have slight implications for social movement or social change. They often occur during a holiday celebration, or during a victory celebration. They begin as merrymaking activities but, often through mismanagement by agencies of law enforcement, degenerate into violent disorders.

Civil disorder and injury to persons and property

An investigation made more than a decade ago indicated that one of the most frustrating tasks in police work is controlling riotous situations. This study of how law enforcement personnel handled a number of riots was done in consultation with the local and state police and with National Guard officials. The conclusions of the study were that most large-city police departments have developed plans and some expertise in handling riot situations, but that small police departments often do not have training in the area of handling unruly crowds.[10] This information is of significance, since it is small-community police departments that are frequently called upon to deal with youthful exuberance.

When a situation gets out of hand and develops into a civil disturbance, it becomes a threat to the social order in a number of ways. Certainly in theory, it can be argued that a riot is a threat to

[8] The President's Commission on Law Enforcement and Administration of Justice, *The Challenge of Crime in a Free Society* (Washington, D.C.: U.S. Government Printing Office, 1967), pp. 118–19.

[9] G. T. Marx, "Issueless Riots," *Annals of the American Academy of Political and Social Science*, 391 (September 1970), 21–33.

[10] President's Commission, *The Challenge of Crime*, pp. 118–19.

the authority of government and consequently to the government itself. From the practical standpoint, many governments have been toppled by riotous actions. The classic example took place from 1789 to 1792 in France. Gustav LeBon described this in his account of the French Revolution, in which violent civil disobedience resulted in the downfall of the reign of Louis XVI.[11] Most acts of rioting do not bring down governments, but they may well cause injury to persons and property.

One of the best-documented studies of civil disorders and their cost was made by a federal commission regarding the civil disorders of the 1960s. The investigation disclosed that about 10 percent of the people killed in civil disorders were public servants—primarily firefighters and law enforcement officers. Ninety percent of the fatalities were civilians, and a great majority of these were black people. Of the injured, approximately 38 percent were public servants and 62 percent were private citizens.[12]

Of course, deaths and injuries are not the sole measure, in human terms, for the cost of civil disorders. For example, the commission found that the dislocation of families and individuals clearly could not be qualified in terms of dollars and cents. Other human costs were fear, distrust, and alienation—these occur in every civil disorder. Finally, it should be noted that even a relatively low level of violence and damage in absolute terms can very seriously disrupt a small or medium-sized community. This is an important consideration, particularly in view of the commission's conclusion that violence is not limited to large cities. (A large city was defined as one having a population of more than 250,000 people.) Besides personal injury, much property damage was incurred in the cities through acts of civil disorder.

Of the twelve cities investigated by the commission, nine reported damages in hundreds of thousands of dollars, the other three in millions of dollars.[13] Where extensive damage occurred, it was generally caused by fire. The other great losses during civil disorders were caused by looting and/or damage to stock inventories, buildings, or both. Suffering the greatest loss through looting, in descending order, were liquor stores, clothing stores, and furniture stores. Generally speaking, public institutions were not the targets of serious attack, although police and fire equipment was damaged in approximately two-thirds of the riots and civil disorders investigated.

---

[11] Gustav LeBon, *The Crowd: A Study of the Popular Mind* (New York: Viking Press, 1960).

[12] *Report of the National Advisory Commission on Civil Disorders* (Washington, D.C.: U.S. Government Printing Office, 1968), pp. 65–66.

[13] *National Advisory Commission*, pp. 66–67.

Not all the listed damage was intentional or caused by the rioters. Some of it seemed to be a by-product of police- and fire-department efforts to control the situation. But even though this damage was largely accidental, it was still of great consequence to businesses in the area where the riot occurred. And none of the damage figures includes an estimate in dollars of the extraordinary administrative expense of municipal, state, and federal government caused by the disorder.

The commission advised that the cost of civil disorder that erupts into rioting is enormous in terms of the threat to peace, persons, and property, and that such disorders should be prevented. Toward this end, it is necessary to be able to reasonably predict when they will happen. This seems very difficult to do, but it may be possible.

IDENTIFYING THE POTENTIALS FOR VIOLENT DISORDER

It is imperative that a police department make preparations long before violence occurs, even before the tension signals that disorder is about to break out. A competent and farsighted police executive assesses the possibility of outbreaks of violence or of the staging of nonviolent demonstrations long before they happen. He or she will be making plans for action to be taken and should be especially involved in creating and developing a sound community-relations program.

The law enforcement administrator is very much interested in maintaining a vigil against the possibility that violence will erupt in the jurisdiction. There seems to be ample warning of potential interracial imbalance long before any large-scale incident occurs.[14] Any government officials, local or state, who believe that events occurring elsewhere are strictly the work of outside agitators and are therefore impossible in their city may well be in for a rude awakening.

Furthermore, disorders are not always racial in origin; labor disputes have often been the rallying point for disorders. In fact, any group that feels strongly that it has been treated unfairly may become involved in a riotous situation. A striking example of this was the disorder of homosexuals and their sympathizers in San Francisco in 1979.

The sign of approaching problems seems to follow a definite

---

[14] "The Police and Community Conflict," in N. A. Watson, ed., *Police and the Changing Community: Selected Readings* (Washington, D.C.: International Association of Chiefs of Police, 1965), pp. 3–12.

pattern. Tensions rise rapidly, and responsible leaders on both sides of the question realize that it may erupt into violent disorder. Law enforcement officers sense more and more hatred directed toward them. Incidents affecting the group in which discontent is rising—perhaps members of an ethnic group from a ghetto—are expanded out of all relation to reality.

Nonviolent demonstrations, on the other hand, tend to occur more spontaneously. This is because the nonviolent demonstration is felt to be—indeed, has legally been found to be—a means of legitimate protest and, as such, a much more likely enterprise for involvement of average citizens. If a sincere, courteous, and honest effort is made to communicate with the leaders of such a demonstration before it takes place, the probability of its turning into a violent disorder will be greatly diminished.

As far as possible, law enforcement personnel should request the leaders of demonstrations to disclose their plans. In most instances, these plans will be given in full. The pertinent laws and official policies that govern the demonstration should be explained. Obviously, no law should be invoked against protesters that would not be directed against any other citizen in the community.

Law enforcement personnel in the jurisdiction in which a demonstration takes place must assume responsibility for the protection of the participants. When arrests must be made, they should be made quickly. Care should be taken that no unnecessary force is used or comments made by the arresting agency. It goes without saying that the arrest should be legally justifiable.

Returning our attention to tension situations capable of exploding into full-scale violent disorders, it should again be emphasized that major disorders are the culmination of a buildup process that is quite observable; they are set off by a final precipitating incident. When the development process is under way, law enforcement supervisory personnel should make an earnest attempt to understand it. If they fail to make a reasonably correct interpretation, the outcome could be disastrous for the community.

It is generally believed that mobilizing constructive community elements to deal with tensions of this sort is, first of all, an informational task.[15] Law enforcement must have knowledge about the tension, its relative state, and where violence is most likely to erupt. Such information can be gathered in a number of ways. By the vast network and coverage of law enforcement agencies, the mood and tempo of the community can be assessed. Each officer should be required to report incidents that might be stress-produc-

---

[15] J. D. Lohman, *The Police and Minority Groups* (Chicago: Chicago Park District, 1947), pp. 104–5.

ing, particularly those involving ghetto or barrio residents. Also, an effort should be made to obtain information from such people as schoolteachers, social workers, ministers, reporters, and employees of the transportation industry. People in these fields can often offer important data regarding the pressure build-ups. Informally obtained information from members of the business community, particularly tavern owners and liquor-store operators, can often be most useful, because incidents reflecting tension often occur in these types of public places.

All information should be screened by supervisory personnel. By evaluating the location and kinds of incidents that have occurred, they should be able to arrive at a conclusion as to the amount of tension present in a given area. As pressure rises, this should be reported to the head of the law enforcement agency and to other government agencies that would be interested in such information and in a position to act upon it.

An important method of observing tensions and, indeed, of resolving or preventing conflict between police and members of the public is through continuing communications.[16] The feeling is that police administrators must open and maintain contact with all sections of the community they serve, particularly with ghetto and barrio residents. Furthermore, law enforcement supervisory personnel such as police captains or inspectors should know the local principals of high schools and junior high schools, the directors of social agencies, and the priests, rabbis, and ministers.

In each police precinct, open house should be held at least quarterly. Law enforcement officers should use these occasions to explain their work to the public. Also, an opportunity should be provided for people to air their complaints to the precinct commander or to a high-ranking officer the department has sent for just such an occasion. Making it possible for people to present their hostile feelings toward the police in this kind of situation, although probably difficult for the officers involved, may be tremendously valuable in dealing with openly antagonistic groups.

Communication with the public not only is valuable in helping to prevent problems; it can also be quite useful in preparing for problems that may arise. Law enforcement officers should be encouraged to attend various functions in the district they ordinarily patrol. Meetings of the PTA, neighborhood associations, block clubs, and the like are the types they should be interested in. At these meetings, the officers might well discuss the problems of law enforcement.

[16] G. Edwards, *The Police on the Urban Frontier: A Guide to Community Understanding*, Pamphlet Series, No. 9 (New York: Institute of Human Relations Press, 1968), pp. 69–71.

Members of an integrated community-relations unit of the police department in Baltimore work on a day-to-day basis with civil-rights organizations.[17] This unit also meets periodically with teen-age groups in an effort to ward off trouble before it starts. Contacts like these may help weaken the picture of the police departments as an "enemy occupation force."

GATHERING AND EVALUATING INTELLIGENCE

Law enforcement officials must have accurate, up-to-date information regarding civil disorders. Such information helps in a determination of whether or not, how, and when to act.

Indications of the tensions mounting in a particular group may be ascertained through intelligence information and the appraisal of written material produced by that group. The intentions of militants and students regarding public demonstrations are most often announced. The grievances are proclaimed rather than concealed. Often within the ghetto, organizations write material setting forth their position. Specifically, attention should be given to the graffiti written on fences and buildings by ghetto gangs. This writing often gives valuable information.[18]

Generally speaking, it is unnecessary to devise elaborate plans to discover information that is quite open to discovery. Most information-gathering techniques do not threaten anyone's privacy. On occasion, such techniques do require the use of undercover police agents, and these do create some dangers. However, in most cases, they are not necessary and should not be used. In fact, simply by means of a daily harvest of leaflets that are distributed, much information can be gathered.

Valuable information may also be obtained from written material from the college campuses and most militant organizations. Frequently, the material produced verges on the libelous and/or seditious. From a law enforcement standpoint, these writings should be examined carefully with the old cliché, "The pen is mightier than the sword," clearly in mind. As a measure of heightening tension, written material, when evaluated properly, can be an important informational asset to law enforcement. Disorders generally do not occur spontaneously; they go through a definite build-up process.

The few cases in which the decision must be made to use un-

---

[17] Edwards, *Police on the Urban Frontier*, p. 72.

[18] From a seminar on "Juvenile Street Gangs," at San Jose State University, San Jose, California, July 9, 10, and 11, 1980.

dercover agents are those in which it is suspected that some people are apparently plotting to burn or bomb, and sometimes to maim and kill. Law enforcement officials must first attempt to determine whether or not such a plot is in progress; if it is, they must attempt to keep it from being carried out. In any case, they must try to identify, locate, and apprehend the participants after the fact. The best and sometimes the only means the police have to effect these purposes, especially the preventive one, is by a careful intelligence operation. However, the following cautions should be remembered about such operations:

> Dangers provide compelling reasons to keep intelligence operations at the lowest possible level consistent with peace and security, to entrust intelligence activities to officers whose sensitivities and integrity are above suspicion, and to allow such activities to be undertaken only under strict guidelines and with close supervision. In the long run, clandestine police work cannot be more scrupulous than the department and men who carry it out.[19]

ROUTINE MINOR POLICE MATTERS
AS PRECIPITATING INCIDENTS

Civil disorders do not result from a single incident. Instead, they are generated out of an increasingly disturbed atmosphere. Typically, over a period of time, a series of tension-heightening incidents become linked in the minds of those who become involved in the civil disorder. "One central fact emerges from any study of police encounters with protestors, antiwar demonstrators, or black militants; there has been a steady escalation of conflict, hostility and violence."[20]

This report goes on to state that the way police handle incidents tends to have a great bearing on whether or not civil disorder then develops:

> In some senses we do demand more of the police than we do of other groups—or more accurately, perhaps, we become especially concerned when the police fail to meet our demands. But this *must* be the case, because it is to the police that we look to deal with so many of our problems and it is to the police that we entrust the legitimate use of force. Moreover, unnecessary police violence can only exacerbate the problems police action is used to solve. Protestors are inflamed, and a cycle of greater and greater violence is set into motion—both in the particular incident and in future incidents. More fundamentally, the misuse of police force violates basic notions of our society concerning the role of police. Police are not supposed to adjudicate and punish; they are supposed to apprehend and take into custody. To the

---

[19] *Report of the President's Commission*, p. 173.
[20] Skolnick, *The Politics of Protest*, p. 183.

extent to which a nation's police step outside such bounds, that nation has given up the rule of law in a self-defeating quest for order.[21]

An investigation directed toward the disturbances that occurred in the ghettos in the 1960s found that at some point in a potentially explosive situation, a further incident—often a routine or trivial one—became the so-called straw that broke the camel's back.[22] And the tension spilled over into civil disorder, with the violence that this entails.

In approximately 50 percent of the disturbances, prior incidents that increased the tension, as well as the incident immediately preceding the outbreak of violence, were actions taken by law enforcement agencies. Two examples follow that will illustrate this point.

The first example was the arrest of a black cab driver on July 12, 1967, in Newark, N.J. According to police reports, he was tailgating a Newark police vehicle. The man appeared to be a hazard as a cab driver. Within a short period of time, he had had a number of accidents and his license had been revoked. When the police stopped him for tailgating, he was in violation of the revocation of his license. As a result, he was arrested and transported to the Fourth Precinct Station at about 9:30 P.M.

When the police arrived at the precinct station with the cab driver, the cabbie either refused or was not able to walk. Therefore, he was dragged by the officers from the car to the door of the station. Within minutes, civil-rights leaders responded to the call from a hysterical women, saying that a black man had been beaten by the police.

Shortly thereafter, crowds began to form across the street from the precinct station. As the people gathered, description of the purported beating grew more and more exaggerated. Three leaders of the black community tried to disperse the crowd or to channel its energies into a nonviolent protest but were unable to do so. Although these men tried gallantly to calm the situation, by the next evening it had erupted into a full-scale civil disorder.

A second disorder that began with a rather routine incident points out another principle regarding civil disorder. On September 28, 1966, a white patrolman in San Francisco saw several black youths in an approaching automobile. When they jumped out of the car and began to run away, the officer became suspicious. He claims that he fired three shots into the air before hitting one of the youths with the fourth shot. The youth—16 years of age—died just a few feet from his home. Four hours after his death, the automo-

[21] Skolnick, The Politics of Protest, p. 188.
[22] Report of the National Advisory Commission on Civil Disorders.

bile he and his companions had been riding in was reported stolen. When other blacks living in this section of San Francisco, who were reportedly members of a juvenile gang, viewed the body, they began breaking windows, looting stores, and burning buildings.[23]

Youths, particularly those who belong to juvenile gangs, are often in the forefront of civil disorders. Therefore, it seems logical for law enforcement agencies to keep a close tab on activities of juvenile gangs. From their activities, many serious incidents occur that increase tension or precipitate incidents of civil disorder.

Once a demonstration or some form of civil disobedience begins, the police can deal with it in a number of different ways. Two extremes in methods of handling such situations will be presented here. From the standpoint of the police and public relations, the first was most unfortunate.

1. During the week of the Democratic Convention in Chicago in 1968, the police were targets of much provocation. Rocks, bathroom tiles, sticks, and even human fecal matter were hurled at the officers by demonstrators. Some officers responded to the extreme provocations in an unrestrained and undiscriminating manner. Considering that it often inflicted violence upon people who had broken no laws, disobeyed no orders, and made no threats, this response was particularly inappropriate. Among the victims were peaceful demonstrators, onlookers, and residents passing through the area where the confrontation between police and demonstrators occurred.[24]

2. By and large, the police objective in a democracy is to handle demonstrations in a nonviolent manner. An example of this was a demonstration against the Vietnam War that occurred in London when a large crowd of people demonstrated in front of the U.S. embassy. A situation of this type could easily have resulted in a violent confrontation between police and demonstrators.

A platoon system was worked out whereby squads of police relieved one another at intervals to avoid frayed nerves and short tempers resulting from being too long on duty. In general, police strategy for handling the crowd was the linking of arms to form a human wall capable of spreading a menacing crowd into harmless fragments. As the spearhead of the demonstration group plunged through, its members were isolated and propelled away from the line. This tussle continued, and the report indicates that it was viewed as a contact sport rather than a bloody riot.

[23] C. Werthman and I. Pelavin, "Gang Members and the Police," in D. J. Bardura, ed., *The Police* (New York: John Wiley, 1967), pp. 56–98.

[24] D. Walker, *Rights in Conflict—Walker Report to the National Commission on the Causes and Prevention of Violence* (New York: Bantam Books, 1970).

At the end of the day, a large group of tired demonstrators were singing "Auld Lang Syne." The British bobbies joined in the singing, which somehow seemed to be a quite fitting tribute to the job well done by the police on this occasion.

Obviously, the social and cultural differences to be found in the United Kingdom are such that this method of handling demonstrators may not be practicable in the United States. However, examinations of how other democracies handle these kinds of demonstrations may give some insight into the handling of protestors per se.

Since the 1968 Chicago convention, the police in the United States have handled protest problems quite well in a number of incidents. One such incident, the so-called "counterinaugural" protest in Washington, D.C., occurred on January 20, 1969. Many of the people who organized this event had been organizers of the protest at the Democratic Convention in 1968, and many who attended the protest in Washington had attended the protest in Chicago. Roughly equal numbers of people attended these two protests, yet the results of the events were markedly different.

In Chicago, the authorities were restrictive in granting demonstration permits, and some of the police, after being goaded by verbal and physical attacks by a small number of militants, responded with excessive force. Their conduct, although it may have won the support of the majority, did polarize a substantial and previously neutral segment of the population against authorities and in favor of the demonstrators. In Washington, the authorities were rather liberal in their issuance of demonstration permits. And although there was provocative violence by some of the demonstrators, the police used only the amount of force that was necessary to maintain order. This tactic could be considered quite successful, in that it produced little criticism of police behavior.

The National Commission on Causes and Prevention of Violence concluded that the amount of violence that occurred during these demonstrations and the resulting effects on public opinion were directly related to the kind of official response the demonstrators received on each occasion:

> As the Chicago and Washington events differed in preparation, they differed in outcome. After minor skirmishes, trouble in Chicago escalated when throngs of demonstrators, having been denied permits to remain overnight, refused to leave Lincoln Park, their main gathering place. Dozens of police attempted to clear the park on three successive nights. In response to serious and deliberate provocation, but without coherent planning, some policemen clubbed and tear-gassed guilty and innocent alike, chasing demonstrators through streets some distance from the park. Particularly on the side streets,

some bystanders who had taken no part in the demonstration were attacked by police officers. Several media representatives were clubbed and had their cameras smashed. Predictably, tension and anger rose. Extremists who would otherwise be ignored began to attract audiences. They urged demonstrators to fight back. The police were exposed to more and more jeers and obscenities and had to withstand heavy barrages of rocks and other missiles. During one of the first nights, 15 policemen were injured; two nights later, 149 were injured.

In Washington, the cycle of escalating violence never got started. Both verbal and physical provocations by demonstrators were frequently intense, but they were met with restraint. Provocation by police was rare; when it occurred, it was terminated by police and city officials who intervened quickly to restore discipline. In general police withstood physical and verbal abuse with great calm. In the end, the behavior of Washington officials and the police won praise in newspaper editorials and from leaders of the demonstration.

There were some radical leaders, however, who were more grateful for the official response in Chicago, for it appeared to validate their characterization of government as being "reactionary" and "repressive" and to increase support for other protesting groups. The chaos of Chicago also gave solidarity to the ranks of those who regarded all demonstrators, however peaceful, as irresponsible "punks." The overall effect was to increase polarization and unrest, not diminish them.[25]

Summary

Anthropologists, sociologists, and psychologists have noted signs of change in the social structure in the United States during the past three decades. These changes tend to highlight people's dissatisfactions. Although there have always been some people who were not satisfied with the social structure, more and more people are now becoming aware of society's inadequacies, probably owing to advances in the field of communications, particularly television.

In a democracy, people are permitted to express their dissatisfactions in approved ways. Law enforcement officers must allow such expressions as long as they are made in a lawful manner. From a practical standpoint, this is a very difficult job, with many implications. The person who demonstrates his dissatisfaction may be any citizen from any social station; when demonstrations are not handled well by the police, the result is

[25] *Final Report of the National Commission on the Causes and Prevention of Violence: To Establish Justice, to Insure Domestic Tranquility* (Washington, D.C.: U.S. Government Printing Office, 1969), pp. 71–74.

a loss of confidence in constituted authority or, worse, civil disorder.

When a threat of this sort gets out of hand, it becomes a threat to the social order. It may become a threat to the government itself, or a threat to person or to property. Identifying those situations that have potential for violent disorder is a must for the well-functioning police department. The signs of an approaching situation seem to follow a certain pattern. Predictably, tensions rise rapidly, and responsible leaders on both sides of a question can perceive this buildup. Generally speaking, at such a time law enforcement personnel become the object of more and more hatred.

To diminish the chances of having a demonstration erupt into violence, a sincere effort should be made by law enforcement personnel to communicate with the demonstration leadership. Further, law enforcement must protect the rights of demonstrators as well as the rights of the majority. Pertinent laws and policies should be explained to the demonstrators so that they can be aware of what constitutes a legally permissible demonstration and what constitutes an illegal demonstration. When and if arrests of demonstrators are made, they should be made quickly, and with as little force as possible.

A check of the buildup of tension is important. Information regarding its rise should be gathered by patrol officers as well as by supervisory personnel and outside persons and agencies. Written material is another measure of heightened tension. When such material is screened, it can give law enforcement agencies important clues.

Police must handle with care a demonstration that is a lawful expression of discontent, or the protest may degenerate into a civil disorder or riot. When tensions are high, poor police handling can be disastrous.

Discussion topics

1. Name several ways that behavioral scientists measure social change.
2. In what way does social change tend to cause civil disorders?
3. Explain what a precipitating incident has to do with civil disorders.
4. Explain what tension has to do with civil disorders.

5. In what way can the police evaluate tension within the community?

6. Why is the study of how other countries handle civil disorders of importance to someone interested in civil disorders in the United States?

7. Discuss the gathering of intelligence as it relates to civil disorders.

8. What do the predatory activities of juvenile gangs have to do with civil disorders?

Annotated references

Bordua, D. J., ed., *The Police: Six Sociological Essays.* New York: John Wiley, 1967. Essays by six sociologists who are concerned with law enforcement in a society in which freedom of the individual is of great concern.

Edwards, G., *The Police on the Urban Frontier: A Guide to Community Understanding.* New York: Institute of Human Relations Press, 1968. This pamphlet outlines relations between the police and the public in a number of situations. It suggests some ways to modernize and improve law enforcement, particularly as it operates within the ghettos of large cities.

Final Report of the National Commission on the Causes and Prevention of Violence: To Establish Justice, to Insure Domestic Tranquility. Washington, D.C.: U.S. Government Printing Office, 1969. This report is concerned with the total problem of violence surrounding civil disorders.

Heaps, W. A., *Riots, U.S.A., 1765–1965.* New York: Seaburg Press, 1966. Covers some of the riots and civil disorders that have taken place during the 200 years of this nation's history.

Hinman, C. F. and K. L. Washburn, "Shoot—Don't Shoot: A Realistic Fire Arms Course," *FBI Law Enforcement Bulletin,* July 1980, pp. 1–5. An interesting article in light of the fact that a shooting on occasion has precipitated a great deal of civil unrest.

King, M. L., Jr., *Why We Can't Wait.* New York: Signet Books, 1964. The late black leader tells about frustrations caused by the lack of black people's participation in the American society. The book gives some insight into Dr. King's decisions regarding nonviolent demonstrations for equal rights.

Report of the President's Commission on Campus Unrest. Washington, D.C.: U.S. Government Printing Office, 1970. Discusses a number of incidents of civil disobedience that occurred on college campuses during the late 1960s. It points out some of the inadequacies to be found in the college situation as well as the inadequacies of law enforcement in its attempt to quell disturbances on the campus.

Skolnick, J., *The Politics of Protest: Task Force Report on Violent Aspects of Protest and Confrontation.* Washington, D.C.: U.S. Government Printing Office, 1969. This report discusses the political aspects of civil disorders, and some of the objectives and goals of militants who become involved in leading them.

Walker, D., *Rights in Conflict: Walker Report to the National Commission on the Causes and Prevention of Violence.* New York: Bantam Books, 1970. This is the report of the investigation into the civil disorders surrounding the Democratic National Convention in Chicago in 1968.

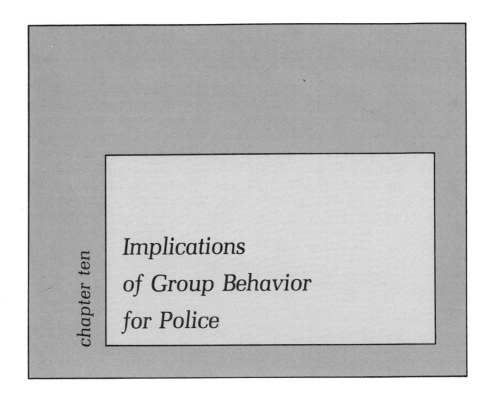

chapter ten

Implications
of Group Behavior
for Police

There seems to be no end to the many books, articles, conferences, speeches, and commissions which have analyzed, diagnosed, counselled, prescribed, or proscribed concerning violence. Violence is clearly a major social problem. Crimes of violence, riots in urban ghettos, and political assassinations have been responsible for the appointment of . . . [a number of] recent national commissions: The President's Commission on Law Enforcement and Administration of Justice (1965), The National Advisory Commission on Civil Disorders (1967), . . . The National Commission on the Causes and Prevention of Violence (1968) . . . [and The President's Commission on Campus Unrest (1970)]. These commissions have engaged the efforts of many distinguished citizens and outstanding scholars.[1]

Investigation by scholars into civil disorders has given rise to concern with the ways knowledge and theories of the behavioral sciences can be applied to training programs and community-relations programs. Because methods of handling civil unrest are of great importance to many people throughout the nation, a brief

[1] J. F. Short, Jr., and M. E. Wolfgang, "On Collective Violence: Introduction and Overview," *Annals of the American Academy of Political and Social Science,* 391 (September 1970), 2.

look at some behavior patterns might suggest alternatives to physical force in controlling unrest.

Traditionally, mob behavior has been interpreted in two widely different ways. One has emphasized the group itself. This interpretation suggests that groups are more or less independent of the individuals of which they are composed. The other emphasizes the behavior of the individuals who make up the crowd.

Gustav LeBon, associated with the first theory, illustrated his point with a description of the behavior of the aggressive mobs of the French Revolution. LeBon felt that a crowd might have a "group mind" that supersedes the minds of the individual participants. He believed that the individuals in such crowds are "swept up" and thereupon lose individuality. The crowd was considered uncivilized and irrational. The participant, no matter how rational or civilized a person, could be reduced to a bestial level in a crowd.[2]

The opposing concept, while recognizing that individual behavior changes in certain respects in the presence of other people, stresses that members of a crowd act as individuals. In most instances, their presence tends to have a restricting effect on behavior. However, under certain conditions, there is a permissiveness about a crowd situation that induces individuals to act in a less restrained way. A man might normally never think of looting a store, but when others are doing so, he may join them. The thought that "everybody is doing it" and the feeling that as an individual he cannot be singled out and punished for his act may be responsible for this change in behavior.

Because police sometimes need to intervene in the activities of groups, a systematic study of the social, psychological, and cultural factors related to the behavior of people en masse should help prepare a police officer to discharge his or her duty more intelligently and effectively.

The crowd

Behavioral scientists generally refer to people en masse as a *collectivity*. They use this term to denote crowds, groups, classes, and the public. Practically all group activity can be thought of as collective behavior. Group activities consist of individuals acting together in some way; in the action there is some fitting together of the different lines of individual conduct.

[2] G. LeBon, *The Crowd: A Study of the Popular Mind* (New York: Viking Press, 1960).

Because the collectivity that police are most concerned with is the crowd, we will examine here the structure and function of crowds, and later the individuals who make up the crowd.

TYPES OF CROWDS

For our purposes, four types of crowds will be discussed.[3] The first type can be identified as a *casual crowd*. A group of people observing a display in a store window is an example. Characteristically, the casual crowd has a momentary existence. More important, it is loosely organized and has very little unity. The members of this crowd come and go, giving temporary attention to the object that has captured their interest. Each member has little association with the others. They are classed as a crowd only because the chief mechanisms of crowd formation are present.

A second type of crowd can be designated the *conventionalized crowd*. An example is the spectators at a football game. Their behavior is essentially like that of the members of the casual crowd, except that it is expressed in established ways. For instance, the crowd at the game probably stands for each kickoff. This established way of being involved in an activity is what sets off the conventionalized crowd from other types.

The *expressive crowd* is the third type. Its distinguishing characteristic is that excitement is expressed in physical movement and, instead of being directed toward an objective, is a form of release. This type of crowd is commonly found in certain religious sects.

The last type that will be considered is the so-called *acting* or *aggressive crowd*. Its outstanding feature is that there is an objective toward which activity is directed. An aggressive crowd could easily be classified as a mob. It is this type of crowd that is of concern to law enforcement personnel.

According to the *theory of collective behavior*,[4] the so-called acting crowd can be divided into two subtypes: (1) "the crowd acting because of panic," as in the case of the reaction of a theater audience to a fire; and (2) "the crowd acting because of a hostile outburst," also known as a riot mob. It should be noted that panic and hostile outbursts frequently occur in sequence. In many cases, panic behavior by a crowd is followed by hostility and attacks on

[3] H. Blumer, "Collective Behavior," in A. M. Lee, ed., *Principles of Sociology* (New York: Barnes & Noble, 1951), pp. 165–222.

[4] N. J. Smelser, *Theory of Collective Behavior* (New York: Free Press, 1963).

persons and agencies held to be responsible for the panic in the first place.

THE FORMATION OF CROWDS

Most social scientists are in general agreement regarding the phases in the formation of a crowd. An exciting event, which catches the attention of people and arouses their interest, seems to be the first step. In the process of being occupied with the event and the excitement generated by it, a person is likely to lose some self-control. Characteristically, impulses and feelings are aroused that tend to press one on to some type of action. A number of people stimulated by some exciting event, therefore, are inclined to behave like a crowd.

The second phase in the formation of a crowd involves a milling process. People who are aroused by some stimulating event are inclined to talk to one another and/or to move about, if this is possible. This tends to increase the excitement, since each person's excitement is conveyed to other people and then reflected back, thereby intensifying the whole condition. The milling process seems to generate a common mood among members of the crowd and also to increase the intensity of that mood. Individuals are inclined to take on a common identity and are therefore much more likely than in other circumstances to act as a unit.

The formation of a crowd may be the culminating or precipitating event in police concern with a group. Because the police objective is to avoid precipitating events, it becomes important for officers to handle crowd situations with good judgment. And because good judgment is much more likely if all the pertinent facts are known, it is of prime importance that police obtain as much information about a group and its composition as possible.

In bygone days when patrolmen walked beats, a good officer knew the people who lived on his beat. He could predict where trouble was likely to occur and who would be involved in it. As often as not, he could prevent an act of violence and avoid the necessity of picking up the pieces afterward or of making an arrest.

No one would suggest that we give up modern police organization and go back to the officer on the beat. However, as we continue to expand and refine our law enforcement techniques and police use of intelligence, we are aware that efficiency may be impersonal. And although people appreciate efficiency, they resent impersonalization; this in itself may cause problems.

We will discuss other aspects of crowd formation in the section specifically dealing with the acting or expressive crowd.

CHARACTERISTICS OF A CROWD

Certain general characteristics apply to all crowds; others apply only to certain types of crowds. Let us examine the general characteristics in turn.

Size   It is obvious that, under certain circumstances, the very size of a crowd may cause problems for police. The thousands of people at an athletic contest necessitate careful planning and organization, particularly regarding orderly movement. Also, police will probably be quite concerned with plans for protecting people in case of an emergency caused by a disaster. However, with the possible exception of traffic control, the size of a crowd generally gives little indication as to the nature and seriousness of the problems law enforcement officers will face. Such problems are usually related to other characteristics of the crowd. And yet, because ineffective handling owing to a lack of adequate police personnel may prove troublesome, it can be seen that the size of a crowd is an important dimension.

Duration   *Duration* means how long a group has been in existence. For example, a group of boys may have existed as a gang for a number of months before they congregate as a crowd on a street corner. Merely to chase the boys off the corner may disperse the crowd, but in actuality, this brings more *solidarity* to the gang. Rather than dispersing a group, social agencies such as police and juvenile probation departments may be more interested in steering it into constructive channels, making it healthy and useful.

Identification   This dimension relates to whether or not a person considers himself a member of a group and/or identifies with it. Identification is a process that occurs within an individual; nevertheless, groups can be distinguished on the basis of degree of identification of the members. Other members of a group are frequently aware of one's membership in that group, especially if there is some kind of formal organization, congregation, or interpersonal communication. Strangers are often able to identify members of a group. An example is police, who are readily identified by their uniforms. A person who is easily identified as a member of a given group on the basis of appearance or behavior is said to be "highly visible."

The tendency of people to identify with groups plays an important part in determining their values and their behavior. Their behavior, in turn, may help to identify them as belonging to a particular group. Knowledge that a person identifies with the Black Muslims, the Black Panther Party, or the Ku Klux Klan may be important. These groups are based on racial prejudice, social avoidance, active discrimination, and hostility; and those who identify with them may be expected to behave in accordance with the group's beliefs.

Polarization   Polarization occurs when members of a group focus their attention upon some object or event. A crowd may be polarized toward a speaker, a movie, or an athletic event, for example.

A group may or may not be polarized. A group of passengers on a commuter train would probably not be; they would be involved in individual pursuits, such as reading or talking. But suppose someone fired a gun into their car. At this point, every passenger in the car would immediately be polarized toward that event.

Polarization is one of the dimensions characterizing the relationship between a leader and his or her followers. In controlling the behavior of masses of people, police may use the tactics of removing the leader from the group. This will change the pattern of polarization.[5]

Often, police manipulate these dimensions in crowd control. The following are examples:

1. The use of *bullhorns* for giving orders in an attempt to command the attention of a crowd is essentially an attempt to change the polarization of that crowd.

2. Taking *photographs* of participants in a mob action often makes people forcibly aware that they are members of a group that is regarded with disapproval. Protective anonymity is lost, and identity with the crowd produces anxiety, causing members to withdraw from the group.

3. *Dispersing* a crowd may well physically terminate its duration.

4. Often police *divide* a mob in two, thereby changing its size and converting it into two smaller groups that can be dealt with more easily and effectively.

A close examination of the acting crowd is in order, particularly in view of its importance to law enforcement personnel.

THE ACTING CROWD, OR THE HOSTILE OUTBURST: A SOCIOLOGICAL VIEW

Often, a hostile outburst or mob action follows a panic situation, apparently because people feel there are a limited number of

---

[5] N. A. Watson, ed., has described the dimensions of a crowd more fully in "Police and Group Behavior," in *Police and the Changing Community: Selected Readings* (Washington, D. C.: International Association of Chiefs of Police, 1965), pp. 179–212.

escape routes and these are closing; escape must be made quickly. An audience rushing to the exits when it believes a theater is on fire is an example of a panic situation.

According to one theory, a hostile outburst usually takes place in the presence of three conditions: *a situation of strain, a structurally conducive setting,* and *a means of communication among the persons undergoing the strain.*[6] These aspects in combination are referred to as *structural conduciveness.*

In the panic situation cited above, the *situation of strain* was physical danger. However, many situations of strain are socially institutionalized, such as strains resulting from differences in class, religion, political outlook, or race.

If hostilities are to arise from conditions of strain, these conditions must exist in a *structurally conducive setting.* This is a setting in which (1) hostility is permitted, or (2) other responses to strain are prohibited, or (3) both. An example would be in strained racial relations, in which hostility to members of another race is accepted by each race, and there are no means to alleviate the strain, such as by discussion between the two racial groups.

The next phase of the process involves *adequate communication,* which must be available for spreading a hostile belief and for mobilizing for an attack. Individuals who do not understand one another and whose backgrounds of experiences differ greatly are not easily molded into a mob. An audience, because it permits rapid communication, common definition of a situation, and face-to-face interaction, has many of the attributes for becoming a mob.

With the spreading of truths, half-truths, and rumors through a group, the possibility that this information will become a generalized belief increases. If the group begins to believe the rumors and half-truths, then, given a reason, it may be ready for a hostile outburst. The term for such a reason is a *precipitating cause.* A precipitating cause may justify or confirm existing generalized fears or hatreds. In a racial outburst, for example, the precipitating cause might be a report—true or false—that a person from the other racial group has committed some unwholesome and/or unsavory act.

With this precipitating cause comes the final stage of the outburst, which is a *mobilization for action.* This does not occur, however, unless *strain, structural conduciveness, generalized beliefs,* and *a precipitating cause* are all present.

Consideration of the stage of mobilization for action calls for examination of leadership and the organization of the hostile outburst. Leadership may take many forms. It may range from the sim-

<hr />

[6] Smelser, *Theory of Collective Behavior,* pp. 222–69.

ple model—such as the first person to throw a stone in a riot—to a recognized organized leader who deliberately agitates a group into action through actions and speech. The organization may be associated with a social or other type of movement. An example of an extreme lack of organization and leadership is the brawl, in which there is no evidence of division of labor or cooperation between individuals involved in the situation. At the other extreme, we find the paramilitary units whose members have specialized roles. These units have acted in certain incidents of civil disobedience.

Once a hostile outburst begins and people become aware that there is a crack in the social order that is conducive to the expression of hostility, an interesting phenomenon takes place. A rash of hostile actions appears, many of them motivated by hostilities that are not related to the conditions or strains that gave rise to the initial outburst of hostility. This buildup effect, in which people capitalize on the fact that an outburst has occurred, is, in a hostile crowd situation, generally followed by a complaint regarding inappropriate use of force by the police.

It is often found that a mob contains not only a number of people who become involved because of the initial strain and/or grievance, but also some people with grievances that are independent of the condition that caused the mob to form. This probably explains why participants in a riot may shift their attack from one object to another.

Ideas for Controlling Hostile Outbursts   Once behavior has erupted into a hostile outburst such as a riot, social control must be exerted. By a reexamination of some of the phases in such outbursts, it is possible to see how and at what point a social agency can intercede to try to avoid the riot.

At the beginning of a buildup of a hostile outburst, there is *strain*. The strain may be economic, caused by poverty; interracial, caused by prejudice; or of other natures, caused by any number of situations. It is quite obvious that social agencies can and should intercede in an attempt to alleviate some of this strain.

A second factor is a setting that is either *permissive of hostility, or prohibits other responses, or both.* For this reason, residents of the ghetto must be able to make complaints about police brutality to a responsible group that will investigate the complaints. Adequate means for registering discontent with police should be built into the police system. But this should never intimidate police in their rightful use of authority. This is most important, for it has been found that inadequate enforcement of law and order also tends to encourage hostile outbursts.

Social agencies can take action to correct *false beliefs* caused by rumors and half-truths. Constant efforts should be made to sustain a dialogue between the parties in discord and the police. By means of such two-way communication, police have the opportunity of showing up half-truths and rumors for what they are and preventing them from crystallizing into generalized beliefs.

In the event that a crowd begins *mobilizing for action,* it may be possible to forestall a hostile outburst by disrupting the organizational process. When there are designated leaders, either personal or organizational, removing them or rendering their leadership ineffective may result in quelling the outburst.

In the last analysis, when a hostile outbreak occurs, the *behavior of social agencies* in the face of the outburst determines how quickly the situation will be resolved. The manner in which force is exercised encourages or discourages further hostility. It has been shown that when authorities issue firm, unyielding, and unbiased decisions in short order, the hostile outburst tends to be dampened.

The individual in the group situation: psychological views

Whereas Gustav LeBon insisted that a crowd had a unique nature distinct from the individuals of which it was composed,[7] Floyd Allport took the other extreme and theorized that there is no real difference in people's behavior whether they are in a crowd or isolated. According to Allport, "the individual in the crowd behaves just as he would behave alone, only more so."[8]

This hypothesis holds that the actions of a crowd express the emotional needs, prejudices, and resentments of the members of that crowd. In a crowd, individuals may do things they would not ordinarily do, but a crowd does only what most of its members would *like* to do. The stimulation of the crowd, coupled with its protection, allows individuals to express hostility they might not be inclined to express in normal circumstances. For example, people often have an impulse to break something; in a riot, a person can do this without feeling guilty. To further support Allport's theory, records show that a high proportion of the people arrested during riots have previous arrest and criminal records. Many of these people were looters, who were taking advantage of the situation.[9]

Mobs constitute a danger to orderly social life because they

[7] LeBon, *The Crowd.*

[8] F. H. Allport, *Social Psychology* (Boston: Houghton Mifflin, 1924), p. 295.

[9] M. E. Wolfgang, "Violence, U.S.A.—Riots and Crime," *Crime and Delinquency,* October 1968, pp. 289–305.

tend to suppress selection among rational alternatives in making a decision regarding intelligent social policy. The circumstances that excite a crowd or increase its excitement are commonly referred to by psychologists as *stimuli*.[10] If a stimulus is to affect the crowd, most of those in the crowd must respond to it. The word "Fire!" shouted in a crowded public place would be a stimulus; it would tend to arouse a common mass action in the people there. Besides the original stimulus, another may be present. A person observing the responses made by others in a crowd may find that these have become an additional stimulus to him. This accounts for people acting "more so" in a crowd.

There is speculation that most people are not punished but are more or less rewarded for acting with a large group. Supposedly, this begins when children in school are disciplined for stepping out of line, while the children who remain in line are not. From childhood on, most people learn to conform to the group and are rewarded for doing so by feeling no fear of punishment.

A number of psychologists believe that when people are in a crowd, their perceptions of past experiences and their subsequent behavior are changed by the special social conditions around them.[11] For example, when life becomes difficult and is full of stress and strain, such as during widespread hunger and unbearable living conditions, individuals in a group may view certain social norms differently. Certainly people who are starving may view the taking of a loaf of bread as something other than theft.

It is probable that most behavioral scientists see a blending of the theory that a person reacts directly to a stimuli and the theory that one sees a situation differently because of past experience. It is generally felt that people learn attitudes, prejudices, and biases, and that these affect how they see a situation and thus how they react to it. This does not mean that behavioral scientists will not continue to talk about individuals reacting to stimuli. It does mean that they are aware that behavior is very complex.

HOW LEADERS MANIPULATE CROWDS

Certain other psychologists concur with Allport's theory of crowd behavior. They feel that crowd behavior is often surprising because so little is generally known about how individuals really act when they are alone. Often people conform on the surface in social circumstances, but they have within them the potential to

[10] N. E. Miller and J. Dollard, *Social Learning and Imitation* (New Haven, Conn.: Yale University Press, 1941), pp. 218–34.

[11] M. Sherif, *The Psychology of Social Norms* (New York: Harper & Row, 1966), pp. 67–88.

act antisocially when the right types of stimulus unleashes an antisocial response. Skillful leaders are frequently able to release such antisocial responses.[12]

Most people have been trained to follow a leader in certain circumstances. Even the rules of a childhood game are based on this concept. However, people have also been taught to follow the crowd under a different set of circumstances. The example of children made to stay in line in school is an appropriate one.

A leader is able to use these two factors. The leader generally tends to be the center of attention by standing alone and speaking. Some leaders use repetition and rhythm to stir a crowd to frenzy. Good examples of this can be found in old newsreels showing huge crowds of Nazis responding to Adolf Hitler at party rallies.

Crowd leaders use such tactics to get an emotional buildup rising in a crowd. They may use emotion-laden verbal symbols such as "rape," or "defense," or any one of a number of derogatory racial or religious terms. These words can stir up high emotions, causing a person to act in a violent manner.

It has been said that individuals in a crowd do not critically evaluate the leader's use of rhythm and repetition for stimulation. To be critical, one must wait and evaluate a number of alternatives in regard to how a situation should be handled. Therefore, one means of controlling a crowd and possibly preventing a violent outburst is to introduce a debate with the crowd leader. This will create a pause for critical evaluation and may check the impulsive activity that can take place under the stimulation of repetition and rhythm within the shelter of the crowd.

Crowd control

We have discussed the fact that when a group of people get together in a crowd, they can be stimulated by the crowd itself to act in a manner that is not typical of their normal behavior. It is obviously in the interests of law enforcement to know the nature of crowds so that they can be controlled or even prevented from forming. Sometimes prevention of potentially dangerous crowd action is effected by declaring martial law and/or by imposing curfew and restrictions against assembly.

Disaster can result if police officers fail to understand crowds and their actions. In ghetto areas, some riotous situations have been touched off when police have made what originally appeared

---

[12] Miller and Dollard, *Social Learning and Imitation.*

How to deal w/ crowds.

to be routine arrests. Here are some ideas on how to deal with this kind of situation:

1. Police officers must refrain from impulsive actions; therefore, they must ascertain the facts first.

2. Once police officers have the facts, they should act quickly. A quick disposition of a matter tends to neutralize the consequences of much interracial hostilities when such emotions are present.

3. A police officer should constantly try to display a fair and professional attitude. This type of behavior commands the confidence and cooperation of the best elements in a gathering crowd.

4. If the people involved in the original incident that the officer was called to investigate are excited and emotionally upset, efforts should be made to separate them from the crowd situation as soon as possible. Such a practice helps prevent the communication of emotions and excitement to the more excitable spectators in the gathering crowd.

5. Generally speaking, indiscriminate mass arrests have a most undesirable effect on public attitudes toward the police. Mass arrests invariably involve some innocent people. This magnifies the difficulty, since the arrest of innocent bystanders creates the impression of excessive and unbridled use of authority, as well as incompetence.

6. When unruly crowds gather, it should be possible to mobilize an adequate number of police quickly. A show of force is preferable to a belated use of force. Once an incident gets beyond the control of the police, it can be brought into control again only with a great deal of difficulty, and the possibility is then quite high of damage to property, and even of the loss of life. A situation should never be permitted to develop wherein control passes from the hands of the police authority to the crowd.[13]

Community relations and group behavior

Besides knowing how to handle direct confrontations, police should keep other community-relations practices in constant operation.

[13] J. Lohman, *The Police and Minority Groups* (Chicago: Chicago Park District, 1947), pp. 102–7. Also see J. A. Sandora and R. C. Peterson, "Crowd Control and the Small Police Department," *FBI Law Enforcement Bulletin*, December 1980, pp. 2–5.

The police are only one of several resources that may be used in problems of human relations and in relieving the consequences of crowd tension. It is true that police are often accused of aggravating and inciting tension. These accusations are often untrue; they probably arise because the police are necessarily constantly involved in incidents involving public order. They will be blamed by a certain segment of the society for what they have done, and they will be blamed by another segment for what they have not done.

Police can do a great deal toward enlisting the cooperation of responsible elements in the community, thereby bringing about adequate public support in crisis situations. To get the cooperation of these people, the police must make known to them possible situations. A police department is in a position to know when tension may lead to unruly crowd behavior. If each patrol officer reports on all incidents that might cause a crowd to gather, a picture of potential reaction can be obtained. Certainly interracial group incidents should be reported.

Incidents nearly always occur in public places. Therefore, schoolteachers, community workers, ministers, transportation employees, housing directors, and social workers will be able to add more information about these situations. Information of this sort can also be obtained from local businessmen, such as poolroom operators and tavern owners. Because crowd situations are sometimes set in motion by the activities of juveniles, it is well to keep close tabs on juvenile gangs. Many serious incidents of friction have begun from the predatory activities of such groups.

The reporting of incidents, however, will be of no value unless the information is assimilated and proper steps are taken to alleviate the tension revealed by the reports. One of the proper steps for doing this is to again enlist the cooperation of neighborhood leaders, particularly in ghetto areas. Such people might serve as an advisory group. They should participate at the planning level, well before their direct appeals to the people are needed during critical periods.

If attempts to resolve the situation have failed and a confrontation does take place between police and a hostile crowd, it should be remembered that excessive use of force is to be avoided. Just enough force should be used to restrain those who need it. Of course, adequate numbers of officers should be called in to try to help quell the disturbance. A large group of police represents a *show* of force, which is usually quite different from an excessive *use* of force. Generally speaking, there is no substitute for judicious and impartial action by all police officers. At the time of an incident, tact may well be the ingredient that prevents the situation from getting out of hand.

Our concern with potentially riotous incidents should not be taken to suggest that the role of the police agency in human relations is basically one of riot control. Rather, it is essentially one of preventing such occurrences, for the very foundations of government are involved in the success of the police in minimizing internal strife. The competence and integrity of the police in their ability to guarantee public order is a cornerstone of government. Riots cannot be tolerated by any nation, for once lawful procedures for the solution of conflicts and redress of wrongs are violated or abandoned, the collapse of society is inevitable.[14]

A number of social scientists feel that a civil disorder is an expression of need on the part of the governed, and that, therefore, most energies should be spent in satisfying that need rather than in formulating plans to quell the disturbance. The government's responsibility in the just, speedy, and effective handling of potential situations of civil unrest is a problem with which the police are genuinely concerned.[15]

The belief that riots are far more structured than many behavior theorists suggest is based on this contention regarding the implications of civil disorders:

> An approach that gives equal emphasis to force and reform fails to measure the unanticipated consequences of employing force; and it fails to appreciate the political significance of protest. If American society concentrates on the development of more sophisticated control techniques, it will move itself into a destructive and self-defeating position. A democratic society cannot depend upon force as its recurrent answer to longstanding and legitimate grievances. This nation cannot have it both ways; either it will carry through a firm commitment to massive and widespread political and social reform, or it will develop into a society of garrison cities where order is enforced without due process of law and without the consent of the governed.[16]

Summary

During the past decade, the federal government has appointed a number of commissions to investigate the causes of violent behavior, particularly civil disorders. Study of the history of

---

[14] W. T. Gosselt, "Mobbism and Due Process," *Case and Comment*, 74 (July–August 1968), 3–6.

[15] E. Currie and J. H. Skolnick, "A Critical Note on Conception of Collective Behavior," *Annals of the American Academy of Political and Social Science*, 391 (September 1970), 34–45.

[16] J. H. Skolnick, *Task Force Report on Violent Aspects of Protest and Confrontation: The Politics of Protest* (Washington, D.C.: U.S. Government Printing Office, 1969), p. 262.

other nations, both past and current, shows that this problem of civil disorder may well be common to mankind in general.

Civil disorders have a number of things in common. With knowledge gained through study, certain patterns and generalized facts about civil disorders emerge, and these can be utilized by the government and law enforcement in particular in managing or quelling these occurrences.

Behavioral scientists begin their study of group behavior by separating people en masse into different groupings. Because the main concern of the police is with the grouping called the *crowd,* types of crowds have been categorized: the casual crowd, the conventionalized crowd, the expressive crowd, and the acting or aggressive crowd.

The formation of a crowd is usually dependent on a common attention-getting event that generates excitement and sometimes causes a loss of individual self-control. According to such crowd characteristics as size, duration, identification, and polarization, people experience varying degrees of commitment to crowd action. Knowledge of these factors enables law enforcement personnel to handle potentially bad crowd situations.

The acting or aggressive crowd, from a sociological frame of reference, usually grows out of three conditions: a situation of strain, a structurally conducive situation, and a means of communication among those undergoing the strain. There is usually a precipitating cause that finally mobilizes the crowd for action. Often a leader can control the crowd by manipulating the generalized feeling of the participants. One good tactic by police is to isolate such a leader from the crowd; another is to physically divide the crowd to dissipate hostile currents of feelings.

There are various theories about the individual in the crowd situation. Some, such as LeBon, believe that the crowd has a unique nature distinct from the individuals within it. Still others are convinced that the individual in the crowd behaves as he ordinarily would, only more so. At any rate, a crowd environment produces actions by individuals that are not typical of their everyday behavior.

Obviously, it is important for law enforcement personnel to understand certain aspects of the crowd, and to seek from community members information about potential crowd causes. This enables them in some cases to prevent crowds from forming and in others to be able to control possibly riotous crowds. A judicious use of force is imperative in crowd control, as are fairness and respect for citizen needs. The function of police in this respect is to maintain public order while making possible the solution of conflicts and the redress of wrongs.

Discussion topics

1. Discuss the idea that different acts of civil disorder have many things in common.
2. List the types of crowds named in this chapter.
3. What does a precipitating incident have to do with a riot?
4. Explain how the characteristics of a crowd may be used by the police in handling the crowd.
5. How does the childhood game of "Follow the Leader" condition people to participate in riots?
6. Based on sociological theory, what are some suggestions for dealing with civil disorders?
7. Based on psychological theory, what are some suggestions for handling civil disorders?

Annotated references

The Annals of the American Academy of Political and Social Science, Collective Violence, 391, September 1970. This issue is devoted to the theoretical considerations of collective violence.

LeBon, G., The Crowd: A Study of the Popular Mind. New York: Viking Press, 1960. One of the first serious treatises on crowd behavior.

Lohman, J. D., The Police and Minority Groups. Chicago: Chicago Park District, 1947. This book is over thirty years old, yet it is still a classic on the subject of civil disorders.

Miller, N. E., and J. Dollard, Social Learning and Imitation. New Haven, Conn.: Yale University Press, 1971. Another classic that applies learning theory to crowd behavior.

Shirley, J., "Stadium Security: A Modern Day Approach to Crowd Control," FBI Law Enforcement Bulletin, August 1980, pp. 22–25. This article sheds some light on the matter of handling a large crowd.

Skolnick, J. H., Task Force Report on Violent Aspects of Protest and Confrontation: The Politics of Protest. Washington, D.C.: U.S. Government Printing Office, 1969. This report makes a somewhat more liberal interpretation of the value of civil disorders than that of most police agencies. For the serious student of law enforcement, this point of view is an important one to know and understand.

Smelser, N. J., *Theory of Collective Behavior.* New York: Free Press, 1963. This book, concerned with the behavior of crowds, has particularly pertinent discussions regarding panic situations and hostile outbursts as these relate to human behavior.

Watson, N. A., ed., *Police and The Changing Community: Selected Readings.* Washington, D.C.: International Association of Chiefs of Police, 1965; and New York: New World Foundation, 1965. Contains articles that provide good reference material for the overall subject of police–community relations.

chapter eleven

Intergroup
Human Relations:
Implications for
Law Enforcement

While it is true that the vast majority of relationships between the groups of a community are of little concern to police, it is also true that many intergroup relationships are of critical concern for law enforcement. Consideration of the groups that draw police interest is indicated.

One of the most consistent views police officers have of groups with whom they must deal is that such groups are often followers of extremists.[1] In effect, this perception focuses to a greater degree on the person or people who appear to be influencing the group than on the group itself.[2]

To consider the causes of problems when attempting to prevent them is, of course, good police practice. However, dealing with the unrest and tensions that create police problems necessitates giving attention also to the problem itself—the group, and the other groups to which that group relates. Because of the nature of

---

[1] See, as one of many examples, N. A. Watson, "The Fringes of Police–Community Relations Extremism," *The Police Chief*, XXXIII, No. 8 (August 1966), 31–38.

[2] Watson, "Fringes."

intergroup activities in a free society, police must deal with certain groups directly even when aware that the source of the problems may be elsewhere.

Consider, for example, police responsibility in the case of continuous high school fighting between students of different races. In these cases that become severe enough to require police involvement, police intelligence, more often than not, is aware of the hostile philosophies of certain leaders that aggravate an inflamed situation. Moreover, police intelligence is frequently aware of the agitation long before such philosophies are transformed into any form of violence. Beyond police intelligence gathering, law enforcement agencies often provide a community-relations program of some sort that tries to head off the potential problem. The two main weapons available to police to combat the growth of such strife are public awareness and intense attention to the potential trouble spot. In a democratic society, police do not have the option of intervening with the "source" if the source is not breaking the law. Of course, there are enforcement options when the source becomes explicit enough to provide a case of inciting a riot, but such instances are rare—police frequently deal with an awareness that cannot be acted upon unless other factors come to bear.

Preventing, or at least reducing, the potential for violence between groups, then, often becomes a matter of how well police use the two main weapons put at their disposal—public awareness and attention to potential trouble spots. These two alternatives may be more than enough when public awareness leads to public education, and when attention to the trouble spots leads to improved relations between groups.

Of course, the police face a far greater challenge than simply coping with potential explosive tensions between youthful high school groups. Indeed, police can scarcely relax the vigilance demanded by an era of societal unrest that has been steadily evolving for several decades.[3] The focus and intensity of the explosive intergroup problems may have appeared to subside in recent years, but law enforcement is by no means in a position to regard the problems as solved. Like the many other factors in police–community relations, intergroup tensions retain a constant potential for law enforcement problems—not to mention problems for the society in general. Consider, for example, the disproportionately high number of people of minority descent receiving police attention:

> *Communication with minority groups.* A critically important communications problem confronts police in urban areas with significant minority pop-

---

[3] See, for example, Eldridge Cleaver, *Soul on Ice* (New York: McGraw-Hill, 1968). See also J. Cohen, *Burn Baby Burn* (New York: E. P. Dutton, 1967); and W. Grier, *Black Rage* (New York: Basic Books, 1967).

ulations. Those areas have been the scene of several disorders in recent years, and they frequently require a disproportionately high percentage of police resources. Inhabitants of those areas frequently feel they have less influence on police enforcement policies and practices than other city residents. Members of minority groups must be convinced that their police service expectations are known and respected by the police. They must be shown that their recommendations are being acted upon.

Many police agencies in cities with large ethnic and racial minority groups have developed programs to ensure consideration of the needs of minorities in the development of policies and operational response. Indeed, some police administrators view this as their primary community relations effort. These programs have included informal advisory groups and special units within the police agency to work with minority groups in developing channels of communication.

A unique example of police–public communication can be found in the Detroit Police Department's "Buzz the Fuzz" Program. The program, which began early in 1971, involves a weekly radio talk show moderated by a local well-known radio personality having appeal to the city's black community. The panel normally consists of the Commissioner of Police, an inspector and sergeant from the Department's Public Information Office, and two citizen representatives from the Chamber of Commerce. The panel answers all questions and complaints telephoned in by members of the public.

The panel acts as a referral resource for other city agencies, channels complaints of consumer fraud to the Chamber of Commerce, and accepts and acts upon complaints of police misconduct. Generally, an answer is provided immediately. If research is required, the answer is delayed until the next show. Cases of substantial police misconduct are referred to the department's citizen complaint section for investigation; however, weekly progress reports are given until disposition is announced.

The program, which started out as a thirteen-week special, has been televised four times and has become a standard means of communication with the community. On occasions, the Police Commissioner or his representative have gone on the moderator's regular daytime program to dispel rumors or to report on significant crime and other community problems. Since local conditions dictate the need and type of response, each chief executive should recognize the special problems presented in communicating with minority groups and strive to develop methods of ensuring that he is in communication with all elements of his community.

Communicating with non-English-speaking minorities. Because it is the responsibility of every police agency to provide service uniformly to every person in its jurisdiction, the problem of communicating with substantial portions of the community who speak little or no English must be solved.

Most police agencies employ officers who speak the most commonly encountered foreign language to answer telephone requests for service. Some agencies maintain files of all officers who speak foreign languages so they may be called upon to interpret calls for service.

San Diego, California, which has a substantial Mexican-American population, teaches Spanish in its Police Academy, identifies Spanish-speaking police officers on name tags, and publishes leaflets describing the police department complaint procedure in both Spanish and English.

In San Jose, California, the police department explains the police function, the law, and legal procedures on a local radio broadcast in Spanish.

It has been suggested that bilingual officers receive a bonus for maintaining fluency in a foreign language. Linguistic ability should at least be a factor in determining the qualification of a police candidate. In Los Angeles, it is considered a compensating factor for candidates who might not otherwise meet a minimum employment requirement such as height.

While local conditions should dictate if the need exists for a police agency to undertake bilingual programs, as a minimum, every police agency having a substantial non-English-speaking minority should ensure that all telephone requests for services can be processed effectively and that the agency programs are modified to ensure adequate communication between non-English-speaking minority groups and the police agency.[4]

It must be stated clearly that the mere existence of minority groups does not necessarily create a police problem—even non-English-speaking minority groups. The problem emerges when unrest leads to tensions of the variety that, in turn, pose the threat of violent intergroup or antigovernment strife. Even the knowledge of group attitudes does not provide police with sufficient indication that the problems necessarily exist. With regard to group attitudes, "community attitude studies do not necessarily tell us what people actually do."[5] That is, one can "think crime" without behaving criminally; and crime, or law violation, is the only interest police have, the only one they *should* have, in group behavior in a free society.

Is there a criminal who does not respect at least some of the laws that he does not break? His attitude toward those laws is possibly just as good as the attitudes of noncriminal groups. Embezzlers, for example, may identify with groups that are appalled by violent crimes. Conversely, many assaulters and perhaps rioters may identify with groups that consider the embezzler or the burglar an unwholesome person. The income tax cheat may well consider himself a member of a group that maintains a generally law-abiding attitude. The reward or payoff that presumably motivates violation of one law may, for any number of reasons, not be rewarding to the violator of other laws. Violation of law, therefore, may not be motivated by "criminal attitude"—particularly if one's *general* attitude tends to correspond with that of the noncriminal group.

To clarify the significance of attitude, consider those attitudes that seem to correspond with "noncriminal grouping." Group attitudes that are essentially noncriminal do more than reduce the

---

[4] *Working Papers for the National Conference on Criminal Justice*, January 23–26, 1973 (Washington, D.C.: U.S. Government Printing Office, 1973), pp. 139–40.

[5] Maxwell Jones, *Social Psychiatry* (Springfield, Ill.: Chas. C Thomas, 1972), p. 32.

chances of potential criminality—they actually form the basis of citizen participation in anticrime programs a police agency might wish to pursue. In reading the material that follows, keep in mind these two factors: (1) a group with noncriminal attitudes, and (2) a group attitude that corresponds with the attitude of criminals.

Every police agency should immediately ensure that there exists within the agency no artificial or arbitrary barriers—cultural or institutional—that discourage qualified individuals from seeking employment or from being employed as police officers.

1. Every police agency should engage in positive efforts to employ ethnic minority-group members. When a substantial ethnic minority population resides within the jurisdiction, every police agency should take affirmative action to achieve a ratio of minority-group employees in approximate proportion to the makeup of the population.

2. Every police agency seeking to employ members of an ethnic minority group should direct recruitment efforts toward attracting large numbers of minority applicants. In establishing selection standards for recruitments, special ability such as the ability to speak a foreign language, strength and agility, or any other compensating factor, should be taken into consideration in addition to height and weight requirements.

3. Every police agency seeking to employ ethnic minority members should research, develop and implement specialized minority recruitment methods. These methods should at least include:

   a. Assignment of minority police officers to the specialized recruitment efforts;

   b. Liaison with local minority community leaders to emphasize police sincerity and encourage referral of minority applicants to a police agency;

   c. Recruitment advertising and other material that depicts minority-group personnel performing a police function;

   d. Active cooperation of the minority media as well as the general media and minority recruitment efforts;

   e. Emphasis on the community service aspect of police work; and

   f. Regular personal contact with the minority applicant from the initial application to final determination of employability.

4. Every police chief executive should ensure that hiring, assignment, and promotion policies and practice do not discriminate against minority groups.

5. Every police agency should continually evaluate the effectiveness of specialized minority recruitment methods so that successful methods may be emphasized and unsuccessful ones may be discarded.[6]

With regard to group attitudes, presumably the noncriminal attitude emerges as an asset to law enforcement. But *attitude* and *behavior* are not the same thing. Police function on the basis of

---

[6] *Working Papers for the National Conference on Criminal Justice*, p. 147.

behavior (or sometimes potential behavior) rather than on the basis of attitude; attitude is important but merely as a causal factor to be considered.

Attitude in this context, then, is certainly less significant than specific behavior to law enforcement personnel. This raises a question regarding the relation of attitude to intergroup behavior. If attitudes within a community are not effectively correlated with the kinds of behavior that concern law enforcement, a method is necessary to anticipate at least some of the problems between groups before disruptive behavior occurs—a method not dependent on attitude or speculation about it.

In short, it is not enough to merely establish ratios of police officers to correspond with a particular group that may or may not have intergroup problems with other groups in the community. Moreover, the deficiency in merely having ratios has to do with a dependence on attitude, over which police have no control, in contrast with behavior, for which police are held responsible when it is in violation of the law.

Perhaps a brief discussion of what the community and community groups actually are might prove valuable before we consider any prediction of behavior by these groups that might make police involvement in intergroup community problems appropriate.

The community and its groups

The accepted classic sociological definition of *community* is "human population living within a geographic area and carrying on a common interdependent life."[7] But the depth and breadth of social problems that ultimately affect law enforcement require some recognition that the "human population" with which police may be concerned are probably not enjoying a "common interdependent life," or at least not perceiving themselves that way. Indeed, for purposes of a discussion of the effect of intergroup activities on law enforcement, it should be recognized that there are generally several "communities," or several "populations."

But if the community has more than one population, and the enforcement goal is to find a method of anticipating behavior that does not correspond to law-abiding attitudes, the first step must be to identify each population sufficiently well to associate with it its

---

[7] G. Lundberg, C. Schrag, and O. Larsen, *Sociology* (New York: Harper & Row, 1968), p. 128.

particular attitudinal traits. Criticisms of "stereotyping" and "generalizing" notwithstanding, sophisticated police effort to anticipate problems requires recognition of specific group orientations.

Although the overriding law enforcement goal of identifying each population has more to do with reducing community tension than with immediate control of crime, clearer identification of citizen population could, in many instances, also be of great use to crime control as such. But in the present context of anticipating rather than controlling criminal behavior, sensitive recognition of the characteristics of particular populations within a community is essential.

A population is a group that might be called by other names, such as the public, a crowd, a mob, a gang, and so on. What the population is called or the kind of group it is becomes important only because this influences both the behavior of the population and the response to the population by other groups, including the group of law enforcers. A population that gathers and calls itself (or is called) a gang or a mob may well behave in a different way from a population labeled "the public" or, more simply, "a crowd." Care then is needed in defining each population, particularly because the label changes when behavior changes.

A particular population may never become a crowd or a mob, simply because its members never gather. But gathering in itself does not create a mob or a crowd. Sociologists commonly refer to gatherings of people as *plurals* or *aggregates* or *aggregations*. These terms are as vague or as specific as the terms *folkways* and *mores*, and depend more on the sociologist using the terms than on any specific connotation.

Gathering together, then, does not necessary imply either a mob or a crowd. When members of a population group gather, the behavior they exhibit is far more significant than the gathering itself. However, sophisticated understanding of the attitudinal characteristics of a particular population may motivate law enforcement to be far more attuned to the behavior in some instances than in others.

In order to move toward an understanding of the kind of population to be considered significant to law enforcement, let us consider the gang, inasmuch as it does more than gather, regardless of its behavior after gathering. And unlike other groups, the gang is usually the same population each time it gathers. It is this sameness that permits law enforcement to examine not only the behavior of the gang but certain influences on the gang's behavior that are often both predictable and controllable.

A gang, like a crowd or a mob, is a group, but it is a group that is distinguished from other groups in terms of sameness. Sameness in a group on a continuing basis is valuable to law enforcement, since, if a certain gang has the same characteristics over and over again, law enforcement can become adept at predicting its behavior well enough to control potentially criminal behavior.

The size of the gang, like the size of a community population group of any kind, is a simple matter of numbers. Complexity emerges when the police are confronted with many gangs. In such instances, it is not only the particular group's activities that must be dealt with, but also the activities of all the groups in relation to one another. Of necessity, the size of the group then becomes extremely significant. Communication within the group is one of the more subtle influences in relation to size; a more dramatic factor is the availability of police resources when violence occurs.

Emphasis on stress and tension between different-sized groups may well create a common ground on which two distinctly different police administrative philosophies can merge, as indicated in the following quotation:

> At the outset, identifying the role of the Chief of Police in the community seemed a rather simple task. I would merely reflect on long-held convictions, reduce them to the simple truths I knew them to be, and write them all down. I would say things such as, "Maintain a meaningful dialogue with (a) youth, (b) their parents, (c) the schools, (d) merchants, (e) everybody," and, "Relate meaningfully to (a) the community, (b) neighboring communities, (c) the state, (d) the nation—everybody."
>
> After awhile, it got pretty bad, and I began to realize that the role of one in public service, like the role in a play, cannot be defined by merely setting down a list of tasks. It must be explored to be understood.
>
> Two kinds of people undertake to define roles: those who speak from the authority of their experience, and those, like myself, who speak from the subjective analysis of their observations. In the first instance, the audience will usually react without suspicion to the pronouncements of the expert. The novice, however, will be shown no such deference. He must prove his contentions, and this is as it should be.[8]

The acknowledgement that both approaches must incorporate the goal of reducing tension between different-sized populations within a community affords a common basis on which law enforcement personnel can approach the changing community uniformly—whether as the "expert" or as the "novice" referred to in the quotation. In the context of this common ground, let us examine the goals of groups that may generate stress and tension.

[8] K. M. Cable, "The Chief and the Community," *The Police Chief*, 38, No. 3 (March 1971), 24.

GROUP GOALS

Although the relationship between the majority and minority groups in a nation or in a community is critical, the minority group is cited here as deserving specific attention for law enforcement. After all, in a voting democratic society, the majority is presumably less motivated to pursue conduct that would require police intervention, since the availability of a majority opinion vote generally satisfies much of the stress of a majority group.

With the obvious exception of a "ruling class," the position of minority groups throughout history has been far less favorable than that of majority groups, even (or especially) in societies controlled by dictators. In more recent times, there have been varying degrees of interest in human rights in various parts of the world, but generally stronger in Western civilizations. As the focus of the world has gradually been directed toward human rights, ever since the Magna Carta and especially since the creation of the United Nations, struggles have taken place between societies considering themselves downtrodden and those more fortunate. Within the "downtrodden societies," struggles between various poulations have also emerged. Thus, the goals and aspirations of one group in a society no longer necessarily reflect the goals and aspirations of any other group.

In America, where individual freedom is proclaimed, it should not be surprising that many claim their freedom to struggle for the same affluence that richer Americans enjoy. To the degree that this is the pursuit, goals do not conflict, even when the method of achieving the goals may. A more difficult phenomenon for law enforcement to address is the conflict in goals themselves—when the goal for a minority group is not affluence but political power that would eliminate affluence. The nebulous indicators of serious tension in such a matter are rarely visible until police find they have a problem. Police attention in such matters, then, is restricted to consideration of the degree to which individual freedom in a democracy is available.

Individual freedom, it has been said, "ends at the other fellow's nose." In terms of different community groups' having the common goal of individual freedom, the end might instead be the other group's dignity or freedom. It follows then that there must be restrictions on the goal of individual freedom or group freedom. Freedom to seek control over one's destiny in such diversified areas as education, economics, and personal respect must, of necessity, be *restricted freedom,* to avoid impingement on the freedom of others.

But the point at which police have the responsibility to enforce such restrictions is not clear, since the rules themselves are vague. The freedom to strike the other fellow's nose, or to deprive the other fellow of freedom or dignity, is not and cannot be permitted if there is to be the orderly environment that is required for orderly government to function.

Meaningful dialogue is a requisite not only between the groups whose goals may conflict, but also between police and groups whose tension may mount. Bringing about such dialogue between groups probably begins with dialogue between police and the total community. Communication—the exchange of viewpoints—is the essential ingredient of success in dialogue. But two-way communication implies a great deal more than points of view. Two-way communication, particularly when geared to clarifying certain restrictions on freedoms of the majority and minority, must first consider the limitations that exist—the limitations that the police are responsible for enforcing. Frustrations resulting from the enforcement of restrictions on freedom cannot be totally resolved, but making clear the police function of ensuring that the freedom of one does not restrict the freedom of another is highly productive in reducing tension.

Recognition must be given to the biases and prejudices that distort communication and hamper dialogue between the majority and minority, or between minorities whose goals conflict. The majority group is usually what sociologists like to call the middle class. This group values steady employment, if for no other reason than the material rewards that are culturally valued or thought to be accessible only through work. The values of those who are not work-oriented are very different, and in many cases, these conflicting values tend to bias each of these groups' perceptions of the other. Dialogue between two such groups is strained tremendously if these biases are not recognized.

The police are not permitted the luxury of evaluating which philosophy is more desirable. They must simply remember that the potential for violence, destruction, and other police problems can be generated by failure by one group to recognize the biased or prejudiced perception of another, particularly if it is a majority perception of a minority.

Two-way communication, dependent as it is on each group's expecting to hear and be heard, also isolates the significance of expectations. A group that does not expect to be heard or to hear is not likely to feel motivated to attempt such communication. The expectation of not being heard is most frequently experienced by minority groups, who, recognizing that their orientation differs from that of the majority, assume the existence of prejudice that would prevent communication.

Complaints from minority groups often resound through the mass media in their coverage of incidents that demonstrate the conflict between members of the community and the police. In many instances, complaints that police are indifferent to the problems of minority communities are accompanied by the observation that this is to be expected—with the expectation that there will be a bias. Sophisticated police come to recognize that understanding the orientation of a group, or of an individual, is not the same as agreeing with it. Enforcement of the law and the anticipation of enforcement problems require an understanding of many orientations that conflict. Failure to grasp sensitively the varied and conflicting orientations of community groups creates much of the enforcement deficit with which the police must ultimately cope.

Ultimately, police recognition of conflicting orientations contributes to successful interracial human relations in a community—an achievement bound to reduce the difficulties of enforcing the law.

Interracial human relations

For those American minorities that are identifiable by racial characteristics, it is much more difficult to elevate their status to that of the majority than it is for minorities identifiable only by language and dress. Indeed, their acquisition of the social behavior, the dress, and the language habits of the majority may only serve to emphasize their racial differences.

The term *interracial human relations,* then, acknowledges a great deal more than the inherent frustration of membership in a relegated minority, the despair that accompanies the witnessing by generation after generation of the elevation of nearly all relegated minorities but theirs, and a system that inflicts severe socioeconomic penalties upon those already penalized by loss of dignity. To be meaningful, interracial human relations must avow the right of every person to be respected as a human being.

Police in particular cannot afford to treat this as an option, for failure to acknowlege right invariably leads to police problems. Moreover, fundamental respect for humanity is a prime requisite of enforcing law in a society in which the only justification for police intervention is the violation of law. In recent decades, police have made a great deal of progress in coming to grips with the reality that all human beings are the highest form of life, and that only the behavior of people can be called good or bad. Bad behavior is subject to modification in proportion to the degree of human dignity accorded; treat a person like an animal and modification of the unacceptable behavior becomes less likely.

This is not to say that the proper behavior by police will completely eliminate the need for force. Law enforcement is, and will remain, a dangerous, often deadly job, in which violence may be thrust upon police regardless of their sensitivity to the nature of human interaction. Nevertheless, it remains true that interracial human relations affords police an avenue for reducing the magnitude of the enforcement segment of their responsibility.

In this sense, interracial human relations differs very little from intergroup relations. After all, both are intergroup human relations. But a sensitivity to all the problems affecting intergroup relations is only the beginning of good interracial relations. With interracial groups comes a sense of urgency, owing to the recognition that time alone did not and cannot resolve problems that it has resolved for other intergroup relations. Time, on the contrary, continues to amplify racial problems and, if those problems are not mitigated, time may be running out.

Summary

The part of human relations having greatest relevance to the enforcement of law is the relations between groups. Police must recognize differences between "populations" within a community. The police function has been conceived of in terms of apprehending criminals or in some other way directly responding to crime, but owing to complexities in a modern society, police must also anticipate problems before they occur. Therefore, the police role must be broadened to encompass the anticipation of problems between the groups within a community.

Attitudes of a group may be to some degree law-abiding even when certain laws are collectively violated by the group membership. Even those defined as criminal retain a quasi-respectful attitude toward certain laws. But a law-abiding attitude is not a good predictor of law-abiding behavior.

A community is not merely a geographical area; more important, it is a collection of populations. It is vital that law enforcement personnel be aware of the various kinds of intergroup relationships in the community in order to actively seek reduction in the stress and tension that generate law enforcement problems.

In discussing law enforcement interests in friction between population groups, we must distinguish between crowds, mobs, gangs, or the like. Sensitivity to attitudinal characteristics of groups can provide a key to their group activity or behavior.

Stress between population groups relates to rights, freedoms, dignity, affluence, goals, and conflicts. Achieving freedom can bring about conflict when such freedom is either gained or maintained at the expense of another's freedom or dignity. This and other potential conflicts make meaningful dialogue resulting from two-way communication a beneficial goal for law enforcement.

Because the racial identity of some minority-group members is relevant to community tensions, particular sensitivity to this aspect of intergroup relationships is a prime requisite for successful police effort to anticipate and, where possible, prevent tensions and conflicts between community groups.

Discussion topics

1. Discuss the view that virtually all human interaction generates tension.

2. Explain the value of expanding the police role beyond the direct response to law violation, to incorporate the anticipation of police problems.

3. Elaborate on the significance of conflict in goals between groups within a community.

4. Discuss factors that would make a group's behavior significant to police efforts to anticipate stress.

5. Discuss the community in terms of "joining" the majority population group; in terms of criteria for distinguishing between the community's population groups; in terms of stress between population groups.

6. Discuss two-way communication and meaningful dialogue in relation to stress and tension between groups.

Annotated references

Bayley, D. H., and H. Mendelson, *Minorities and the Police: Confrontation in America*. New York: Free Press, 1968. An excellent elaboration of long-standing militancy in intergroup tensions affecting police.

Coffey, Alan R., *Police Intervention into Family Crisis.* Santa Cruz, Calif.: Davis Publishing, 1977. Explores in detail the process of police involvement in family matters prior to commission of crimes.

Kuykendall, J. L., "Police and Minority Groups: Toward a Theory of Negative Contacts," in *Police.* Springfield, Ill.: Chas. C Thomas, 1970. Elaboration of the disproportionately high police contacts with members of minority groups.

McDowell, Charles P., *Police and the Community.* Cincinnati, O.: W. H. Anderson, 1975. Chapters 3 and 4 provide a general context for the topic of population grouping.

Reasons, C. E., and J. L. Kuykendall, eds., *Race, Crime, and Justice.* Pacific Palisades, Calif.: Goodyear, 1972. An excellent elaboration of the disproportionate representation of minority groups in the justice process.

Watson, N. A., *Issues in Human Relations.* Gaithersburg, Md.: International Association of Chiefs of Police, 1973. A sharply focused examination of police perspectives on most of the matters dealt with in this chapter.

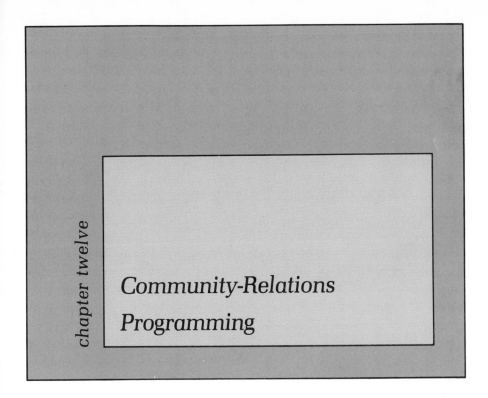

chapter twelve

Community-Relations Programming

If there were a standard, or even a set of standards, for establishing a program for community relations, this chapter would examine particular programs that "meet" the standards. But in truth, the incredible variation in needs, realities, and circumstances between cities, counties, and states, prevent a standard for community-relations programming. Nevertheless, there are many common factors among jurisdictions, and this chapter will address some of the more significant.

Future law enforcement careers will probably experience even greater emphasis on the relations between criminal justice and the community served. Programs that are administered for the specific purpose of improving such relations are likely to grow—perhaps in some jurisdictions, to the point that all police careers will, at one time or another, include active experience in a community-relations program. It is already a standard police practice to acknowledge the public-relations (PR) responsibilities of police officers. Community-relations programming, however, is a great deal more than public relations.

In a sense, any effective police program could be made to

serve as good PR. But in the case of community-relations programs, PR may be the least of many goals. Ideally, community-relations programs afford police the opportunity to *anticipate* law enforcement problems and, more important, gain public support in heading them off before they develop. The process through which such ideal community support occurs so thoroughly intertwines PR and specific community-relations activities that it might be useful to consider the difference between the two.

There is, of course, a distinct difference between PR as such and community relations if the program is geared to anticipating specific law enforcement problems; PR may or may not aid in such anticipation. However, neither this distinction nor any other provides universal agreement among police administrators with regard to the often subtle differences between the two.

Both PR and effective community-relations programs have to do with improving the police image, but PR usually sets that as the goal. Community relations goes further by seeking to head off police problems within the community. Ideally, of course, successfully anticipating potential problems and working within a community to head them off would improve police image and therefore be good PR as well as good community-relations programming; perhaps it would also increase the availability of resources.[1] From the perspective of the *intent* of a police administrator, however, there is a distinct difference between PR and community-relations programming efforts.

Another perception of the distinction has to do with change, or improvement. Generally, programs geared totally to PR assume neither change nor improvement in police activities; the task at hand is merely to present a more favorable image of what police activities are. Community-relations programs assume an improvement in the police function and certainly entail some change in certain police functions.

There are conflicting viewpoints on whether or not police *can* be "changed" or "improved."[2] From the positive orientation, community relations offers a goal for law enforcement that does not necessarily have to emphasize either change or improvement—it merely emphasizes that successful anticipation and correction of any police problem constitutes good police work. If community-relations programs accomplish this, such effort in the community would be additionally rewarded with an improved public image of police.

---

[1] See, for example, A. R. Coffey, *Police Intervention into Family Crisis* (Santa Cruz, Calif.: Davis Publishing, 1977). Chapter 9 covers a wide range of resources needed by police in dealing with community problems.

[2] See, for example, A. C. Germann, "Changing the Police—The Impossible Dream," *Journal of Criminal Law, Criminology and Police Science*, Vol. 62, No. 3 (September 1971).

Recruitment

It is true that some police agencies retain a good public image without vigorous community-relations programming, but it is not true that good public relations anticipates and prevents major police problems. On the other hand, good PR can be just as useful as good community-relations programming in the important area of recruiting qualified candidates for police careers. Indeed, successful recruitment of the most qualified often requires a combination of PR and sophisticated community-relations programming, since highly qualified candidates are unwilling to settle for either poor-image or totally reactive law enforcement.

As the trend increases toward college-prepared police careers, the sophistication of the police recruit also increases. As we noted earlier, police in a democratic society react to crimes already committed far more often than they actively anticipate and prevent crime. But more and more today, police education includes the concept of relating to the community in such a manner that at least some of the causes of crime can be altered by anticipation and correction, even in a democratic society.

The sophisticated candidate readily recognizes the advantage of working in an agency actively seeking a reduction in police problems, and also recognizes programs for community relations as one of the more effective methods to reduce those problems. It would scarcely be realistic to hope to attract the most qualified candidates in the future without addressing this very real influence.

Of course, the community-relations program of a given agency may not function under the title of "community relations." As a matter of fact, the program may take the form of a policy that every police officer perform some particular task, or that a group of specialists handle most of the tasks, or some combination of both. Even the most knowing career candidate might be amazed at the variety of approaches to community relations.

The focus of community relations

Often a PR program is mistaken for an agency's community-relations program, which suggests the need to clarify the difference. Programs designed to improve the public's attitude toward police can be thought of as PR. Programs designed to anticipate problems and to head them off through vigorous community work can be thought of as community relations. A combination of both can be effected through programs designed to improve the public's attitude toward police and simultaneously to work within the community to ensure that specific problems are being dealt with. It should be emphasized, however, that the problems should be those that are of significance to the enforcement of law, not those over which police have no influence or legitimate concern. That is, any police program intended to deal with the community should do so on the basis of potential police problems rather than political or other unrelated problems.

By confining the problems to which police address themselves to the area of law enforcement, community-relations efforts can be more sharply focused, geared to specific problems. This would not only focus more clearly on particular goals but also afford a method of determining whether too much or too little police effort is being expended. Vague, all-inclusive political or economic problems afford no reference point; specific community-relations goals provide the constant reference point.

Program example: family crisis intervention

As an example of specific law enforcement problems to which a community-relations effort might be directed, imagine a police jurisdiction experiencing a constant rise in family fights in which violence and injuries occur. Further imagine that the goal is simply to reduce the injuries associated with police calls to family disturbances. A claim could be made that community-relations programming worked if there were fewer injuries. A more ambitious goal might be to reduce not only the injuries but also the number of calls for police assistance in these matters.

Police intervention into family crisis is only one of many examples that could be used to clarify police–community relations. But it serves as a good example, because police officers are greatly aware of the high proportion of family fights in the typical police patrol function, and of the community-relations implications. Moreover, the potential for violence and possible bodily harm inherent in family-fight situations clearly establishes domestic difficulties as a continuing police problem, requiring continual attention in most jurisdictions. And changes in lifestyles with regard to marital status, as well as a host of other variations in the living arrangements in society today, have not significantly altered the reality that domestic calls often carry high risk for police officers.

In view of this fact, it is significant that community relations has great potential for providing effective aid to families having problems, and for promoting social influences to encourage voluntary law enforcement—a clear case for success in community relations. Police understanding and use of family-crisis-intervention methods as tools can encourage positive attitudes toward law enforcement, as well as reduce police problems. In that way, peace officers may conceivably be producing as much PR as community relations. In this context, consider the following:

> Attempting to distinguish between "intervention" by police and "intrusion" by police is, in many ways, meaningless. The virtual ease with which it can be established that *all* police control of human behavior constitutes *intrusion* underpins the contention that police "intervention" into family strife *is* "intrusion." In other words, the term "intervention" is simply "intrusion" by another name *because* police are seeking to control human behavior. This intent to *control*, whether or not the control is welcome, can serve as a persuasive argument for calling police efforts to intervene in family strife "family-crisis-intrusion" instead of "family-crisis-intervention."

> But while it remains true that *any* police effort to control human behavior *is* intrusion, it is also true that there is an extremely wide variation in both the nature of such police effort, and the intended outcome of such police effort. This wide variation appears to more than justify distinguishing between *intruding* for the purposes of enforcing law, and *intervening* to prevent law violations. In short, the distinction between police "intrusion" and police "intervention" is a matter of intent to "enforce law" as opposed to intent to "prevent law violation."

> This distinction, however, loses a great deal of significance in many, if not most, of the family disturbances in which police involvement is *perceived* as intrusion, regardless of police intentions. This reality suggests emphasis upon recognition that even the most sensitive *intervention* on the part of police tends to come across as intrusion. Such emphasis also permits easier recognition of the *risk* involved in police efforts to intervene in family strife—that how police are perceived may be far more significant than the police intentions. In other words, understanding the *risks* involved in police contact with family strife suggests emphasis upon the intruding nature of *all* police effort and behavior, with only secondary emphasis upon police intentions.

> Recognizing the intruding nature of police involvement in family strife also affords a basis for defining the actual nature of police risks during such intrusion—intrusion into crisis defined as "one or more family members unable to cope with stress." The first dimension of this general nature has to do with the *reaction* to intrusion—a reaction that might be thought of as "we-versus-they."[3]

Prevention vs. control

We have emphasized throughout this text that law enforcement in a democratic society can justify intrusion into the private lives of the citizens only on the basis of law violations, and that the term

---

[3] Coffey, *Police Intervention into Family Crisis*, p. 30.

enforcement relates to the degree of force necessary to enforce the law. Among police officers who oppose community-relations programs on philosophical grounds, frequent reference is made to the constraints placed on police in constitutionally formed governments. However, since "pure" enforcement would require tens of thousands more police officers than are currently employed, consideration should be given to the *preventive* nature of a great deal of the enforcement already in existence.

Assume for a moment that the discussion is police intervention, or "intrusion," into gang activity in a city rather than family troubles. The concerns with how police are perceived in the context of family crisis intervention are virtually the same concerns that would be applied to community-relations programs geared to gang activities, if the object is to *prevent* rather than to *control*.

The patrol division in any law enforcement agency is probably equipped with distinctively marked automobiles, usually displaying large badge decals, and frequently with prominent emergency lights. Most would agree that these easily discernible vehicles have a deterring influence on at least some law violations, notably speeding laws. The offenses that are deterred have also been prevented—prevented in the same sense to which community relations is geared.

At any given moment, however, the patrol car can switch from a preventive function to a "pure" enforcing function—intercepting a law violator who was not deterred. And in the case of community-relations programming, a police officer diligently working with gangs to prevent criminal activity may also switch to the enforcement function if the criminal activity occurs in spite of such efforts.

In this context, community-relations programs are no different from the patrol function and other functions of a police agency. Automobile or foot patrol is usually geared toward preventing (or deterring) crime more than apprehending criminals. A community-relations program conducted by the law enforcement agency is also geared to preventing police problems before they occur.

Each program's uniqueness

The similarity between community-relations programs and traditional police programs suggests that community relations can, and perhaps should, be unique in terms of tailoring its efforts to the overall police responsibility. Problems relating to crime vary as much from one community to another as the penal statutes vary from one state jurisdiction to another. But just as there is considerable similarity in penal codes, there can be great similarity in goals and even methods of community-relations programs. However, the difference between communities in problems, resources, economies, and politics requires a community-relations program to be unique to the community involved if it is to gain optimum success. This question—whether optimum success is to be achieved—requires further consideration, from the point of view of future candidates for police careers and also in terms of the evolution of American police science.

During the emergence of a more widespread police interest in community relations a few decades ago, there seemed to be more similarities than dissimilarities between programs. This apparent uniformity among widely separated jurisdictions probably had to do with the massive federal and, in many cases, state funding for local law enforcement efforts. Government grants for nonexperimental purposes frequently require that the program funded follow certain guidelines, and the result is often a kind of inbreeding in which most successful applications for funding have a great deal in common. Of course, not all early community-relations programs were grant-funded; but the influence of the many programs that were was enormous, because literature and legislation alike often held up successful programs as models.

Similarities, to perhaps an inordinately high degree, continue to this day—depending upon the kind of comparisons made, and upon the general characteristics of jurisdictions compared—between organized efforts to integrate community relations into law enforcement. This similarity, however, is no longer as massive, nor as perpetuated, as when federal funding created the general appearance of uniformity. Gradual but steady change continues in the salient characteristics of community relations and law enforcement.

A reasonable argument can be made that there never was an actual uniformity in anything other than certain training, certain techniques, and perhaps certain organizational characteristics of community-relations programs. Jurisdictions vary widely not only in size, economy, and crime problems, but even more widely in political and economic characteristics. Moreover, two seemingly identical communities may have entirely different levels of public tolerance of criminal behavior—a critical factor in the incentive for law enforcement to be concerned with community relations. Most would agree that the never-ending conflict between safe streets and individual rights forces differences, even between police programs within the same department.

Much of what was once identified and labeled as community

relations a decade or two ago is frequently now performed by police without a specific label, leading some to believe that community relations no longer exists in certain jurisdictions. But where this evolution has occurred, community relations has simply been blended with local police functions. Similarly, police administrators who claim to have done away with the early programs have, in many instances, merely integrated them into staff-training programs—that is, moved them from a small group of specialists into the mainstream of police operations through staff training. Far from doing away with community relations, such a powerful move to integrate into overall law enforcement is the optimum application of the concepts dealt with throughout this volume. In such instances, the agency has gone well beyond the restrictive limitations of a small number of specialists who perform activities that are different from the other law enforcement resources.

In police agencies where a group of specialists still represent the police community-relations effort, uniqueness of programming peculiar to the local jurisdiction has also emerged. More often than not, the relationship between local police problems and community-relations efforts is becoming the most salient program feature—which is particularly significant in view of the earlier emphasis on techniques and organization. The more the emphasis is placed on local problems, the more the salient features of the program are unique—and, of course, the more local, the greater the potential for effectiveness.

The gradual trend toward conceiving of police–community relations as uniquely local permits bringing to bear on local problems the concepts presented in this and previous chapters, without concern for particular organizational requirements, format, or even techniques. Recognition that uniqueness can, when handled correctly, enhance police–community relations permits more imaginative use of even the most limited police and community resources. Indeed, it may well be that the mere perception of a need for community relations is the most critical factor in programming.

Such a perception can emerge in many ways, from police wishing the public would consistently report a particular offense, to crowd intervention into police efforts to make street arrests. Probably the common denominator of all perceptions of a need for community relations is the recognition that not only is law enforcement far easier with community support; *full* law enforcement is impossible without it.

Perceiving the need for community relations may well be the most critical factor in starting, but another factor is just as important in making it pay off. That added factor is not the program design. In the final analysis, the factor of programming efforts have more, far more, to do with police *attitude* than with program design or organizational configurations. For, indeed, police who *want* community relations already have at least the beginning of a program, even if they do nothing beyond wanting it. A law enforcement organization that wants the benefit of community relations is bound to permeate with that desire all contacts with the community it serves.

Summary

The distinction between public relations and community relations for police is primarily that effective community relations affords PR, but PR does not necessarily afford community relations.

Community relations has enormous influence on all police functions, particularly recruiting, family crises, and intergroup conflict. Law enforcement cannot be successful without support from the community, and this support depends greatly upon a good community-relations program.

Early community-relations programs were quite similar, but more recently, programs have been tailored to meet the needs of local police agencies and have frequently been integrated into the functions of the specific organization.

The recognition of the need for a community-relations program, and the desire for it, are far more critical factors in the development of these programs than are their design or the technique applied in them.

Discussion topics

1. Elaborate on PR as presented in this chapter.
2. Discuss community relations in contrast to PR.
3. Discuss how an effective community-relations effort can achieve PR.
4. Why is effective PR not necessarily good comunity relations?
5. What is the advantage of seeking to make community-relations efforts unique to a local jurisdiction?
6. What is the advantage of integrating community-relations efforts into the overall police function?

Annotated references

Bayley, D. H., and H. Mendelson, "The Policeman's World," in E. Reasons and J. L. Kuykendall, eds. *Race, Crime and Justice*, Pacific Palisades, Calif.: Goodyear, 1972. An elaboration of the context in which police apply community relations.

Coffey, Alan R., *Police Intervention into Family Crisis*. Santa Cruz, Calif.: Davis Publishing, 1977. Detailed analysis of family crisis intervention.

———, *The Prevention of Crime and Delinquency*. Englewood Cliffs, N.J.: Prentice-Hall, 1977. A broad perspective for viewing police as the initial community contact point on a continuum of justice processes.

Keiley, J. A., and T. W. O'Rourke, "An Appraisal of the Attitudes of Police Officers toward the Concept of Police–Community Relations," *Journal of Police Science and Administration*, 1, No. 2 (June 1973), 224–31. A good general commentary on some of the police reaction to what this chapter proposed.

McDowell, Charles P., *Police and the Community*. Cincinnati, O.: W. H. Anderson, 1975. A broad-perspective coverage of the subject matter of this chapter.

Sarason, Seymour B., *The Psychological Sense of Community: Prospects for Community Psychology*. San Francisco: Jossey-Bass, 1976. Broad-based discussion of the overall context in which the matters presented in this chapter are carried out.

The National Advisory Commission on Criminal Justice Standards and Goals, *Community Crime Prevention.*, Washington, D.C.: U.S. Government Printing Office, 1973. Affords a broader perspective for specific achievements in community relations.

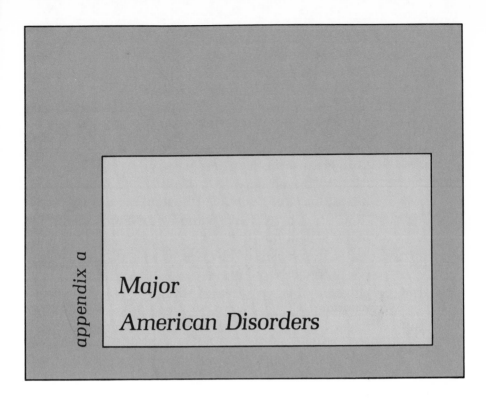

appendix a

Major American Disorders

Major american disorders[1]

1765	Stamp Act riots in Boston and New York
1771	The Regulators
1772	Burning of the *Gaspee*
1774	Resistance to the Boston Port Bill
1784	Revolt against North Carolina
1786	Shays' Rebellion
1788	Doctors' Riot, or Anti-Dissection Riot
1794	Whiskey Rebellion in Pennsylvania
1795	Demonstrations against the Jay Treaty
1798	Virginia and Kentucky Resolutions

[1] Adapted from V. G. Strecher, *The Environment of Law Enforcement: A Community Relations Guide* (Englewood Cliffs, N.J.: Prentice-Hall, Essentials of Law Enforcement Series, 1971), pp. 35–49. By permission of the publisher.

1799	Fries Rebellion
1832	Tariff Nullification
1842	Dorr Rebellion
1844	Anti-Catholic riots in Philadelphia
1849	Astor Place riot in New York City—31 killed, 150 wounded, 86 arrested
1851	San Francisco Committee of Vigilance
1854	Struggle in Kansas over slavery
1855	German tavern-keepers' revolt in Chicago—many killed, hundreds wounded by gunfire
1863	Conscription riots in Boston and New York City—many killed, hundreds injured
1871	Anti-Chinese riot in Los Angeles—23 Chinese killed (18 in one afternoon)
1871	Orange riots in New York City—33 killed, 91 wounded
1877	Great labor strikes in West Virginia and Pittsburgh, Pa.—in two days, 16 soldiers and 50 strikers killed; 125 locomotives, 2,000 freight cars, and a depot burned and destroyed; many killed and wounded in Chicago
1913	Ludlow Massacre—more than 50 killed
1919	Chicago race riot—38 killed, 537 injured
1921	Tulsa race riot—30 killed, several hundred injured
1943	Detroit race riot—34 killed, 700 injured
1964	Race riots in New York City, Rochester, Philadelphia, Jersey City, Paterson, Elizabeth, and Chicago—6 killed, 952 injured
1965	Los Angeles (Watts) race riot—36 killed, 895 injured

BOSTON—1765

Incident: Stamp Act riots[2]
Year: 1765
Location: Boston (concurrently in other colonies, less destructive riots)
Protagonists: British government vs. Sons of Liberty
Generational Issues: Presence of British troops in the colonies; oppressiveness of colonial government

[2] W. A. Heaps, *Riots, U.S.A., 1765–1965* (New York: Seabury Press, 1966), pp. 9–18.

Transient Issues: Sons of Liberty movement; tactless commands of the government

Precipitant: Appointment of Stamp Distributor; organized agitation by the Sons of Liberty; a hanging in effigy from the "Liberty Tree"

Police Involvement: Chief justice and sheriff of Suffolk County were stoned when they attempted to persuade a mob to disperse. The mob destroyed the home of the newly appointed Stamp Distributor. On another day, a law officer read the riot act to a mob forming under the Liberty Tree. This mob left to destroy the office of the vice-admiralty court, where they burned all records, and also the new home of the comptroller of customs; here they "enjoyed the contents of his wine cellar." Later that day, the mob completely demolished the mansion of the chief justice. He had opposed the Stamp Act but, as noted above, had previously sought to dissuade the mob from violence. At least 11 violent disorders occurred in this general pattern.

Disposition: The Stamp Act was never enforced; it was repealed in 1766. Six or seven arrestees were released by the rioters, "who had forced the jailer to give up the keys."

NEW YORK—1788

Incident: Doctors' Riot, or Anti-Dissection Riot[3]

Year: 1788

Location: New York City

Protagonists: Medical students and faculty of the New York Hospital vs. neighborhood workmen

Generational Issues: No legitimate means of obtaining human bodies for medical studies; growth of medical science, development of scientific method in medical education

Transient Issues: Medical students stole bodies, at first from the potter's field and Negro graves, later from a church graveyard. Newspapers criticized the activity, and public anger grew.

Precipitant: A curious boy, peeping into the dissection

[3] Heaps, *Riots,* pp. 19–29.

class, was chased off by a student who held up a human arm, telling the boy it was his mother's. By grisly coincidence, the boy's mother had recently died; her husband discovered that her grave had been opened and the body removed. He gathered a mob of more than 1,000 and demolished much of the medical school. Parts of human bodies were paraded by rioters to recruit a larger mob, which now included "sailors, loafers, criminals and motley mischiefmakers."

Police Involvement: The sheriff, accompanied by the mayor, rescued four medical students in the initial incident. Lacking sufficient officers and unable to disperse a mob surrounding the hospital medical school, the sheriff organized an 18-man military detachment and marched on the crowd. The mob mocked them and threw dirt and stones at them. The force withdrew and then returned, whereupon the mob smashed their muskets, chased off the troops, and stormed the jail, where the doctors had taken refuge. There followed ten additional confrontations of mobs (now numbering some 5,000) and military units. At least seven persons were killed and nine seriously injured. Most injuries were not recorded. The militia finally used armed force to quell the major disorder.

Disposition: Grand-jury recommendations for penalizing doctors and students were dropped by the court. Hospital authorities dismissed from the staff those doctors and students who had been in the dissecting room when the precipitating incident occurred, and fined each offender $20. A law was enacted to supply a limited number of cadavers for medical education.

PHILADELPHIA—1844

Incident: Anti-Catholic Riots[4]
Year: 1844

[4] Heaps, *Riots,* pp. 30–38.

Location:	Philadelphia (concurrently in many other cities during the 1840s and under the Know-Nothing movement of the 1850s)
Protagonists:	American Republicans (Nativists) vs. Irish Catholic immigrants
Generational Issues:	Religious intolerance, based on the belief "that the loyalty of Irish immigrants would be owed to Rome and the Pope rather than to their new country and that cheap Irish labor would lower the American standard of living
Transient Issues:	The bishop asked the school board to excuse Catholic children from reading the King James version of the Bible so that they could be instructed in the Catholic translation. Nativists attacked this request (approved by the board) as a move to take the Bible out of the classroom.
Precipitant:	Huge gathering of Nativists in the middle of the Irish section of the city. A fight started and moved into the street. Guns were fired from buildings into the crowd by Irish residents. Nativists fought back with bricks; one of them was killed and many wounded.
Police Involvement:	First the militia, then the citizen police and a sheriff's posse intervened in the three major pitched battles between the Irish and Nativists. The mob fired cannon into the military force and sniped from upper-story windows and rooftops. Nativist rioters engaged military and police units in pitched battles. Twenty to 24 were killed, more than 100 seriously injured. One arrest.
Disposition:	Two grand-jury hearings blamed the Catholics for the riot, citing their efforts to exclude the Bible from public schools.

NEW YORK—1849

Incident:	Astor Place riot[5]
Year:	1849
Location:	New York City
Protagonists:	Anti-British theater patrons vs. English actor McReady and Astor Place Opera House

[5] Heaps, *Riots,* pp. 39–60.

Generational Issues: Anti-British feeling generated over a long period by critical articles written about America by British travelers. Native American movement generated national hatreds.

Transient Issues: National feelings focused on the prime British actor and the prime American actor of the time; each was treated rudely in the other's land. A downward spiral to violence occurred in the United States.

Precipitant: A McReady performance of *Macbeth* at the Astor Place Opera House was greeted with, "Down with the English hog!" and then continual catcalling; a shower of pennies, fruit, and finally chairs. The following night, McReady was persuaded by 48 leading citizens to appear again. Nativists circulated handbills citing a (fictitious) threat to McReady's detractors by British seamen then in port. Nativists attended the performance to disrupt it. Audience included 1,800 men and 6 women. Police removed the riotous 10 percent of the audience. Nativists rioted outside the theatre, where a great crowd had gathered through curiosity. Many windows were broken, and stones hit the audience. The outside mob was swelled by ruffians. Police and infantry fought the mob without gunfire for some time, but they sustained many serious injuries from paving blocks and bricks. Then a pistol shot from a rioter hit a troop commander; a bayonet charge was ordered, warning shots were fired, and finally, three volleys were fired into the mob. Despite many deaths and injuries, the mob continued the fight until two cannon were loaded with grapeshot and aimed; the rioters then dispersed. Thirty-one were killed, 150 seriously injured, and 86 arrested.

Disposition: A Nativist resolution censured the police and military for their "barbarous treatment of peace-loving citizens." A coroner's jury found police and military action justified. Ten rioters were finally tried, found guilty, and sentenced to varying jail terms. Before the Astor Place riot it was the legal opinion

that no one could be prosecuted for a riot, as it was presumed to be "the natural effect of political passion." Judge Daly's charge completely reversed this concept, and prosecution for rioting became accepted under American law.

CHICAGO—1855

Incident: German tavern-keepers' revolt[6]

Year: 1855

Location: Chicago

Protagonists: Native American, Know-Nothing political party vs. German immigrants and tavern-keepers of the North Side

Generational Issues: Election of Native American mayor and his commitment to suppress immigrants and drive them out of business. Nativist reaction to great migrations from the British Isles and Germany during the 1830s and 1840s.

Transient Issues: Nativist-inspired high liquor-license fees, which would have driven out of business the hundreds of small beer dealers of Chicago, nearly all of whom were German immigrants

Precipitant: The arrest of more than 200 German saloon-keepers for violation of a previously unenforced Sunday-closing law. A test-case criminal trial was disturbed by a demonstration of 500 Germans and a counterdemonstration at Clark and Randolph Streets.

Police Involvement: Captain Nichols, who headed the police department, cleared the streets and dispersed the mob upon orders from the mayor. A few men who resisted were arrested and taken into custody. That night, North Side Germans decided to cross the river and "rescue the prisoners. The rioters armed themselves with shotguns, rifles, pistols, clubs, knives, and every species of weapon. . . ." The spirit of revolt was heightened by rumor of a "raid" and by speeches exhorting immigrants to revolt against impending "slavery." ". . . the bridge opened, and the rioters

[6] J. L. Flinn, *History of the Chicago Police* (Chicago, Ill.: W. B. Conkley, 1887) pp. 72–79.

swarmed across, only to be met by a solid body of policemen. . . . A collision was expected, and it came. Cries of 'Shoot the police,' 'Pick out the stars,' rose from the mob, accompanied by the cracking of guns and pistols. The police replied without waiting for orders, and for several minutes there was a hot engagement in the vicinity of the Sherman House. A German, whose name is lost, levelled a double-barrelled shotgun at Officer Hunt and blew off his left arm. Sheriff Andrews . . . ordered a young man named Frazer . . . to return the fire. He did so, shooting the German dead. A large number were wounded on both sides, and several mysterious funerals occurred on the North Side within the next few days. . . ."

Disposition: Sixty prisoners were added to those already being held, and the mayor ordered two military companies to protect the courthouse with their artillery. But the riot was over, and "nearly all the cases against the imprisoned rioters were dismissed. . . ."

BOSTON—1863

Incident: Conscription riot[7]

Year: 1863

Location: Boston (concurrently in New York City, two days before)

Protagonists: Citizens opposed to lottery-type draft vs. Provost Marshal's serving draft notices in Boston

Transient Issues: General opposition to the conscription, "as unconstitutional, unjust, and oppressive . . . ," especially the provision that a man was entitled to exemption if he paid a $300 fee or furnished a substitute. Hourly newspaper specials on the New York conscription riot.

Precipitant: A woman attacked two marshals, who she mistakenly thought had come to take her husband into the army. She was joined by

---

[7] Edward H. Savage, *Police Records and Recollections* (Boston: John P. Dale and Co., 1873), pp. 347–70.

neighbors and passersby, and finally the entire crowd watching the draft lottery became involved.

Police Involvement: Several policemen were attracted to the disorder and beaten by the crowd; more were sent in, with the same results. The rioters then surrounded one of the police stations and were seen to be armed. That night, several armed mobs moved about the city, beating strangers, police, and members of the military forces. There was window smashing and looting in the commercial districts, and several cases of arson occurred. At least eight were killed, many were seriously injured, and approximately a dozen persons were arrested.

Disposition: Then, as now, there were serious questions about the causes. The police historian reported: "Whether the Conscription riot ... was the result of regular and extensive organization, reaching far beyond the limits of our own city or State, for the purpose of aiding the Rebellion, or whether it was only composed of a combination of men limited within the bounds of Boston and the suburban towns, or whether it was only a spontaneous outbreak, which is at any time liable to happen in all thickly populated places, is a question not well understood." No arrests or prosecutions are recorded.

LOS ANGELES—1871

Incident: Anti-Chinese riot[8]
Year: 1871
Location: Los Angeles (concurrently in San Francisco, 1877; Denver, 1880; Wyoming, 1885)
Protagonists: White residents vs. Chinese community
Generational Issues: A shortage of manpower in the mining and railroad industries inspired the importation of shiploads of indentured coolies. Even though profits increased for company owners, there was a reduction of wages for whites; racial prejudice followed.

[8] Heaps, *Riots*, pp. 61–71.

Transient Issues: To avoid payment of the bride-price, a young man from one tong (a Chinese family society or organization) married, in a civil ceremony, a girl owned by a rival tong. Tong warfare ensued among the Chinese of Los Angeles. There was some gunfire between the rival clans.

Precipitant: A policeman, one of the six-man Los Angeles force, intervened in an intertong exchange of gunfire and was wounded. Soon after, a rancher assisting another policeman was fatally wounded. A large crowd (at least 10 percent of Los Angeles' population of 6,000) gathered at the false report that Chinese were "killing whites wholesale."

Police Involvement: The marshal deputized guards and surrounded the courtyard of the large building in which most of the city's Chinese lived. A lynching occurred shortly afterward, and the mob shot 18 Chinese during the afternoon and hung their bodies in various places in the town. Others were hanged outright, many were multilated. The police assisted in securing many Chinese in the jailhouse, even though some of the policemen were found to have participated in the shootings and others were intimidated and prevented from interfering with lynching parties. Twenty-three Chinese are known to have been killed, and $30,000 was looted from Chinese quarters.

Disposition: Arrests were variously reported at 30, 39, and 150. Ten men were brought to trial for the killing of a Chinese physician; eight were found guilty and given sentences of two to six years. A year later, the California Supreme Court reversed the verdict, stating that the indictment charged only the killing of the Chinese, not murder.

NEW YORK—1871

Incident: Orange riots[9]
Year: 1871

[9] Augustine E. Costello, *Our Police Protectors* (New York: Police Pension Fund, 1885), pp. 244–48.

Location:	New York City
Protagonists:	The Orange Societies vs. the "green" (Catholic) Irish
Historical Issues:	Two-hundred-year quarrel between Orange Protestant Irishmen and Catholic Irishmen, carried over from Ireland to New York
Transient Issues:	Orangemen applied for a parade permit to celebrate an anniversary date of William of Orange, first Protestant monarch of Ireland. Permit at first refused on public safety grounds, later issued.
Precipitant:	During the parade, along a route lined by hostile Irish Catholics, a shot was fired from a window.
Police Involvement:	Police, in addition to a military regiment, were accompanying the Orangemen in large numbers. When the shot was fired from the window, without awaiting orders, the regiment fired into the crowd. Their first volley killed policemen as well as bystanders. Thirty-three were killed and 91 seriously injured.
Dispositon:	Much indignation was expressed at the action of the troops for firing without waiting for an order, and firing so wildly as to wound and kill some of their own men.

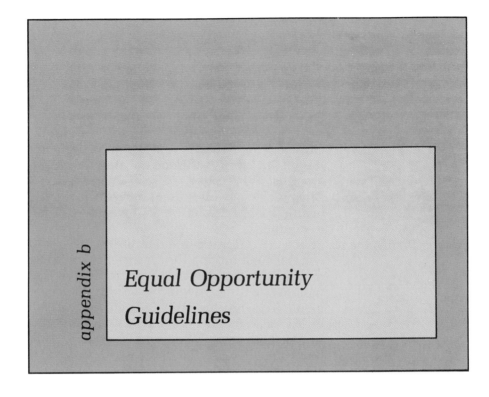

appendix b

Equal Opportunity
Guidelines

On March 9, 1973, the Law Enforcement Assistance Administration of the Department of Justice (LEAA) promulgated equal employment opportunity guidelines (28 CFR 42.301, et seq., Subpart E). The second paragraph of those guidelines reads as follows:

> In accordance with the spirit of the public policy set forth in 5 U.S.C. 553, interested persons may submit written comments, suggestions, data or arguments to the Administrator, Law Enforcement Assistance Administration, U.S. Department of Justice, Washington, D.C., 20530, Attention: Office of Civil Rights Compliance, within 45 days of the publication of the guidelines contained in this part. Material thus submitted will be evaluated and acted upon in the same manner as if this document were a proposal. Until such time as further changes are made, however, Part 42, Subpart E as set forth herein shall remain in effect, thus permitting the public business to proceed more expeditiously.

In accordance with the preceding paragraph, written comments, suggestions, data, or arguments have been received by the administrator of the Law Enforcement Assistance Administration. Material submitted has been evaluated and changes deemed by

LEAA to be appropriate have been incorporated into revised equal employment opportunity guidelines, the text of which follows:

By virtue of the authority vested in it by 5 U.S.C. 301, and section 501 of the Omnibus Crime Control and Safe Streets Act of 1968, Pub. L. 90–351, 82 Stat. 197, as amended, the Law Enforcement Assistance Administration hereby issues Title 28, Chapter 1, Subpart E, of Part 42 of the code of Federal Regulations. In that the material contained herein is a matter relating to the grant program of the Law Enforcement Assistance Administration, the relevant provisions of the Administrative Procedure Act (5 U.S.C. 553) requiring notice of proposed rulemaking, opportunity for public participation, and delay in effective date are inapplicable.

SUBPART E—EQUAL EMPLOYMENT OPPORTUNITY GUIDELINES

Sec.

42.301   Purpose.

42.302   Application.

42.303   Evaluation of employment opportunities.

42.304   Written Equal Employment Opportunity Program.

42.305   Recordkeeping and certification.

42.306   Guidelines.

42.307   Obligations of recipients.

42.308   Noncompliance.

AUTHORITY: 5 U.S.C. sec. 501 of the Omnibus Crime Control and Safe Streets Act of 1968, Pub. L. 90–351, 82 Stat. 197, as amended.

42.301 PURPOSE

(a) The experience of the Law Enforcement Assistance Administration in implementing its responsibilities under the Omnibus Crime Control and Safe Streets Act of 1968, as amended (Pub. L. 90–351, 82 Stat. 197: Pub L. 91–644, 84 Stat. 1881), has demonstrated that the full and equal participation of women and minority individuals in employment opportunities in the criminal justice system is a necessary component to the Safe Streets Act's program to reduce crime and delinquency in the United States.

(b) Pursuant to the authority of the Safe Streets Act and the equal employment opportunity regulations of the LEAA relating to LEAA-assisted programs and activities (28 CFR 42.201, et seq., Subpart D), the following Equal Employment Opportunity Guidelines are established.

42.302 APPLICATION

(a) As used in these guidelines, "Recipient" means any state, political subdivision of any state, combination of such states or subdivisions, or any department, agency or instrumentality of any of the foregoing receiving Federal financial assistance from LEAA, directly or through another recipient, or with respect to whom an assurance of civil rights compliance given as a condition of the earlier receipt of assistance is still in effect.

(b) The obligation of a recipient to formulate, implement, and maintain an equal employment opportunity program, in accordance with this subpart, extends to state and local police agencies, correctional agencies, criminal court systems, probation and parole agencies, and similar agencies responsible for the reduction and control of crime and delinquency.

(c) Assignments of compliance responsibility for Title VI of the Civil Rights Act of 1964 have been made by the Department of Justice to the Department of Health, Education and Welfare, covering educational institutions and general hospital or medical facilities. Similarly, the Department of Labor, in pursuance of its authority under Executive Orders 11246 and 11375, has assigned responsibility for monitoring equal employment opportunity under government contracts with medical and educational institutions, and non-profit organizations, to the Department of Health, Education and Welfare. Accordingly, monitoring responsibility in compliance matters in agencies of the kind mentioned in this paragraph rests with the Department of Health, Education and Welfare, and agencies of this kind are exempt from the provisions of this subpart, and are not responsible for the development of equal employment opportunity programs in accordance herewith.

(d) Each recipient of LEAA assistance within the criminal justice system which has 50 or more employees and which has received grants or subgrants of $25,000 or more pursuant to and since the enactment of the Safe Streets Act of 1968, as amended, and which has a service population with a minority representation of 3 percent or more, is required to formulate, implement and maintain an Equal Employment Opportunity Program relating to the employment practices affecting minority persons and women within 120 days after either the promulgation of these amended guidelines, or the initial application for assistance is approved, whichever is sooner. Where a recipient has 50 or more employees, and has received grants or subgrants of $25,000 or more, and has a service population with a minority representation of less than 3 percent, such recipient is required to formulate, implement, and maintain an Equal Employment Opportunity Program relating to employment practices affecting women. For a definition of "employment practices" within the meaning of this paragraph, see 42.202(b).

(e) "Minority persons" shall include persons who are Negro, Oriental, American-Indian, or Spanish-surnamed Americans. "Spanish-surnamed Americans" means those of Latin American, Cuban, Mexican, Puerto Rican or Spanish origin. In Alaska, Eskimos and Aleuts should be included as "American Indians."

(f) For the purpose of these guidelines, the relevant "service population" shall be determined as follows:

(1) For adult and juvenile correctional institutions, facilities and programs including probation and parole programs, the "service population" shall be the inmate or client population serviced by the institution, facility, or program during the preceding fiscal year.

(2) For all other recipient agencies (e.g., police and courts), the "service population" shall be the state population for state agencies, the county population for county agencies, and the municipal population for municipal agencies.

(g) "Fiscal year" means the twelve calendar months beginning July 1, and ending June 30, of the following calendar year. A fiscal year is designated by the calendar year in which it ends.

42.303 EVALUATION OF EMPLOYMENT OPPORTUNITIES

(a) A necessary prerequisite to the development and implementation of a satisfactory Equal Employment Opportunity Program is the identification and analysis of any problem areas inherent in the utilization or participation of minorities and women in all of the recipient's employment phases (e.g., recruitment, selection, and promotion) and the evaluation of employment opportunities for minorities and women.

(b) In many cases an effective Equal Employment Opportunity Program may only be accomplished where the program is coordinated by the recipient agency with the cognizant Civil Service Commission or similar agency responsible by law, in whole or in part, for the recruitment and selection of entrance candidates and selection of candidates for promotion.

(c) In making the evaluation of employment opportunities, the recipient shall conduct such analysis separately for minorities and women. However, all racial and ethnic data collected to perform an evaluation pursuant to the requirements of this section should be cross-classified by sex to ascertain the extent to which minority women or minority men may be underutilized. The evaluation should include but not necessarily be limited to the following factors:

(1) An analysis of present representation of women and minority persons in all job categories;

(2) An analysis of all recruitment and employment selection procedures for the preceding fiscal year, including such things as position description, application forms, recruitment methods and sources, interview procedures, test administration and test validity, educational prerequisites, referral procedures and final selection methods, to insure that equal employment opportunity is being afforded in all job categories;

(3) An analysis of seniority practices and provisions, upgrading and promotion procedures, transfer procedures (internal or vertical), and formal and informal training programs during the preceding fiscal year, in order to insure that equal employment opportunity is being afforded;

(4) A reasonable assessment to determine whether minority employment is inhibited by external factors such as the lack of access to suitable housing in the geographical area served by a certain facility or the lack of suitable transportation (public or private) to the workplace.

42.304 WRITTEN EQUAL EMPLOYMENT OPPORTUNITY PROGRAM

Each recipient's Equal Employment Opportunity Program shall be in writing and shall include:

(a) A job classification table or chart which clearly indicates for each job classification or assignment the number of employees within each respective job category classified by race, sex and national origin (include, for example, Spanish-surnamed, Oriental, and American Indian). Also, principal duties and rates of pay should be clearly indicated for each job classification. Where auxiliary duties are assigned or more than one rate of pay applies because of length of time in the job or other factors, a special notation should be made. Where the recipient operates more than one shift or assigns employees within each shift to varying locations, as in law enforcement agencies, the number by race, sex and national origin on each shift and in each location should be identified. When relevant, the recipient should indicate the racial/ethnic mix of the geographic area of assignments by the inclusion of minority population and percentage statistics.

(b) The number of disciplinary actions taken against employees by race, sex and national origin within the preceding fiscal year, the number and types of sanctions imposed (suspension indefinitely, suspension for a term, loss of pay, written reprimand, oral reprimand, other) against individuals by race, sex and national origin.

(c) The number of individuals by race, sex and national origin (if available) applying for employment within the preceding fiscal year and the number by race, sex and national origin (if available) of those applicants who were offered employment and those who were actually hired. If such data is unavailable, the recipient should institute a system for the collection of such data.

(d) The number of employees in each job category by race, sex, and national origin who made application for promotion or transfer within the preceding fiscal year and the number in each job category by race, sex and national origin who were promoted or transferred.

(e) The number of employees by race, sex and national origin who were terminated within the preceding fiscal year, identifying by race, sex and national origin which were voluntary and involuntary terminations.

(f) Available community and area labor characteristics within the relevant geographical area including total population, workforce and existing unemployment by race, sex and national origin. Such data may be obtained from the Bureau of Labor Statistics, Washington, D.C., state and local employment services, or other reliable sources. Recipients should identify the sources of the data used.

(g) A detailed narrative statement setting forth the recipient's existing employment policies and practices as defined in 42.202(b). Thus, for example, where testing is used in the employment selection process, it is not sufficient for the recipient to simply note the fact. The recipient should identify the test, describe the procedures followed in administering and scoring the test, state what weight is given to test scores, how a cutoff score is established and whether the test has been validated to predict or measure job performance and, if so, a detailed description of the validation study. Similarly detailed responses are required with respect to other employment policies, procedures, and practices used by the applicant.

(1) The statement should include the recipient's detailed analysis of existing employment policies, procedures, and practices as they relate to employment of minorities and women (see 42.303), and, where improvements are necessary, the statement should set forth in detail the specific steps the recipient will take for the achievement of full and equal employment opportunity. For example, the Equal Employment Opportunity Commission, in carrying out its responsibilities in ensuring compliance with Title VII, has published Guidelines on Employee Selection Procedures (29 CFR Part 1607), which among other things, proscribes the use of employee selection practices, procedures and devices (such as tests, minimum educational levels, oral interviews and the like) which have not been shown by the user thereof to be related to job performance and where the use of such an unvalidated selection device tends to disqualify a disproportionate number of minority individuals or women for employment. The EEOC Guidelines set out appropriate procedures to assist in establishing and maintaining equal employment opportunities. Recipients of LEAA assistance using selection procedures which are not in conformity with the EEOC Guidelines shall set forth the specific areas of nonconformity, the reasons which may explain any such nonconformity, and, if necessary, the steps the recipient agency will take to correct any existing deficiency.

(2) The recipient should also set forth a program for recruitment of minority persons based on an informed judgment of what is necessary to attract minority applications including, but not necessarily limited to, dissemination of posters, use of advertising media patronized by minorities, minority-group contacts and community-relations programs. As appropriate, recipients may wish to refer to recruitment techniques suggested in Revised Order No. 4 of the Office of Federal Contract Compliance, U.S. Department of Labor, found at 41 CFR 60–2.24(e).

(h) Plan for dissemination of the applicant's Equal Employment Opportunity Program to all personnel, applicants and the general public. As appropriate, recipients may wish to refer to the recommendations for dissemination of policy suggested in Revised Order No. 4 of the Office of Federal Contract Compliance, U.S. Department of Labor, found at 41 CFR 60–2.21.

(i) Designation of specified personnel to implement and maintain adherence to the Equal Employment Opportunity Program and a description of their specific responsibilities suggested in Revised Order No. 4 of the Office of Federal Contract Compliance, U.S. Department of Labor, found at 41 CFR 60–2.22.

42.305 RECORDKEEPING AND CERTIFICATION

The Equal Employment Opportunity Program and all records used in its preparation shall be kept on file and retained by each recipient covered by these guidelines for subsequent audit or review by responsible personnel of the cognizant state planning agency or the LEAA. Prior to the authorization to fund new or continuing programs under the Omnibus Crime Control and Safe Streets Act of 1968, the recipient shall file a certificate with the cognizant state planning agency or LEAA regional office stating that the equal employment opportunity program is on file with the recipient. The form of the certification shall be as follows:

I, _____ (person filing the application) certify that the _____ _____ (criminal justice agency) has formulated an equal employment opportunity program in accordance with 28 CFR 42.301, et seq., Subpart E, and that is on file in the _____ (name of office) _____ (address), _____ (title), for review or audit by officials of the cognizant state planning agency or the Law Enforcement Assistance Administration, as required by relevant laws and regulations.

The criminal justice agency created by the Governor to implement the Safe Streets Act within each state shall certify that it requires, as a condition of the recipient of block grant funds, that recipients from it have executed an Equal Employment Opportunity Program in accordance with this subpart, or that, in conformity with the terms and conditions of this regulation no equal employment opportunity programs are required to be filed by that jurisdiction.

42.306 GUIDELINES

(a) Recipient agencies are expected to conduct a continuing program of self-evaluation to ascertain whether any of their recruitment, employee selection or promotional policies (or lack thereof) directly or indirectly have the effect of denying equal employment opportunities to minority individuals and women.

(b) Post award compliance reviews of recipient agencies will be scheduled by LEAA, giving priority to any recipient agencies which have a significant disparity between the percentage of minority persons in the service population and the percentage of minority employees in the agency. Equal employment program modification may be suggested by LEAA and, accordingly, recipient agencies are encouraged to develop recruitment, hiring or promotional guidelines under their equal employment opportunity program which will correct, in a timely manner, any identifiable employment impediments which may have contributed to the existing disparities.

(c) A significant disparity between minority representation in the service population and the minority representation in the agency workforce may be deemed to exist if the percentage of a minority group in the employment of the agency is not at least seventy (70) percent of the percentage of that minority in the service population.

42.307 OBLIGATIONS OF RECIPIENTS

The obligation of those recipients subject to these Guidelines for the maintenance of an Equal Employment Opportunity Program shall continue for the period during which the LEAA assistance is extended to a recipient or for the period during which a comprehensive law enforcement plan filed pursuant to the Safe Streets Act is in effect within the State, whichever is longer, unless the assurances of compliance, filed by a recipient in accordance with 42.204(a)(2), specify a different period.

42.308 NONCOMPLIANCE

Failure to implement and maintain an Equal Employment Opportunity Program as required by these Guidelines shall subject a recipient of LEAA assistance to the sanctions prescribed by the Safe Streets Act and the equal employment opportunity regulations of the Department of Justice (Sec 42 U. S. C. 3757 and 42.206).

Effective date—This Guideline shall become effective on
August 31, 1973.

Dated August 24, 1973.
DONALD E. SANTARELLI
Administrator, Law Enforcement
Assistance Administration
[FR Doc. 73–18555 Filed 8–30–73;8:45 am]

Dealing with
Community Tensions
and Civil Disturbances
*—a Checklist**

I. *Factors Contributing to Community Tensions and Civil Disturbances*
   A. Social Factors
      1. Racial or minority-group injustices, whether real or imagined, create an atmosphere of distrust and fear.
      2. Religious differences can often create schisms in the community just as serious as racial differences.
      3. Normal community activities, involving crowds, could deteriorate into serious disorder under certain conditions (e.g., large crowds outside, hot weather, an "incident").
      4. Existence of a matriarchal society prevalent in Negro areas can present unusual problems to police and the larger community.
      5. Adult attitudes towards conduct of young people, teen-agers, etc., may vary due to different cultural values and attitudes. These may be in conflict with the norms of the community.
   B. Economic Factors
      1. Extreme poverty can breed crime and perpetuate barriers to social advancement.

* Taken from California Commission on Peace Officers Standards Training Post (CONDENSED).

2. Unemployment and/or unfair hiring practices tend to confirm for minority-group persons that they are facing a "stacked deck" in their efforts to improve their lot.
3. Poor housing conditions and discrimination in the sale of real estate create dislike for the "power structure," and the policeman who symbolizes the establishment.
4. Affluence of large parts of the community create unawareness and insensitivity so that no desire to cope with "minority-group" problems exists.

C. Political Factors
  1. Power struggles:
    a. Efforts by the majority, legal and otherwise, to maintain the status quo.
    b. Efforts, legal and otherwise, by minority groups to upset the balance of power; to share, dominate, or alter the political system.

D. Absence or Failure of Constituted Authority
  1. Failure of law enforcement to act:
    a. In a crowd or arrest situation, due to indecision, or lack of appropriate laws.
    b. In certain situations due to a lack of manpower, or inadequately trained manpower.
    c. Because of a fear of adverse public reaction.
  2. Absence of law enforcement:
    a. Serves as a contributing factor to disorder because members of the crowd (or mob) feel they can act with impunity.
    b. Some in minority-group areas feel they are not receiving adequate police services.

E. General Factors
  1. Minority-group struggles for full enjoyment of civil rights.
  2. Inequitable law enforcement, real or imagined, toward minority groups.
    a. Demonstrated bias or prejudice on the part of police.
    b. A feeling in some areas that they are "overpoliced."
  3. Lack of meaningful communication between police and the minority community.
  4. Stereotyping:
    a. Of minorities by police and other city officials.
    b. Of police and city officials by minorities and the larger community.
  5. Rumors and sensationalism:
    a. Inflammatory statements and stories based upon distortions and/or half-truths.

  b. May be originated by police, city officials, minority groups, religious and lay groups, news media.
 6. Absence of organization and leadership among the masses of minority-group members.
  a. Self-proclaimed leaders much in evidence.
  b. Leaders selected by the white majority to represent the minority much in evidence.
  c. General lack of opposition among the minorities against the radical elements (tacit approval).
  d. No real leadership for the minority community.
 7. General public apathy towards the issue of civil rights and impartial law enforcement.
 8. Outsiders who capitalize on local problems as a means of promoting their own goals.

II. *Warning Signs of Community Tensions*

 A. Early Manifestations
  1. A greater frequency of resisting arrest in certain areas. Gathering of crowds when arrests are made.
  2. An increase in charges of alleged police brutality, an increased distrust or resentment of law enforcement.
  3. A rising volume in the number of incidents of violence, or threats of violence.
  4. Increasing rumors and statements of dissatisfaction, public name-calling and other attempts at provocation.
  5. The appearance of "hate" literature, threatening or derogatory signs, leaflets, pamphlets.
  6. A stepping-up of gang activity, characterized by antisocial activity on the part of minority-group members; acts of vandalism and malicious mischief, particularly on public property.
  7. Progressively overt attacks upon constituted authority through:
   a. Protest meetings.
   b. Speeches and literature.
   c. Sit-ins, lie-ins, etc., in commercial and public buildings.
   d. Disruption of and interference with police activities.
  8. Apprehension or fear on the part of police officers.

III. *Policy Re Community Tensions and Civil Disturbances*

It is the department head's responsibility to formulate sound policies that will serve as guidelines to members of his agency in their contacts with the public. It is suggested that thoughtful consideration be given to the following areas of police policy:

 A. Administrative Policy
  1. This involves a stated position on the issues of police–community relations, human relations, and civil disturbances.

This position would recognize the right of peaceful demonstration, and at the same time point out the responsibilities of those who demonstrate. It should contain a pledge of fair and impartial enforcement for all members of the community.

2. Policy statements should be reduced to writing.
3. Obtain concurrence of other city officials.
4. Provide appropriate dissemination through:
    a. News media.
    b. Departmental orders.
    c. Staff meetings.
       (Releases to the public would consist of a statement of general principles. Material distributed to the department would be specific and detailed.)
5. Policy Inspection
   There should be an affirmative answer to each of the following questions:

    a. Is middle management selling it?
    b. Does everyone understand it?
    c. Are they demonstrating that they believe in it, and are following policy?
    d. Is someone officially designated to make such inspections and report back to the chief?

B. Organizational Policy
1. Considerations:
    a. The size of the department and the magnitude of the problem will determine whether community relations will be an assignment for one individual, or a special unit should be formed.
    b. The person or unit should operate in a staff capacity, and should report directly to the chief.
    c. A summary of collected intelligence should be furnished the department head on a regular basis for review and analysis.
2. Special operations dealing with civil disturbances:
    a. The field commander (designated in advance) will be in complete charge.
    b. A second-in-command and an alternate should be chosen to provide 24-hour continuity.
    c. In the event of a major disturbance, the field commander would relieve the district and/or shift commander, and would assume charge.
    d. The field commander, subject to the approval of the chief of police, would have authority to mobilize and request mutual aid.
    e. The field commander would maintain liaison for legal advice in the field with the District Attorney.

f. The field commander would be responsible for public information releases.

C. Operational Policy for Disturbances

  1. Personnel:
    a. All personnel would be required to "report in," upon hearing announcements on radio or TV, or upon notification to their residence.
    b. An adequate supervisory ratio should be maintained.
    c. Training and re-training should be continuous.
    d. Assignment of men should be commensurate with the size and seriousness of the situation.
    e. Overtime limitations should be kept in mind in routine operations.

  2. The Field Commander:
    a. He should specify the geographical area that contains the problem and then assume complete charge of that area.
    b. Headquarters and communications should be advised of the perimeter established.
    c. The community-relations unit and headquarters will act in a staff capacity to the field commander.

  3. External Relations:
    a. Policy should be preestablished that would clarify the involvement of other city departments' personnel, as well as outside law enforcement agencies.
    b. The public should be kept informed but steps should be taken to keep curiosity-seekers out of the area.

  4. Use of Force:
    a. The use of force, particularly individual combat, should be avoided. There must be a great deal of restraint on the part of police, and when action is taken it should be by units, not individual officers.
    b. Chemicals, such as smoke or tear gas, should be used only when authorized by the field commander. When it is used, there should be a more than adequate supply available at the designated location in the field. Provisions should be made for escape routes for the crowd and first aid for rioters, when requested.
    c. Dogs frequently create a negative reaction in crowds when they are used for crowd control and /or arrest. They should be used only in extreme situations.
    d. The use of firearms should be avoided and the practice of firing "warning shots" is not advised. The use of firearms should be considered as a last resort, and then only when necessary to protect the lives of citizens and officers.
    e. Insulting language is often construed as a form of "harassment" and "brutality." Care should be given to

avoiding terms and names that would antagonize the group being dealt with.

(1) Officers should expect to receive abusive language and should avoid being baited into making imprudent remarks and/or arrests.

5. News Media:

a. A public information officer should be part of the field command staff. He should have a counterpart at headquarters (in disturbances of major proportions) to whom he will feed information as it becomes available.

b. The P.I.O. should arrange for a specific schedule for press releases and a point of dissemination. He should not deviate from this procedure unless a major event occurs.

c. The P.I.O. should act as a "buffer" between the press and the field commander, so that the commander can devote maximum time and attention to the problem.

d. Reasonable limitations should be set for the press re-entry into high hazard areas. Contacts by the press with police personnel in the field, in the form of personal interviews, should be minimized. Efforts should be made to confine such interviews to the command post area, and with the approval of the officer in charge.

e. News media representatives should be required to produce bona fide credentials in order to enter the area. In major distrubances, consideration could be given to the issuance of special press cards by the P.I.O.

6. Arrests:

a. When demonstrations are known in advance, meetings should be held with the head of the organization against whom the demonstration would take place, and his counsel. Policy should be agreed upon as to at what point arrest would be in order, and that the firm or organization would be willing to prosecute.

b. Similar meetings should be held with the leaders of the demonstrating groups. Ground rules should be formulated that both the demonstrators and police understand.

c. Whenever possible, it should be decided in advance whether physical arrests and the bail procedure would be used, or whether arrestees could simply be released on citation or summons following the booking.

d. Alternatives should be decided upon to handle prisoners in the event custodial facilities are saturated.

7. Emergency Funding:
   a. Certain staff members should be authorized to sign emergency requisitions.
   b. These requisitions could be for food, lumber, gasoline, vehicle parts or repair, guns, ammunition, etc.
   c. Major purchases should be with the knowledge and approval of the logistical commander, and normally through his office.

IV. *Prevention—The Key to Coping with Community Tensions*
Experience of many law enforcement agencies indicates that most civil disturbances can be prevented, or if not prevented, their negative effects can be minimized. One of the best prevention tools is the reputation of an agency in terms of fair, impartial, and efficient law enforcement, and the knowledge that the agency possesses an interest in and knowledge of the problems of the community.
The following factors have been shown to be important in the development and maintenance of a good prevention program:
A. The Selection Process
   1. Recruiting standards at the entrance level should stress the selection of intelligent and stable individuals who react well under stress. It is most desirable to select persons:
      a. Who are able to deal effectively both in group and individual relationships.
      b. Who possess a background that helps equip them to deal with a variety of people, and changing social, cultural, and political conditions.
   2. An inventory of existing staff should be made to identify those individuals who can be assigned to important posts in sensitive areas.

B. Training and Its Role in Prevention
   1. The benefits of good training should be stressed to individual officers.
   2. Basic concepts of community relations should be covered at the recruit level. In-depth training should be administered at the in-service and re-training levels.
   3. Legal training, in addition to its normal implications, should include study of laws specifically relating to community problems and disturbances. This would include:
      a. Local and county ordinances
      b. State and Federal statutes
      c. Other laws governing public assembly, constitutional rights, etc.
   4. Field tactics and techniques of self-defense should be taught as part of the continuing curriculum.

a. Basic training should be on a department-wide basis, with provisions for periodic re-training.

b. Special and intensive training of a continuous nature should be provided to crowd control units.

5. Decision making is difficult at all levels. An effective exercise of this skill can be developed through role-playing in problem solving sessions wherein individuals must evaluate situations and decide on courses of action.

6. Department policies and procedures are subject to change. There should be particular emphasis on keeping all personnel aware of changes or modifications relative to:

   a. Court decisions
   b. Community-relations programs
   c. Standards of conduct for officers
   d. Collecting and reporting intelligence
   e. Coping with disturbances
   f. Post-disturbance recovery

7. In order to have an effective liaison with the community, there must be good two-way communication. This can often be facilitated through training in:

   a. Understanding minority-group cultures and their problems.
   b. The importance of semantics (slang, colloquialisms, "trigger words," etc.)
   c. Developing the ability to listen and comprehend, and to speak and be understood.
   d. The need to explain (not defend) changes in enforcement policies and actions.

C. Community-Relations Programs as a Vehicle for Prevention

1. The term "Police–Community Relations" too often is defined in narrow terms. It would appear more appropriate to refer to *all* relationships between the police and the community rather than in terms of relationships with racial minority groups. The emphasis should be on special group problems within the larger community, regardless of their nature. It would be advisable to maintain contact with *all* groups, regardless of whether or not their viewpoints are compatible with those of the department.

2. Specialization in community relations offers advantages in all but the smallest department. Ideally, a specialized unit would deal with all relations with all the community. Its secondary purpose would be to deal with special groups within the community.

3. Important to the formation of such a unit would be the criteria

for selecting its staff. There should be assurance that those selected:

   a. Possess a sound background in general law enforcement, with a demonstrated record of good conduct, and stability.
   b. Have a record of having made good arrests, resulting in a high rate of convictions, with a minimum of resisting arrest charges involved.
   c. Have a suitable academic background.
   d. Have a substantiated reputation for fairness, good judgment, and an absence of any crippling bias or prejudice.

4. The head of the community-relations unit would report directly to the department head and would act in a staff capacity to the rest of the organization. At the same time it would be important to stress that members of the unit must not discard their identity and responsibilities as policemen. Regardless of how deeply involved they become in their assignment, their primary responsibilities are still to the department. There must be a correlation between their goals and objectives, and the goals and objectives of the agency they serve.

5. A continuous and effective liaison should be maintained between this unit and special-interest community groups, and the human relations commission. This bond between the police and the community can be formed by:

   a. Making good community relations the responsibility of everyone in the department, from the patrolman to the chief.
   b. Actively seeking out and making the acquaintance of individuals and associations, not waiting for them to "make the first move."
   c. Keeping the public fully informed.
   d. Demonstrating a continuing interest in community problems; seeking citizen reaction and advice.
   e. Being willing to listen to citizen complaints about the community, the police, the city government. Being willing to make referrals, or institute a police follow-up when appropriate.
   f. Frankly stating the police position (when there is one) on community issues, and being willing to change positions that experience and common sense indicate need modification.

6. Press relations and publicity efforts of this unit should be within the framework of departmental policy. Major releases should always be cleared with the chief of police in advance. It would be ideal to use a professional public relations man in

this unit, but in any event it would be desirable to utilize a staff member with special training in journalistic and public relations techniques.

7. Program goals of the community-relations unit should be the result of extensive planning and receive department head approval before attempts are made to implement them. Generally the program goals will be to bring about better understanding and mutual trust between the community and the police. Such programs are:
   a. Those aimed at the entire community.
   b. Those designed to reach children and teenagers, in and out of school.
   c. Those designed to deal with problems presented by special groups.

D. Complaint Procedures
1. The organizational structure should be geared to accommodate the processing and disposition of citizen complaints. One satisfactory method is to:
   a. Set up specific channels and procedures.
   b. Supplement this with means of disseminating knowledge of this system to the public and members of the department.
   c. Receive complaints made about departmental policies and/or procedures, as well as against individuals.
   d. Establish procedures to insure prompt follow-up and feed-back to the complainant.
   e. Have a policy to issue public statements regarding false reports that have been maliciously and intentionally filed against an officer.

2. Establish channels to receive *complaints by police officers re the public.* Make it a policy to bring these complaints to the attention of the appropriate community group and the press to generate some responsible action on their part. Complaints by officers might include:
   a. Assaults on police officers.
   b. Verbal abuse, provocation, "baiting."
   c. Defiance of authority, interference with arrests and other police action.
   d. Lack of respect for constituted authority.
   e. False accusations.
   f. Preferential treatment for minorities.
   g. Apathy, lack of support for law and order.
   h. Untrue and/or unfair treatment of police by news media.

E. Some Consequences of Poor Police–Community Relations
1. There is reduced morale, efficiency, and attention to duty

in the police department. Consequently, there will probably be higher crime rates and detrimental effects on dealing with crime and delinquency generally.

2. There is reluctance on the part of the community to participate or assume responsibility in the process of law enforcement. This will result in less success in preventive and investigative police work.

3. There is an increased likelihood of abuse and injury to policemen in the field.

4. There is increased likelihood of abuse, injury, and infringement of the rights and liberties of citizens.

5. The potential for large-scale violence between the police and segments of the community is greatly increased.

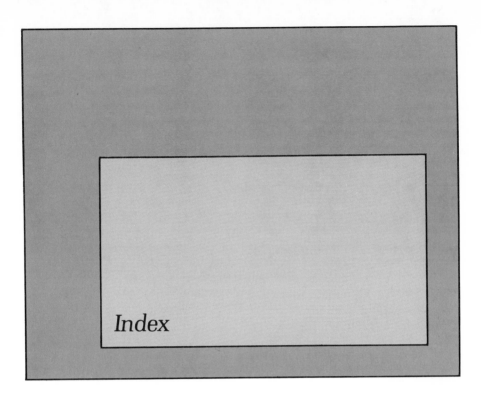

Index

LeBon, 195, 209, 216, 223
Lee, A. M., 210
Leisure, 69
Lewis, O., 135
Lohman, J. D., 116, 119, 127, 152–53, 197, 219
    223
Lomax, L. E., 17

M

Mack, R. W., 6
MacNew, V. J., 158
Manning, P. E., 158, 193
Manpower, lack of, 106
Margolis, J., 21, 27
Marx, G. T., 194
Mayhall, P. D., 21–22, 27, 151
McDowell, C. P., 66, 78, 162, 238
McKay, H. D., 123
Mendez, et al., 47
Mexican-American Education Study, 39–40
Middle class, 193
Militants, 176, 192–93, 199–200, 203
Miller, N. E., 216, 218, 223
Miller, W. B., 85, 97
Mindelson, H., 125, 129–30, 237
Minority groups, 11–16, 20
    Attitudes, 84–86
    Blacks, differential treatment, 102–04
    Demonstrations, 105
    Districts, 104–06
    Improper policing, 105
    Overpolicing, 104–06
    In police, 21–22
    Police representing, 20–21
Misner, G., 127, 152, 157
Mobs, 209, 214–16
Moore, S. A., 95
Morality, 166
Mores, 15, 167
Moynihan, D. P., 138–39

N

National Advisory on Civil Disorders, 29–35,
    37, 48, 195, 201, 208
National Commission on the Causes and Pre-
    vention of Violence, 32, 34–35, 38,
    189, 203, 206, 208
National Conference on Criminal Justice, 229

O

Oberg, K., 145
Orderly environment, 56
Organizations, 15
    Anti-defamation League, 15
    NAACP, 15
    Urban League, 15
O'Rourke, T. W., 125

P

Parole, 167
Peterson, R. C., 219
Plessy vs. Ferguson, 200
Police, attitudes, 86, 90–91
    Authority symbol, 163–69, 173–75, 177
    Brutality, 48, 102–03, 127, 169–170
    Civil rights, 170–71
    Confidence, 106–07
        Lack of, 106–07
    Criticism of, 160–62
    Demonstrations, 179
    Harrassment, 48–49, 102–06, 169–170,
        175
    Hostility, 170–74
    Image, 159–80
        Distorted, 128–30
        With minority groups, 128–156, 159–
        179
        Negative, 159–61
        Positive, 159–60
        Problem of, 160–75
    Power, 163–64
    Professional approach, 174, 175
    Relations in community, 24–25, 128–31
    Roles, 160–65
        Controversy over, 160
        Urban police officer, 161–64
        Variety of, 161–64
    Social problem symbol, 165–70
    Support, 166
Policeman, black, 105–06
Pope, C. E., 125, 151
Porter, B., 117
Power, 64
Prejudice, 7–27
    Character conditioned, 12–14
    Characteristics, 9–10
    Culture-conditioned, 9–12
    Definition of, 8–10